Breaking
the Silence

REDRESS AND JAPANESE
AMERICAN ETHNICITY

Yasuko I. Takezawa

Cornell University Press

Ithaca and London

First published 1995 by Cornell University Press.

Library of Congress Cataloging-in-Publication Data

Takezawa, Yasuko I., 1957–
    Breaking the silence : redress and Japanese American ethnicity / Yasuko I. Takezawa.
       p. cm. — (Anthropology of contemporary issues)
    Includes bibliographical references and index.
    ISBN 0-8014-2985-4. — ISBN 0-8014-8181-3
    1. Japanese Americans—Washington (State)—Seattle—Ethnic identity. 2. Seattle (Wash.)—Ethnic relations. I. Title.
II. Series.
F899.S49J38 1994
305.895'60797772—dc20   94-29600

Printed in the United States of America

⊗ The paper in this book meets the minimum requirements of the American National Standard for Information Sciences–Permanence of Paper for Printed Library Materials, ANSI Z39.48-1984.

Breaking the Silence

A volume in the series

Anthropology of Contemporary Issues

EDITED BY ROGER SANJEK

A full list of titles in the series appears at the end of the book.

One of the oldest living survivors of Japanese American internment receives his letter of apology and redress check. Photo by Akio Yanagihara.

To those who died,
their ordeal not acknowledged,
and
to future generations of
Japanese Americans

Breaking the Silence
honored by our ancestors
is a lamentation;
not of battles lost or won,
but a remembrance of the lives of those
    who have passed before us. . . .
Breaking the silence
is also a tribute to their perseverance. . . .
We do this,
not to rake up old coals,
but to see with new eyes:
the past
can no more be denied.

—Nikki Nojima Louis,
Breaking the Silence

Contents

Illustrations, Maps, Figure, and Tables

Illustrations

Maps

Figure

Tables

A Note to the Reader

All my interview subjects, except those who were already public figures, have been given pseudonyms to protect their privacy. Minor details may be changed. Persons who are quoted from public documents and other published sources bear their true names.

Preface

In 1918 Samuel Rea, president of the Pennsylvania Railroad, declared that in order to become good American citizens, immigrants "must be induced to give up the languages, customs, and methods of life which they have brought with them across the ocean, and adopt instead the language, habits, and customs of this country, and the general standards and ways of American living" (Rea 1918 in Hill 1974: 33). Today, descendants of the immigrants who have streamed into the United States have indeed generally adopted American ways: they speak English, watch the fireworks on the Fourth of July, observe Thanksgiving, and display habits and norms that mark them as "Americans." Japanese Americans are no exception.

Contrary to earlier expectations, however, not only do boundaries continue to demarcate ethnic groups in American society, but the issue of ethnicity has grown more important. Resurgent ethnicity is not a phenomenon unique to the United States. All over the world, political integration of different tribes and ethnic groups into new states and their migration into urban settings, which it was once believed would reduce their differences and unify them, have in fact had the reverse effect of stimulating ethnic consciousness. Especially since the reunification of Germany, many states or societies have been forced to reconfigure according to ethnic group.

After World War II some predicted that Japanese American communities would eventually disappear. Japanese Americans had a remarkable record of acculturation and upward social and economic mobility, and they showed a significant tendency to leave geographical enclaves. Moreover, there has been a rapid increase in marriages outside their ethnic groups. Today, however, community ties and a sense of ethnic identity have been revived among Japanese Americans. Their reaffirmation seems closely related to the redress movement of the 1970s and 1980s, which won from the government an official apology and payments to individuals who had been evacuated and interned during World War II.

In this book on Japanese American ethnicity, I do not take the position that, as the immigration experience recedes in time, ethnic groups assimilate into American society and ethnic identity weakens—that is, the "assimilationist" perspective, which is one of the two poles of the debate on American ethnicity (e.g., Sandberg 1974; Hetcher 1978). I assert the reclamation of ethnicity among Japanese Americans, but I do not base my argument on the retention of cultural attributes or the persistence of structural plurality as many of the "pluralists," the other pole of the debate on American ethnicity, have done (e.g., Glazer and Moynihan 1963; Yancy et al. 1976). Neither do I propose the idea of "symbolic" ethnicity, the sense that ethnic identification is a matter of an individual's voluntary choice (e.g., Gans 1979; Alba 1990; Waters 1990), a position heavily based on studies of white ethnics. Instead, I emphasize historical experience to demonstrate that in the Japanese American case ethnicity has been transformed and reconstructed through reinterpretation of past experience in the American social context.

The Japanese American community in Seattle has been well studied and documented. *Social Solidarity among the Japanese in Seattle* by S. Frank Miyamoto (1939) is a brilliant pioneering work on the pre–World War II period. Miyamoto examined the various types of community organizations and their functions to compare the tight social network of the Japanese community with the segmented social life of the larger society. Referring to the orthodox sociological distinction made by Ferdinand Tonnies, Miyamoto argued that the organization of the Japanese community, though not kinship based as in traditional societies, is characterized by the gemeinschaft sentiment of collective responsibility, in contrast to the more gesellschaft-driven larger society. Miyamoto's introduction to the 1984 edition of his book adds a few new aspects to the picture. For example, he connects Japanese American social solidarity with the wartime evacuation. Surmising that the evacuation was ultimately attributable to prejudice, he describes a causal loop wherein prejudice in the mainstream society forced the segregation of the Japanese minority, which bred their particular behavior system, which in turn generated misperceptions by the majority and exacerbated its prejudice (1984: xxiii–xxiv).

Another important work on Japanese Americans in Seattle is *Transforming the Past* (1985), in which the anthropologist Sylvia Yanagisako analyzes the symbols employed for cognitive opposition between Japanese culture and American culture among Japanese Americans. She describes how Japanese Americans reinterpreted and transformed their kinship relations in their own way, constructing their own model from models of the "Japanese" past and the "American" present.

Other significant works (e.g., Leonetti and Newell-Morris 1982; Ito 1984 [1973]), along with a novel (Okada 1976), autobiographies (Sone 1953; Kodaira 1980; Uchida 1982), and a biography (Kikumura 1981), have further enriched the literature on the Japanese Americans in Seattle. In this book, however, my main concern involves the transformation of Japanese American ethnicity at what I perceive to have been two major turning points, internment during World War II and the redress movement of the 1970s and 1980s. To be sure, an abundant literature on internment already exists, but to my knowledge none of these works also examines the cultural and social impact of the redress movement on the ethnic identity of Japanese Americans. Here, I discuss these effects not only on the Nisei but on the Sansei as well, the generation not usually studied.

I owe a debt of gratitude to many people whose assistance made this work possible. I express my deepest appreciation to the Japanese Americans whom I interviewed. This book could not have existed without their frankness, openness, and willingness to share their personal, often painful, experiences with me. I have deep and fond memories of each of them. Having been trained not to express my opinions or feelings, I responded to their stories with my eyes. And there were many times when my sight became blurred with tears as soon as I touched the steering wheel of my car to drive away from the interview. I *must* leave their voices in this world: that feeling was my fundamental motivation to write this book. Now that I have accomplished my silent but firm promise to them, I feel relief more than anything else. Unfortunately, because I had to organize the transcripts to fit the framework of this book, I could use only a tiny portion of the entire body of interview material, but I hope I will have the chance to record the rest in the future. I also heartily appreciate the warm friendship, encouragement, and moral support of my friends in Japanese American communities, whether I interviewed them or not. With many I have developed a lifelong friendship.

My colleagues at the University of Washington continually gave me moral support and intellectual stimulation. I am most indebted to Charles F. Keyes, academically demanding yet personally warm, for his insightful comments on an earlier version of the manuscript, for pointing the way through the mazes of theory, and for unflagging encouragement. Steve Harrell was unfailingly supportive and offered helpful suggestions. I owe a great deal of gratitude to S. Frank Miyamoto, now professor emeritus of the University of Washington, who read my entire manuscript very closely and provided me with pages and pages of constructive criticism and thoughtful comments. I am most grateful to Donna Leonetti, Noel Chrisman, and Tetsuden Kashima for their suggestions and moral support. Roger Sanjek, the general editor of this series, commented insightfully and usefully on the manuscript. Rainer Baum of the Department of Sociology at the University of Pittsburgh and Yuji Ichioka of the Asian American Studies Center at UCLA also provided helpful criticism. I sincerely thank Eugene Kumekawa for his careful reading. Cherry Kinoshita was indispensable in gathering information on redress, especially after I left Seattle. Linda McPeters offered editorial comments on an earlier version.

At various stages, Dale Watanabe and Roger Martin helped with transcribing tapes, and Makoto Arakaki gave me invaluable assistance in typing the revisions and making final checks. My thanks go to them and to Dan Benson, who developed a special Macintosh Hypercard application for this project, and to Sally Yamasaki, who helped me collect community pictures.

I deeply appreciate my colleagues at the University of Tsukuba for their understanding and for allowing me to visit the United States frequently for follow-up research. I also thank my colleagues at the University of California, Santa Barbara, and UCLA, for friendship and encouragement.

This work was supported by a two-time grant from the Toyota Foundation and a grant from the University Research Fund at the University of Tsukuba. I also received a grant from the Minoru Masuda Memorial Foundation at an early stage of the research. I thank the Fulbright Commission, which enabled me to come to the United States and pursue my graduate work at the University of Washington.

Part of the discussion and data in this book appeared in my article "Children of Inmates: The Effects of the Redress Movement among Third-Generation Japanese Americans," *Qualitative Sociology* 14 (1991): 39–56. The Japanese edition of this book, *Nikkei Amerikajin no Ethnicity: Kyosei Syuyo to Hosyoundo niyoru Hensen* (The transformation of Japanese American ethnicity: The effects of internment and redress), was published by Tokyo University Press in 1994.

Finally, I express my deeply felt appreciation to my husband, Koichi Takezawa, who remained unstinting in his encouragment even after moving back to the other side of the Pacific Ocean.

To all again, I express my sincere thanks.

Yasuko I. Takezawa

Tsukuba, Japan

[1]

Introduction

On November 25, 1978, Thanksgiving weekend, more than two thousand Japanese Americans and their friends gathered at the Puyallup Fairgrounds near Seattle, Washington, to reenact and remember the evacuation and internment of Japanese Americans during World War II. For many of the participants this was the first time since internment that they confronted a part of their history they were too ashamed to remember. These fairgrounds were one of the temporary assembly centers where Japanese Americans on the West Coast were collected and detained for several months before being sent to hastily built internment camps, where many were imprisoned for the duration of the war. A poster distributed to announce the commemoration, printed over a replica of the government's evacuation notice of 1942, which was addressed "To all persons of JAPANESE ancestry," carried the added note:

> To all persons of JAPANESE ancestry and FRIENDS
> The Memory of One Hundred Twenty Thousand Three Hundred and
> Thirteen Issei, Nisei, Sansei and others of Japanese ancestry request
> the pleasure of your company for A DAY OF REMEMBRANCE

Kathy Hashimoto, a thirty-five-year-old Sansei (third-generation Japanese American), wondered in her childhood why her mother, Sumi, always declined to accompany her and her father to the

Puyallup Fair. Sumi was one of many Nisei (second generation) who were determined not to see the fairgrounds again. But on that "Day of Remembrance," thirty-six years later, Sumi, accompanied by her daughter, chose to return.

At the gathering site, the participants were given yellow name tags, and former evacuees wrote their identification numbers from World War II on them. Then about three hundred cars and buses, escorted by military trucks, drove in procession with their headlights on down the interstate highway to Puyallup Fairgrounds, site of Camp Harmony, where military trucks had brought the evacuees more than three decades before. After the ninety-minute procession, participants entered a symbolic "Camp Harmony" through barbed-wire fence.

The re-enactment of the evacuation induced vivid memories of that time in the participants. Barbara Yamaguchi debated whether she should attend the event or not, until her daughters offered her a ride and encouraged her to go. "After we parked the car, as we were walking towards the gathering place, I saw these cowboy trucks and things. I said, 'That's what we used to ride in, that's what you used to do this and that.' I started just talking about all the things, and reminded me, and tears started coming out." She continued: "It was, I think—, a sort of healing took place after that, because it reopened the old wounds. I think it helped. A lot of people said that was the first time they cried. When they were evacuated, nobody cried. But they were able to think back and cried over it."

For the Sansei present, the re-enactment provided their first opportunity to experience an evacuation, even an "ersatz" one, and to observe the exhibition with their parents and other Japanese Americans. David Hayama described his silent but momentous interaction with his father:

It was the first time that I had been involved in anything directly related to the redress movement. What impressed me the most was that my father was there and he is a very quiet man, a very solitary man. I went up and got a name tag for him, and it really meant something for me to acknowledge to him that I understand what you went through. And for them it must have been very, very difficult. I

[2]

guess that really did, when I think about it, bring to life that this was a tragic moment in the history of Japanese Americans, for my parents and grandparents.

This first Day of Remembrance thus broke the silence that had lasted for nearly forty years and was a turning point in the national movement to seek an apology and monetary redress from the United States government for the suffering inflicted on innocent people.

This book is about the life experiences and ethnic identity of second- and third-generation Japanese Americans in Seattle, Washington, particularly as they relate to wartime internment and the eventually successful redress movement. It is no longer a secret of American history that over 110,000 people of Japanese ancestry on the West Coast were forcibly removed from their homes and spent the wartime years behind barbed wire. In October 1990 the American government began distributing an apology letter and twenty thousand dollars in monetary redress to each surviving victim (or to the heirs of those who were still alive when redress legislation was enacted). But why was redress achieved so late, after nearly half a century? Perhaps more important, why was it achieved at all? How did these people, once labeled "quiet Americans" (Hosokawa 1969), whose cultural traditions are counter to the very idea of monetary redress come to stand up and make it happen? How did 0.3 percent of the population manage to appeal to the rest of America? What transformed this group from Japanese to Japanese Americans? This book attempts to solve these puzzles.

The Japanese American Community in Seattle

Redress was achieved through cooperation among a large number of organizations and individuals both within and outside the Japanese American communities across the country. The Seattle community was one of the earliest to promote the campaign enthusiastically. It is therefore a suitable context in which to examine the development of the movement and its effects on people. Seattle has one of highest concentrations of Japanese Americans on the West Coast, and the majority of these families lived in Seattle before the war and returned to the area after internment. Their historical experiences, perceptions, and lifestyles, as Silvia Yanagisako (1985: 2–9) points out, in many ways parallel those of Japanese Americans in other West Coast cities, and there is a significant body of literature on the Seattle community. Thus, it seems an ideal focus for a study of the transformation of Japanese American ethnicity over a long time span.

The Japanese American community in Seattle is one of the oldest in the United States. The very first Japanese immigrant on record came to Seattle in 1883 from Portland, Oregon, followed by a dozen or so others in the next few years. There were only about 200 Japanese immigrants in Seattle in 1887, but by 1900 the number had swelled to 3,900. The sudden expansion of the population can be attributed to the opening of a direct shipping line to Seattle by the Nippon Yusen Kaisha (Japan Mail Steamship Company, later known as the N.Y.K. Line) in 1896. In addition, the Oriental Trading Company, which served as a labor contractor for railroad companies, began operations in 1898 (*North American Times* 1928: 79; Ichioka 1988: 58).

Most of the early immigrants were young men from farms in southwestern Japan, who came to the United States to make money. They intended to stay only three to five years, long enough to save a thousand to three thousand dollars, before returning to Japan (Ito 1984: 41). During this "frontier period," as Miyamoto calls it, the sex ratio was highly unbalanced. Miyamoto reports 507 males per 100 females in 1900 (1984: 31), and the ratio in the state of Washington was even higher: 3,294 per 100. Under these conditions, prostitution thrived, though numerical estimates vary.[1] One of several Japanese books on the history of local immigrants gives a figure of more than one hundred at the "peak" in 1985 (Takeuchi 1929: 43).

During this period, nearly one-third of the Japanese in Seattle

---

[1] Yuji Ichioka states that 71 of the 250 to 260 Japanese residents were employed in prostitution houses, most of which were located on or near King Street in Japantown in 1881 (1988: 34–35). Kazuo Ito believes that about 200 prostitutes were operating at the turn of the century (1984 [1973]: 912–13).

[4]

A grocery store in Japantown in the 1920s. Photo courtesy of Sharon S. Aburano.

were domestic workers; the others operated small businesses, such as restaurants, hotels, grocery stores, and barber shops (Takeuchi 1929: 27).[2]

The composition of the Japanese community in Seattle changed after the Gentlemen's Agreement of 1907–1908 between President Theodore Roosevelt and the government of Japan. Under threat of immigration legislation aimed at the Japanese, Japan agreed to restrict emigration of laborers. Earlier in 1907, Roosevelt had banned entry of Japanese from the interim destinations of Canada, Mexico, and Hawaii. Suddenly the flow of male laborers all but stopped. At the same time more women came into the country as picture-brides. Men already in the United States chose wives from pictures sent from Japan. Families arranged the marriages, and the

[2] See also JACL 1971: 40; Suguro 1989: 1.

women were allowed to enter as the legal wives of previous immigrants. Thus began what Miyamoto calls the "settling period."

In 1924 Congress passed the Immigration Act (the Japanese Exclusion Act), which resulted in the complete cessation of Japanese immigration to the United States.[3] The Issei, the first generation, were ineligible for citizenship under the naturalization law, which was not repealed until 1952, and were prohibited from owning or leasing land. These discriminatory laws promoted a "sojourner" mentality, so that in 1925, 36.5 percent of the Japanese families in Seattle planned to return to Japan, and none ruled out the possibility (Miyamoto 1984: 31). The second generation, however, the Nisei, were American citizens by birth, and they had much less inclination to "return" to a country they had never seen. As their numbers grew, from 6 percent of the Japanese population in Seattle in 1910 to 61 percent in 1940, they began to play an important role in the community and to form their own social organizations (Miyamoto 1984: xii). The Seattle Progressive Citizens League was organized in 1928 and joined the newly formed Japanese American Citizens League (JACL) in 1930 (Hosokawa 1969: 197–98).[4]

The economy of the Japanese in Seattle before World War II was strongly oriented toward small entrepreneurship. Around 1935, 74 percent of the Japanese labor force in Seattle was in some way connected with the trades, hotels and grocery stores being the two major ones (Miyamoto 1984: 18). Japanese women were involved in small-scale enterprises, and were either clerical and sales personnel, proprietors and managers, or service workers outside private households (Glenn 1986: 78).[5]

[3] The effect of the immigration act in Seattle was reflected in the decrease of the Japanese population soon after its enactment. The *North American Times* recorded that the population, which had previously been rapidly increasing, dropped from 9,066 in 1920 to 7,783 in 1926 (1928: 79).

[4] Jerrold Takahashi says it was the more privileged and middle-class-oriented "Old Guard" who led the JACL. They pursued American democratic ideals and urged the Nisei to become loyal Americans, in contrast to, for example, the progressives, who were in a younger age cohort, working class, and less privileged (Takahashi 1980: 152–56). This differentiation did not arise in my interviews with Nisei subjects in Seattle, most of whom seem to have had less political consciousness in the prewar years.

[5] This pattern differs significantly from that in San Francisco, where over half of

Furuya Company picnic, 1930. Photo courtesy of Shosuke Sasaki.

The prewar Japanese community was clustered around *Nihon-machi* (Japantown), with its high concentration of Japanese residences, small businesses, community organizations, and social and cultural activities. Evacuation and internment depopulated Japantown, and the area never regained its prewar vitality. In 1945 when the evacuees started to return to the West Coast, only 60 to 70 percent of what Donna Leonetti calls the nuclear population of the prewar residents returned to the enclave (Leonetti 1976). By that time Japantown was occupied by other minorities, and the Japanese

---

the Japanese women in the labor force were engaged in domestic service (Glenn 1986: 78).

consequently dispersed to other areas. There was a substantial Japanese influx from other parts of the country, such as from Hawaii and California, and by 1950 Japanese Americans residing in the area numbered 6,837 persons, equivalent to the prewar population (Leonetti and Newell-Morris 1982: 23).

As discrimination decreased Japanese Americans gradually became successful and integrated into the wider society. Their occupational patterns changed to reflect this success. In the late 1930s, 46 percent of the income earners in the Japanese population in Seattle worked in independent small businesses, and another 25 percent—including stenographers, clerks, and salesmen—were occupied in support services for those entrepreneurs. By 1970, the white-collar employment of Japanese American males reached 52 percent, compared with 41 percent for white males (Miyamoto 1984: 70; Leonetti and Newell-Morris 1982: 24). Likewise, the percentage of Japanese women in Seattle performing professional and technical work in 1970 was 14.9 percent, whereas in 1940 only 3.8 percent of the Issei women and 5.4 percent of the Nisei women in Seattle had professional or semiprofessional occupations (Glenn 1986: 78, 93). Also in this period, interracial marriage drastically increased. Donna Leonetti and Laura Newell-Morris (1982) report that the Japanese outmarriage rate in Seattle in 1970 was over 50 percent, in sharp contrast to less than 1 percent during the period between 1930 and 1942.[6]

According to the 1990 U.S. Census, the Japanese constituted the second largest Asian group in Washington state (34,366), following the Filipinos (43,799), who in 1980 had been the second largest next to the Japanese. The remaining Asian population included the Chinese (33,962), the Korean (29,697), and the Vietnamese (18,696). In Seattle, however, the Japanese rank third, following the Chinese and the Filipinos, whereas until 1980 the Japanese formed the largest Asian group in the city (see Table 1). Unlike the rapid population growth among other Asian groups in Seattle, the Japanese population has increased slowly in the postwar period. In fact, the

---

[6] Kitano et al. (1984: 180) says the outmarriage rate was as high as 63.1 percent in Los Angeles County in 1977. Lee and Yamanaka, using the 1980 U.S. Census, report a significantly lower figure (34.2 percent) (1990: 291).

Table 1. Asian population trends in Seattle

	1900	1910	1920	1930	1940	1950	1960	1970	1980	1990
Japanese	2,990	6,127	7,874	8,448	6,975	5,778	9,351	10,441	9,762	9,847
Chinese	438	924	1,351	1,347	1,781	2,650	4,076	6,230	9,916	15,084
Filipino			458	1,614	1,392	2,357	3,755	5,830	9,510	14,689
Korean								475	2,199	3,909
Vietnamese									2,601	5,309

Source: US Bureau of the Census.

number of Japanese in Seattle decreased between 1970 and 1980, while the number in surrounding King County increased (from 13,492 in 1970 to 16,391 in 1980). These data suggest that many Japanese Americans moved to the suburbs as their employment opportunities improved and housing discrimination declined.

According to the 1980 U.S. Census, 89.7 percent of the Japanese population of Washington had completed high school, in comparison to 79.0 percent of the Chinese, 71.0 percent of the Filipinos, 87.8 percent of the Koreans, and 79.0 percent of the total population.[7]

The Japanese, according to the 1990 census, accounted for 1.9 percent of Seattle's total population, and 1.4 percent of King County's; Asians and Pacific Islanders as a whole constituted 11.8 percent of Seattle's population and 7.9 percent of King County's. Nationwide, Asians are the fastest growing group with a 160 percent increase during the last decade (see Table 2). At the state level their proportion doubled (*Seattle Times*, March 7, 1991). The Japanese show the slowest growth among Asian groups.

In King County, the Japanese population has traditionally been concentrated in southeastern Seattle, particularly around Beacon Hill, but many of the third generation (Sansei) are moving out to growing suburban areas, even if they continue to work in Seattle. Only around Main Street South and Sixth Avenue South, the prewar heart of Japantown, is there still some atmosphere of a Japanese

[7] The socioeconomic and educational data from the 1990 census are not yet available.

Table 2. Asian population trends in the United States

	1900	1910	1920	1930	1940
Japanese	85,716	152,745	220,596	278,743	285,115
Chinese	118,746	94,414	85,202	102,159	106,334
Filipino	NA	2,767	26,634	108,424	98,535
Korean	NA	5,008	6,181	8,332	8,568
Asian Indian	NA	2,546	2,495	3,130	2,405
Vietnamese	NA	NA	NA	NA	NA

	1950	1960	1970	1980	1990
Japanese	326,379	464,332	591,290	716,331	847,562
Chinese	150,005	237,292	436,062	812,178	1,645,472
Filipino	122,707	176,310	343,060	781,894	1,406,770
Korean	7,030	NA	69,150	354,593	798,849
Asian Indian	NA	NA	NA	361,531	815,447
Vietnamese	NA	NA	NA	245,025	614,547

Source: US Bureau of the Census.

neighborhood, with Japanese restaurants, small businesses, the Nippon-kan Theater, the Seattle chapter of the JACL. Churches, the Nisei Veterans Hall, the Keiro Nursing Home, the *Nikkeijin-kai* (Japanese Community Service), various *kenjin-kai* (prefectural associations), and other community institutions and organizations are dispersed from Beacon Hill through the area known as the International District (see Map 1).

People in the Japanese American community often boast of the harmonious relationship among Asian Americans in the area. As evidence they mention the International District, unique in the nation, in which many different Asian groups are blended. The district seems to have developed from the proximity of Chinatown (west of the district) and Japantown (within the district) since the late nineteenth century. In the early 1900s Filipinos began settling in the south, adding to the mix. The district has been maintained by the numerical balance of these groups in recent decades. Not until around 1970, however, did the International District become the focus of Asian life in the city, as it was revitalized (Santos 1983:

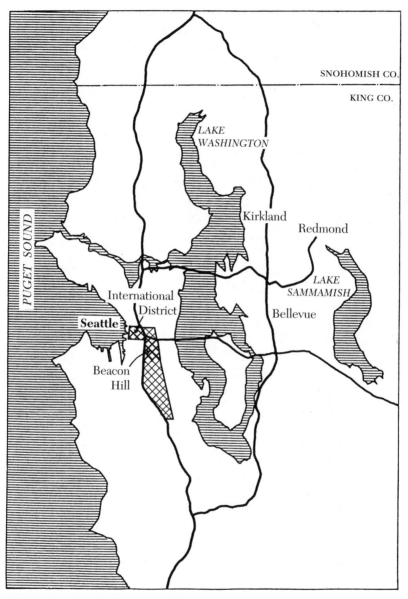

Map 1. Seattle, Washington, and environs

3–4). Today, the district serves the Japanese Americans only as a symbolic community, for very few reside or work there. Nonetheless, it stands for the integrated interethnic relationships among different Asian groups in Seattle and affects the perceptions of Japanese Americans about other Asian Americans.

Despite residential dispersal and the lack of an ethnic enclave, Japanese Americans in Seattle maintain a tight-knit network. Nisei and Sansei from other parts of the nation often mention how fast and thoroughly gossip spreads in the community. It seems true when people say, "Everybody knows each other," especially among those who were locally born and raised.

Political activists in the community say that Seattle is renowned as a "renegade" among Japanese American communities in the nation. The Seattle chapter of the JACL, certainly, has often taken the leadership in controversial issues and in social and political movements. It is this political soil that yielded early interest in and zeal for the redress movement.

The Reconstruction of Ethnic Identity

To understand the transformation of ethnicity among Japanese Americans and to analyze its complexity we must adapt and, if necessary, revise the existing theoretical approaches to fit the case. Let me first briefly discuss some relevant theoretical concepts surrounding ethnicity.

At one time, there was wide agreement among scholars that the members of an ethnic group share common cultural traits, such as language and religion, and physical characteristics based on the common blood line or "race," which are distinctive enough to separate them from others. The characteristics that identify an ethnic group were assumed to be objectively observable, and the persistence of such a group in time was taken for granted. This objective approach is represented by Raoul Naroll (1964), who proposed the concept of a "culture-bearing unit." Although this static perspective has lost favor among students of ethnicity, many anthropologists are often still bound by the basic idea.

[12]

Fredrik Barth's influential work, *Ethnic Groups and Boundaries* (1969), challenged the exclusive use of objective criteria to define ethnicity. Instead, he emphasized subjective ascription and identification by members themselves in defining ethnic boundaries. He shed light on the dynamic and flexible nature of ethnic groups. Barth's notion of ethnicity provides a basis for the argument in this book, since it focuses on how Japanese Americans interpret the meaning of being Japanese Americans, how they draw the boundary between themselves and others through interaction with other groups in the dynamic race and ethnic relations of American society.

Barth's view of ethnic groups has shifted the focus of research toward the source of individuals' subjective identification with their ethnic group—whether from primordial ties or from political and economic (i.e., instrumental) interests that are disguised within cultural symbols. Although in this book, I do not exclude the instrumental aspect of ethnicity from analysis—in fact, it is to some extent pertinent to understanding pan–Asian American identity—primordial ties are more important to Japanese American ethnicity, especially in its earlier stage.

Clifford Geertz has defined a primordial attachment as "one that stems from the 'givens'—or, more precisely, as culture is inevitably involved in such matters, the assumed 'givens'—of social existence" (1963: 259). Among the "given" attributes that form the force of primordial attachment are contiguity and kin connection, blood, language, religion, and custom—all of which, Geertz maintains, are ascribed at birth. Similarly, Harold Isaacs sees primordial affinities as the foundation of what he calls "basic group identity," that is, "the ready-made set of endowments and identifications which every individual shares with others from the moment of birth by the chance of the family into which he is born at that given time in that given place" (1975: 38). According to Isaacs, this type of identity, powerful enough to serve as a foundation of nationhood, should be detached from the many secondary identities that people acquire. An extreme view that is in line with but not the same as primordialism is the sociobiological approach (e.g., Freedman 1979; van den Berghe 1981). Pierre van den Berghe reduces ethnic and racial identification to "extensions of kinship sentiments" (1981: 80). Thus, the key point of the primordialist approach lies in its emphasis on the affective potency of primordial attachments over rational or instrumental forces in the formation and maintenance of ethnic groups, and on the "givens" ascribed by birth into a particular ethnic community.

Primordial attachment operates most powerfully when a culturally homogeneous group becomes integrated into a new political and social unity or first encounters another ethnic group. The primordial sentiment is a basic force that emotionally binds members of an ethnic group within their native social context. As interactions with other people from different cultural backgrounds increase, the members of the ethnic group develop an intense consciousness of sharing certain cultural and physical features that they associate with being born into the group. The Issei, though they possessed considerable regional variations of language or dialect, food, and custom, *became* an ethnic group in the United States, when they were forced to recognize their "given" cultural backgrounds as relatively similar to each other and significantly different from those of the new society they had entered.

Although primordial attachment constitutes, in my view, *one* of the most fundamental of the forces that drive people to form or maintain an ethnic group, it does not explain well how ethnicity persists and is maintained as social conditions change. Increased interaction with other ethnic groups as time passes naturally leads to cultural fusion and acculturation, which tend to weaken, cultural homogeneity, not strengthen it. Since the primordial sentiment is based on givens such as contiguity and kin connection, language, and practices, it would seem that as the givens change, as descendants are further removed from those forebears who developed the primordial sentiment in the new encounter, ethnicity would be lost. Indeed, some U.S. sociologists posit this "straight-line" theory of ethnic relations (Sandberg 1974), that is, that ethnic groups are eventually absorbed into the larger society by means of acculturation.

Study of empirical situations, however, tells us that ethnicity does not necessarily wane proportionately with acculturation. Ethnicity in the United States and throughout the world persists not merely as residues of culturally homogeneous groups but because it functions and has meaning in the present social context.

I place great importance on historical experience, because what separates Japanese Americans from Japanese is, after all, their ethnic experience in American society. Some students of ethnicity see the historical continuity of an ethnic group—its sense of shared history and the symbolic interpretations of that history—as an important factor in maintaining identity. George De Vos contends that "ethnicity . . . is in its narrowest sense a feeling of continuity with the past, a feeling that is maintained as an essential part of one's self-definition" (1975: 17). De Vos, who employs a psychological perspective, underscores the subjective sense of belonging, which must be examined by means of an emic, not simply a behaviorist, approach. "Ethnicity," he asserts, "is determined by what a person feels about himself, not how he is observed to behave." The individual sense of survival, he says, is the essence of ethnicity at the deepest psychological level. In this book, De Vos's point is relevant, for I focus on Japanese Americans' own feelings and perceptions.

Charles F. Keyes, elaborating on De Vos's perspective, suggests that the experiential foundation for ethnic identity is provided by knowledge that a people's ancestors experienced intense suffering (1981: 9–10). This insight helps us to understand why and how the experience of internment forms one basis of Japanese Americans' ethnic identity. When such an experience lasts a long time without being repudiated or without achieving "triumph," however, ethnicity often becomes stigmatized. In this respect, De Vos and Lola Romanucci-Ross note (1975: 365), collective ritual can play a significant role in restoring ethnic pride, permitting members of an ethnic group to celebrate their history.

S. N. Eisenstadt discusses how intellectuals in modern societies reconstruct traditions to formulate collective identity and to integrate emerging groups within a common institutional framework. He argues that certain traditional symbols are transposed to create new central symbols and that the members of the group or society "tend to be predisposed to making a positive connection between their personal identity and the symbols of the new political, social,

[15]

and cultural order" and to accept these symbols "as the major collective referents of their personal identity" (1973: 23). In the case of the Japanese Americans, the redress movement employed certain symbols, derived from past experience, to link personal identity to collective identity.

When ethnicity is transformed through internal evolution, rather than by external influence, the transformation takes place neither suddenly nor without prior foundation. I believe that in this kind of circumstance, the transformation of ethnicity often involves ambivalence about ethnic identity, which is related to the distinction drawn by George Devereux (1975) between ethnic personality and ethnic identity, and to the similar distinction made by Howard F. Stein and Robert Hill (1977) between behavioral and ideological ethnicity. What Devereux calls ethnic identity and Stein and Hill call ideological ethnicity is self-conscious, and what Devereux calls ethnic personality and Stein and Hill call behavioral ethnicity is prior-unselfconscious. Although this dichotomy tends to suppress the complexity of actual self-identifications, the distinction is nevertheless important, especially when ethnicity is stigmatized. In such a case, members of a stigmatized ethnic group try to suppress their ethnic identity and, at the conscious level, choose to identify with an ideologically preferable group in the society, especially if such "passing" is possible. Under such conditions, the ideological aspect of ethnicity determines some aspects of behavioral ethnicity. At the same time, even when ethnicity is stigmatized, some deep-seated, authentic ethnic behaviors and norms are transmitted, without conscious socialization, to descending generations. Transmission is more unconscious when ethnicity is suppressed, and ethnic personality (or behavioral ethnicity) becomes the foundation of ethnic identity (or ideological ethnicity). When the stigma is repudiated and a transformation of ethnicity occurs, this unconscious or subconscious side of ethnic identity, based on common experiences and practices, comes prominently into play. In such cases, certain cultural markers, which had previously been suppressed and had existed only at the subconscious level, suddenly become expressions of positive ideological ethnicity.

We must bear in mind the multidimensionality of ethnic identity.

[16]

The sense of being Asian American, for example, exists among many Sansei, but not all. A number of scholars discuss shifts of ethnic identity according to social context (e.g., Nagata 1974; Patterson 1977; Despres 1975; Keyes 1976). Keyes warns us that "if whatever cultural attributes are associated with particular ethnic groups are taken to be entirely situational, then the identification of a group as being an ethnic group is entirely arbitrary and without analytical value" (1976: 203). Nevertheless, as Orlando Patterson and Leo Despres maintain, members of ethnic groups select or shift their ethnic identity in a given situation to further their own social and economic interests. Judith Nagata, defining the ethnic group as a special kind of reference group, believes that "some individuals may . . . oscillate rather freely from one ethnic reference group to another, without, however, becoming involved in role conflict or marginality" (1974: 333). A close review of her ethnography reveals that the switches take place according to the negative or positive valuation attached to certain ethnic stereotypes or the competition for scarce resources. The instrumentalists, thus, agree that individuals tend to select one ethnic identity over another, reducing or extending their distance from their ethnic group, according to the direct benefits they hope to derive.

The shift of ethnic identity is not necessarily always governed by instrumental forces; nor is it entirely arbitrary. Some have pointed out different "levels" of ethnic identification among members of a society (Leach 1954; Moerman 1965). Ivan Light speaks of "ethnic scope" and maintains that "the nested segments that make up ethnic consciousness need not exclude one another and typically do not" (1981: 71). He proposes four different levels of ethnic scope, namely, continental, national, regional, and local. According to Light, one can identify oneself as, for example, Asian, Chinese, Cantonese, or from a specific place in Canton. Ethnic scope gives a broader and more liberal view of ethnicity than conventional notions of the ethnic group. Light goes so far as to extend scope to the level of worldwide, and he gives supranational (European) consciousness as an example of "a more inclusive level of ethnic awareness in Western Europe" (1981: 72).

Although I do not necessarily agree with all the uses to which the

[17]

notion of ethnic scope has been put, it helps to explicate the multi-dimensional inclusiveness of ethnic identity. It explains how members of an ethnic group can switch their ethnic allegiance or identity depending on the situation but not necessarily out of regard for direct or immediate self-interest. The identity shift does not operate arbitrarily or at random, however. It requires two conditions: the cognitive contrast between ethnic groups as social organizations must be relevant, and a sense of shared experiences and social and cultural characteristics must operate.

I agree with Sandra Wallman that "ethnicity is the recognition of significant differences between 'them' and 'us'." It is "the process by which 'their' difference is used to enhance the sense of 'us' for purposes of organization or identification" (1979: 3). Assuming that fixed cognitive images of these inclusive groups exist at different levels, I believe that individuals select a level of ethnic scope (in Light's term) and shift their identity so as to fit themselves to a given situation. This kind of identity shift may not take place as easily as membership changes in some other types of social organizations or groups, however. Unlike associations that come into existence for specific purposes and dissolve after achieving them, people perceive ethnic groups as rooted in history and, hence, not susceptible to arbitrary or instant changes.

Members of ethnic groups find a psychological niche by belonging to the group. Therefore, when individuals are not accepted by certain ethnic groups and can find no other group to identify with, identity becomes problematic and creates a dilemma. In such cases, it may be necessary to reinterpret the situation and find allegiance in a larger segment of the hierarchy. Those who do so need no longer concern themselves with cultural definition of the kind required for membership in a narrower segment. I believe, in fact, that this factor is important in the emergence of pan-Asian identity among the Sansei.

In addition to the theories of ethnicity developed by cultural anthropology, there are sociological views of ethnicity in American society to consider. Here I want to mention briefly where this book stands in respect to these.

There is a classic debate between those who contend that ethnicity in American society is on the wane because of increasing acculturation and assimilation (e.g., Warner and Srole 1945; Park 1950; Sandberg 1974; Hetcher 1978) and those who maintain that ethnicity has persisted or has been revived (e.g., Glazer and Moynihan 1963; Novak 1972; Stein and Hill 1977). The idea of ethnic revival was popular in the 1970s; it has since been criticized for overestimating the degree of cultural and structural differentiation among ethnic groups (e.g., Steinberg 1981; Yinger 1985; Alba 1990). Assimilationists, however, tend to reduce the concept of ethnicity to Raoul Naroll's meaning, limiting it to shared cultural features different from those of the larger society. We must not ignore other elements, most important, the sense of identity among members of an ethnic group. Ethnicity persists in the United States and in many other places in the world not merely as a residue of original cultural homogeneity but because of its active functioning. Members of ethnic groups respond to various external factors, especially to any threat to the status of the group. Members strengthen their sense of group identity by reconstructing and reinterpreting the past and their tradition to find meanings relevant to the present.

The debate between acculturation and persistence of ethnicity has been gradually reassessed and modified. One contemporary perspective stresses the "symbolic" nature of ethnicity (e.g., Gans 1979; Alba 1990; Waters 1990). These studies, however, draw their theoretical orientation mostly from white American ethnic experience. Other scholars (e.g., Reitz 1980; Fugita and O'Brien 1991) illustrate the persistence of ethnic cohesiveness in spite of progressive structural assimilation. As Milton Gordon's classification exemplifies, assimilation is multidimensional. In this study I describe how ethnic identity resurfaces while Americanization in cultural, behavioral, and identificational terms progresses.

Ethnicity is expressed differently over time. It is continually being constructed and reconstructed by interpretation of the past as related to the present. Japanese Americans, the subjects of this book, have had experiences that make them a uniquely suitable group to examine this thesis.

The transformation of ethnicity among Japanese Americans is both a historical and a generational phenomenon. Japanese Ameri-

[19]

cans have experienced drastic changes in their lives. The Nisei in particular began life in a homogeneous ethnic enclave, endured wartime internment, achieved much after the war, and finally won redress for unjust imprisonment. Also of great interest is the distinct generational character of Japanese American ethnicity. Japanese Americans are one of only a few ethnic groups in the United States to have developed special terminology to denote their distance from the Issei, or first generation, the immigrants.[8] Their children are known as the Nisei, sometimes called the Jun-Nisei (literally, genuine Nisei) to distinguish them from the Kibei (literally, returnees), also, occasionally called Kibei-Nisei, those born to Issei but sent to Japan as children to be raised and educated there. Because of this rearing, the Kibei, as Japanese Americans acknowledge, tend to bear much the same cultural identification as the Issei and form their own special subset. The Sansei, Yonsei, and Gosei form the third, fourth, and fifth generations. Terminology can be further refined if both parents are not from the same generation. An individual may say, for example, "I am actually Nisei-han" (literally, two and a half generations) or "I am San-han" (three and a half). Since a primary function of the terminology is to indicate experience of a specific time span, generational identification is more strongly tied to age-sets than to actual generational lines.[9]

This distinctive form of self-categorization, originating from historical conditions of immigration, helps to magnify and delineate the shifts in ethnicity from one generation to another. Ethnic identity, resulting from cultural reinterpretation of historical experience, differs between generations and is expressed differently. Although this book, with its focus on internment and redress, necessarily includes issues of racial prejudice, discrimination, and exclusion, Japanese Americans here are regarded as an ethnic group, not simply a minority. Some social scientists apply the term

---

[8] Korean Americans also use generational terminology, but because the overwhelming majority are more recent immigrants, their generational categorization is not as developed as that of the Japanese Americans.

[9] See Lyman 1972 and Miyamoto 1986–87, for the discussions of generational character, and Maykovich 1972; Kendis 1979; Hosokawa 1978; Gehri 1973; and Israely 1976; for Sansei ethnic identity.

ethnic group only to minorities, but I believe the two terms embrace different aspects of social and cultural relationships. The term *minority* is attentive to power relations in a society, whereas *ethnic group* identifies cultural distinctions in relation to context, as observed from outside the group and as perceived from within it. As Joan Vincent points out (1974: 377), an ethnic group is mutable and "constantly subject to redefinition."

Thus, by examining the unique history and generational differences of Japanese Americans, I hope to shed light on the mutable and dynamic nature of ethnicity and to discover how this group has reinterpreted its history to make sense of the present world and in the process reconstructed and transformed its ethnicity.

Fieldwork and Methodology

My research is based on several different forms of evidence. The most important were participant observation and personal interviews with fifty-five Japanese Americans. I have also relied on the literature, documentary films, and published and unpublished documents related to the redress movement, including the testimony of more than a hundred Japanese Americans at the hearings conducted in Seattle by the Commission on Wartime Relocation and Internment of Civilians in 1981.

I lived in Seattle from 1982 to 1990. Beginning in my second year of residence, I began to engage in participant observation in the Japanese American community as an anthropologist. This book is based on my fieldwork during my residence in Seattle and a few short-term, follow-up studies in the following years. It was only after I saw the play *Breaking the Silence* early in 1986 that I decided to study the effects of the redress movement.

During my years of fieldwork, the questions I constantly encountered were how I came to have an interest in Japanese Americans, and why I focused on redress. Contrary to the assumption of many Americans, there is little social interaction between Japanese nationals from Japan—including businessmen, students, and new immigrants —and Japanese Americans who have been in this country over three generations. It seemed indeed unusual to them for a young woman from Japan to walk into the Japanese American community without knowing anyone and to stay for an extended period, attending community events and meetings and conducting interviews regarding camp and redress experiences. Nor were these experiences familiar to me or to my relatives.

When I first landed in Seattle, on a typical rainy day in the fall of 1982, I was full of ambition and anxiety about starting graduate work in anthropology in the United States. The proposal I had submitted to the educational institution with which I was about to be affiliated on a Fulbright scholarship stated that I would study "acculturation" among third-generation Japanese Americans. I was interested in doing a comparative study of Japanese and American culture.

Because my fieldwork took place in the same community where I resided throughout my graduate training, I was able to continue it for much longer than the limited session typical in anthropology. This continuity enabled me to establish strong rapport with a wide range of community residents and gave me time to understand the significance of the camp experience and the redress movement to them. This fieldwork also disabused me of my misperception that Japanese Americans lay somewhere on a cultural continuum between the two poles of Japanese and Americans.

My acceptance into the Japanese American society and the larger American society also reassured me regarding my selection of the topic of research. As the years passed and as many people began to remark how "Americanized" I had become, the cultural differences between me and the Japanese Americans diminished. And yet, one decisive difference remained: my family and I lack the historical experience of internment.

My outsider status, I believe, often helped me to obtain detailed and frank answers from Japanese Americans in interviews. They felt less inhibited about telling me personal stories that they said they had not shared with their own children or friends in the community, and they tended to express their views on rather sensitive ethnic and racial issues more openly. It seems to me now that had I been from a completely different cultural background, I might have learned more about precisely how they interpreted traditional Japanese phrases and concepts, such as *shikata ga nai* (it can't be helped; there is no way out), which they considered relevant to their cooperation with the evacuation order.

My interview subjects were selected through personal references from Japanese Americans and others in the local area during my residence in Seattle and also during follow-up studies in the city. Of the fifty-five interviewees, the primary group consisted of sixteen Nisei and sixteen Sansei, balanced in sex. The Nisei subjects had been raised in the greater Seattle area and had spent most of their lives there. All had been sent to a camp during the war and were in their sixties or seventies at the time of the interviews. The Sansei subjects, too, were raised in greater Seattle and had been residents for most of their lives. Their ages ranged from the late twenties to the early forties, and none were elligible for redress payments. I excluded the few Sansei who were born in the camps or spent their early childhood there because their statistical representation in this generation is too small to register in my relatively limited group of interview subjects.

Although the selection of the subjects was not random, a great effort was made to include a range of people: those who were active in the community, those who were not active but maintained strong ethnic ties, and those who had little contact with the community or whom others viewed as more "assimilated." I also considered the distribution by current residence and by area of upbringing in my selection.[10]

[10] Nine of the Nisei in the primary group were still married to their first spouse; five were widowed; two were divorced. Eight of the Sansei were unmarried; seven were married; and one was divorced. All but one of the Nisei had children, and five of the Sansei were parents. Most of the Nisei had retired. Their former occupations varied from housekeeper, sales clerk, and secretary to engineer, general office worker, company employee, and small business owner. Sansei occupations were housekeeper, company employee, government employee, teacher, artist, general office worker, and engineer. All primary subjects were high school graduates, and ten of the Nisei and thirteen of the Sansei had completed a four-year university degree. Four of the Sansei also had postgraduate degrees. Two of the people in the primary group were married to each other and there were four parent-child pairs. There was also one married couple in the secondary group of interviewees and one parent of a subject in the primary group. All the primary subjects have been given

In addition to this primary group of thirty-two subjects, I inter-viewed twenty-three other Japanese Americans from various back-grounds. Through these additional interviews, with Nisei and San-sei who grew up in rural areas, with Kibei, with Nisei veterans, and with several national leaders of the redress movement from outside Washington state, I gained a wider perspective on the community as a whole. This firsthand information was enriched by interviews for other projects and by informal conversation with hundreds of Japanese Americans over my eight years' residence in Seattle.

My nonrandom selection of lifelong Seattle residents, to the ex-clusion, for instance, of those who did not return to the West Coast after internment, may generate some bias in my sample. Similarly, exclusion of the Kibei from the primary group reduces the ability of my sample to represent all second-generation Japanese Americans. Nevertheless, I believe that this bias does not undermine my con-clusions about the evolution of the ethnicity among Japanese Ameri-cans.

I conducted ethnographic interviews, asking open-ended ques-tions following the individual's life course (Sanjek 1990). This meth-od is particularly useful for studying the transformation of ethnicity since it permits discovery of how critical incidents affected the sub-jects' self-identity and of how perceptions of other ethnic groups changed through time. The Nisei were asked questions about their childhood lives and experiences, their evacuation and internment, their postwar lives and experiences, their responses to the redress movement, and their current ethnic experiences and perceptions of other ethnic groups. The Sansei were asked about their childhood and adolescent lives and experiences, their discovery of the intern-ment history, their responses to the redress movement, and their current ethnic experiences and perceptions of other ethnic groups. In both cases I made a special effort to elicit details of their environ-ment, discrimination experience, association and contact with other ethnic groups, and ethnic identity.

The interviews ranged from one two-hour session to four visits

pseudonyms, and each parent-child and married pair shares the same pseud-onymous last name.

totaling eight to nine hours, but most took place in two sessions totaling four to five hours. All the interviews, except those with Kibei and one with a Nisei who switched between English and Japanese, were conducted in English, the subjects' primary language. I took minimal notes, preferring to use a tape recorder in order to provide a more natural atmosphere and to allow me to maintain eye contact. Although tape transcription is very time consuming and costly, as Roger Sanjek notes (1990: 114–15), it has the advantage of providing "instant texts" and accurate accounts. It also gives vivid immediacy to the subjects' perceptions and feelings.

After interviews with each subject were completed, the name was immediately changed to a pseudonym. The transcribed texts from the interviews totaled over a thousand single-spaced pages. The texts of interviews were first divided according to generation, and then transferred to the Macintosh Hypercard program, which in turn classified the texts into about forty categories, according to generation. At the same time, critical incidents applicable to Japanese Americans as a group as well as to individuals were examined and attention given to how those incidents shaped my subjects' perceptions. I also investigated whether perceptions of these incidents differed within the group and, if so, how.

The open-ended question format, in which subjects are encouraged to express and discuss their feelings, experiences, and perceptions freely, does not provide the numerical data to be obtained from the survey method, in which subjects choose answers on a questionnaire constructed by a researcher beforehand. Rather than quantify data that may or may not be clearcut, I reorganized and classified the data into dominant perceptions and experiences, deviations from the main components, and unique perspectives, in order to point out similarities and diversities among different subjects. This is why I used such expressions as "the majority of," "some Nisei," or "a small number of" in my ethnographic text. I present actual quotations from the personal interviews, but for the interpretation and judgment of how representative any story is, I relied on my participant observation and other informal interviews in my fieldwork. The investigation of congruity between the interviewees' responses and their socioeconomic and educational background is beyond the scope of this study, for such a correlational study requires a survey method. Moreover, in this case, one variable (for example, an opinion, a feeling, a perspective on one's life) is difficult to measure as opposed to the other variable (for example, educational background, socioeconomic background). To do so would require a large-scale study that employs both qualitative and quantitative methods, which this book is not intended for.

In comparison to typical survey research studies, a study of this kind is based on a relatively small number of interviews. Quantitative studies in the field of ethnicity are undoubtedly valuable, but some aspects can be satisfactorily examined only by a qualitative approach. Certainly, ethnic identity cannot be understood without an emic perspective. Therefore, questions that will bring out ethnography are more suitable than those designed to test a specific hypothesis. Moreover, open-ended questions permit the anthropologist to observe the subject not just as an isolated individual but as linked to family, friends, and other people in the community. Since I am concerned with collective memory as well as individual memories of the past and with the sense of shared experience, this research method was effective. Furthermore, in my opinion, ethnic identity is a matter not of quantity but of quality, especially since feelings that shape ethnic identity, such as pain, shame, pride, and joy, are not measurable in figures. In addition, it is possible to learn how and why ethnicity is transformed only through qualitative research. In these respects, I hope to cast light on aspects of ethnicity that have been neglected in other studies of Japanese Americans.

The next chapter describes the chronological development of the redress movement in Seattle as part of the national campaign. Chapters 3, 4, and 5 have an ethnographic emphasis. Chapter 3 investigates the Nisei experiences of ethnic identity, including racial discrimination and other incidents and feelings, from their childhood in the prewar era up to the beginning of the redress movement. Chapter 4 turns to the next generation, the Sansei, to explore their experiences and feelings related to ethnic identity from childhood in the postwar era through the rise of Asian American movement. Chapter 5 describes how the dialogue on internment started between Nisei parents and Sansei children, both generations' reactions to redress events, and the effects of the redress movement on their ethnic identity. The concluding chapter analyzes the transformation of ethnicity among Japanese Americans over time and compares and contrasts the two generations with regard to their experiences and how they reinterpreted them and expressed the reinterpretation through the redress campaign. The chapter concludes with a discussion of the relationship between the reaffirmation of ethnicity and Americanization among Japanese Americans.

[2]

The Redress Movement
in Seattle

On October 9, 1990, the oldest living survivor of internment, Mamoru Eto, 107 years old, received a letter of apology and a check for twenty thousand dollars from the U.S. attorney general who knelt beside his wheelchair. Eto was the first of approximately eighty thousand Japanese American victims of evacuation and internment to receive redress after the law authorizing it was enacted on August 10, 1988. The letter of apology, signed by President George Bush, acknowledged, "A monetary sum and words alone cannot restore lost years or erase painful memories. . . . But we can take a clear stand for justice and recognize that serious injustices were done to Japanese Americans during World War II."

The story begins with Japan's attack on Pearl Harbor and the subsequent outbreak of war. Within several hours, the Federal Bureau of Investigation began arresting persons of Japanese ancestry, mostly Issei community leaders whose names were on the "dangerous enemy aliens list," or the custodial detention list, different government agencies had developed from as early as the first half of 1930s. By that evening, agents, without warrants, had searched homes and arrested 736 Japanese on the mainland.[1] The number

[1] In January 1942 General John L. DeWitt sought an opinion on the legality of these searches. Assistant Attorney General James Rowe, Jr., replied in a memorandum, "In an emergency where the time is insufficient in which to procure a warrant, such premises may be searched without a warrant" (Daniels 1988: 206).

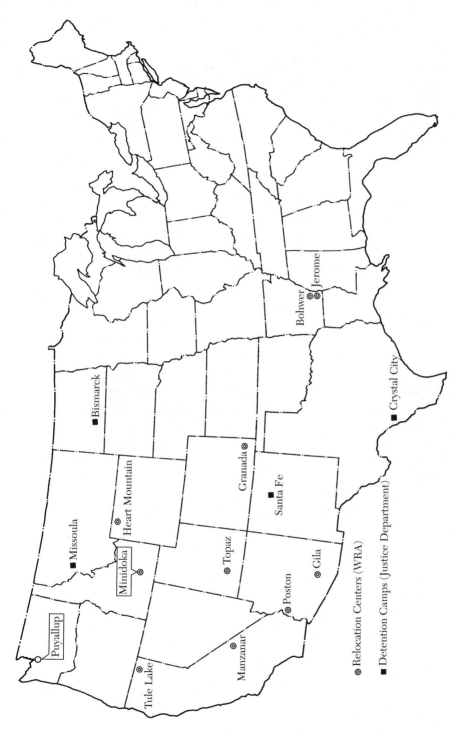

Map 2. Relocation and detention camps, World War II

increased to 2,192 by February 16, 1942. These people, mostly Issei men, were detained at detention camps operated by the Justice Department (Kashima 1984: 393).[2] On February 19, 1942, President Franklin D. Roosevelt issued Executive Order 9066, authorizing the evacuation of people from designated areas on the West Coast. Subsequently, nearly all people of Japanese ancestry (127,000 were in the continental United States in 1941, and over 112,000 resided in the three Pacific Coast states of Oregon, Washington, and California [Weglyn 1976: 36]) were uprooted from their homes and imprisoned for up to three and half years behind barbed wire. More than two thirds of them were American-born citizens, and the rest were immigrants who had been classified as "aliens ineligible for citizenship" under Asian exclusion laws. They were given so little warning before evacuation that they either felt compelled to sell their businesses, furniture, and other belongings for degrading prices or simply lost everything.

The evacuees spent the first few months in "assembly centers" until ten more permanent "relocation centers" in desolate areas became available (see Map 2). By October 1942 all had been transferred to one of these centers, run by the War Relocation Authority (WRA). The government justified evacuation and internment as a "military necessity," even though not a single act of espionage or sabotage was ever documented among persons of Japanese ancestry. The famous investigative report by Curtis B. Munson, a special representative of the State Department, which was carried out in October and early November 1942 at the order of President Roosevelt, noted a remarkable degree of loyalty among people of Japanese descent and indicated the absence of any problem (Weglyn 1976: 34). Moreover, although Executive Order 9066 did not specify Japanese residents or Japanese Americans, nationals of other enemy countries and their descendants were never subject to mass evacuation and internment. Several hundred German and very few Italian American naturalized citizens were also interned, but they were examined individually (Tetsuden Kashima, personal communication, May 3, 1994). Japanese Americans received no such individual

[2] A few Nisei were also arrested, but because of their American citizenship, they were soon released and never sent to detention camps.

examination nor did they have attorneys to represent them; they were simply rounded up and incarcerated.

"Relocation centers" were surrounded by barbed-wire fences. Armed soldiers watched from guard towers. On a number of occasions internees, including children, were shot, sometimes fatally, when they were collecting scrap lumber or retrieving a ball.

In the hurriedly built camps, a single bare room was allocated to each family. The largest was only twenty by twenty-four feet. Sound carried easily in the flimsy barracks, and privacy was impossible to achieve. Meals were provided at central mess halls, and bathrooms, laundries, latrines, and recreation halls were all communal.

In January 1943 the War Department started seeking Nisei volunteers for a special all-Nisei unit later designated the 442d Regimental Combat Team. The team gave highly distinguished service. It was, in fact, the most decorated combat unit of the war. The largest number of decorations, however, also reflected the highest sacrifice of lives.[3]

Many Nisei were allowed to leave camp during the war if they obtained permission to attend college or to work, but they were not permitted to return to the West Coast until early 1945. On December 17, 1944, the commanding general of the Western Defense Command announced the recision of the West Coast exclusion. Just hours later, on December 18, the Supreme Court ruled that detention of evacuees against their will was unconstitutional since there was no longer any "military necessity" involved. Japanese Americans started to return to their hometowns, although some migrated to the East Coast or the Midwest instead and settled there permanently.[4]

[3] The team liberated the town of Bruyeres, France. Years later the residents returned the favor by sending the U.S. president a petition bearing about one thousand signatures in support of redress for Japanese Americans.

[4] There is abundant literature on evacuation and internment. For historical accounts, see Weglyn 1976; Myer 1971; Daniels 1972; Girdner and Loftis 1969; Spicer et al. 1969; Bosworth 1967. Out of the Japanese American Evacuation and Resettlement Study (JERS), came Thomas and Nishimoto 1946; Thomas 1952; and ten Broek et al. 1954. Ichioka 1989 reassesses this JERS project. See also Starn 1986, for the involvement of anthropologists hired by the WRA. For the all-Nisei 100th Battalion and 442d Regimental Combat Team, see Duus 1987. For autobiographies, see Uchida 1982; Modell 1973; Kitagawa 1967. Okubo 1966 [1946] is a book of

Nearly half a century passed before the injustice of the incarceration was publicly acknowledged. The Civil Liberties Act of 1988, which authorized redress for the unjust wartime evacuation and internment, states: "The Congress recognizes that . . . a grave injustice was done to both citizens and permanent resident aliens of Japanese ancestry by the evacuation, relocation, and internment of civilians during World War II. . . . [T]hese actions were carried out without adequate security reasons and without any acts of espionage, or sabotage . . . and were motivated largely by racial prejudice, wartime hysteria, and a failure of political leadership" (102 U.S. Statute at Large 903–4).

Japanese Americans had suffered tremendous economic losses and psychological pain because of evacuation and internment. Nonetheless, for a long time the U.S. government insisted on "military necessity," and the issue of internment was buried in American history. The redress movement was a campaign to correct and "redress" the injustice in the past. Until the bill was actually signed into law by President Ronald Reagan in 1988, however, redress seemed "an impossible dream" to many Japanese Americans. It was achieved through the tireless efforts of the Japanese American Citizens League (JACL) and other Japanese American organizations— such as the National Council for Japanese American Redress (NC-JAR), the National Coalition for Redress and Reparations (NCRR), and coram nobis legal teams—and Japanese American congressmen.[5] Many individuals, not only Japanese Americans but also politicians in the larger society and leaders of other minority and civil rights organizations, joined the effort. It is beyond the scope of my book to document the entire redress campaign. Rather, the purpose of this chapter is to show how the movement and other related events involved and affected Japanese Americans in the greater Seattle area. The Seattle community played a vital role in initiating the

---

drawings with text on camp life. John Okada's novel *No-No Boy* is an excellent portrayal of the agony of the Nisei during internment.

[5] Coram nobis is a writ of error or a writ of review. A person convicted of a crime may challenge the conviction by petitioning for coram nobis when crucial evidence has been omitted or suppressed. Three Japanese Americans convicted during World War II for violating the curfew and evacuation orders filed such petitions in 1983.

movement, proposing a concrete individual payment plan, and advancing it at the national level. While the national drive is relatively well recognized and documented, little is as yet known about the initial efforts of the movement, in which Seattle played a key role.

The redress movement in Seattle falls roughly into four periods: emergence of the idea (1970–1978), the breakthrough (1978–1983), growth of the movement (1983–1988), and legislative appropriation and distribution of redress (1988–1994). Together with political activism, related events took place during these periods, including hearings by the Commission on Wartime Relocation and Internment of Civilians, Days of Remembrance, plays, and local government redress. All these events of the movement helped in the long process of establishing a legal foundation for redress, psychologically readying Japanese Americans for the action, and educating the general public.

Emergence of the Redress Idea (1970–1978)

The first compensation of Japanese Americans for property losses due to evacuation was authorized by the Evacuation Claims Act of 1948, signed into law by President Harry Truman. Despite the Supreme Court decision in the Korematsu case that the evacuation was constitutional,[6] the American government for the first time recognized its "moral" responsibility (Chuman 1976: 240). Under this act, those who suffered monetary loss because of evacuation could file claims for partial compensation. By the time payment was completed in 1965, the federal government had paid a total of $36,874,240 on 26,558 claims. The amount was trivial compared to estimates of actual losses. The Federal Reserve Bank of San Francisco believed Japanese Americans had suffered $400 million in property losses in 1942 (Kato 1961), and the Commission on Wartime Relocation and Internment of Civilians would later estimate

[6] Fred Korematsu and two other young men violated the evacuation order and were prosecuted and convicted. Korematsu challenged his conviction in the Supreme Court. In the case of *Korematsu v. U.S.* (December 1944) the Court upheld the constitutionality of the order. Similar court decisions were made against the other two in 1943.

income losses of $108 million to $164 million and property losses between $11 million and $206 million for which the act made no compensation (CWRIC 1983: 27).

The Evacuation Claims Act had many serious shortcomings. Among the most important were limitations on the amounts that could be paid and how the money was to be appropriated. The Attorney General's Office had discretion in paying claims of $2,500 or less, but the money for larger claims had to be directly appropriated by Congress. Many claimants, unwilling to wait through such a cumbersome process, claimed only the amount that could be disbursed relatively quickly. Moreover, the amended law required that original claims of less than $2,500 be reduced by 75 percent, or the claimant accept the statutory maximum of $2,500, unless they chose to wait, perhaps indefinately, for further appropriations from Congress. Claims had to be supported by documentary evidence of ownership and subsequent financial loss, evidence that in many cases had been lost because of evacuation. Nor were the evacuees compensated for such property as business supplies or furniture or for the loss of income while they were incarcerated or for psychological damage resulting from internment (Chuman 1976: 241–44). As the Legislative Education Committee of the JACL later noted, the Evacuation Claims Act was "never meant to be redress for injustices" (JACL-LEC 1987: 1).

No further action was taken toward redress until 1970. In the interim the JACL participated in a related movement. It joined with other concerned organizations and political activists to persuade Congress to repeal Title II of the Internal Security Act of 1950, or the Emergency Detention Act, as it was known. Under Title II, enacted in the politically tense climate of the cold war with the Soviet Union, the president was authorized to apprehend and detain any persons involved in espionage or sabotage when the country is invaded, officially at war, or victimized by domestic insurrection (Takasugi 1974; Chuman 1976: 327–31). The Justice Department designated six sites, among them the former Japanese American relocation center at Tule Lake, California, for the "detention camp program."

From the beginning, political activists feared this "concentration camp law." In the late 1960s their fears escalated as the African

American civil rights movement and antiwar protests grew, and police reacted with violent repression. Some government officials alluded to the possibility of using detention camps to quiet political protest. The chairman of the House Committee on Un-American Activities, Edwin E. Willis, for instance, declared on May 6, 1968, that communists and black nationalists had essentially declared war on the United States: "Therefore they lose all constitutional rights and should be imprisoned in detention camps" (Chuman 1976: 329).

A small group of Japanese American activists, most of them from California, began to campaign for repeal, being seriously concerned that internment of any minority could legally happen again. The JACL was not initially enthusiastic, but in 1968 it was persuaded to make a resolution supporting repeal. During the next three years the JACL worked with other organizations and politicians both within and outside of Japanese America. Their efforts finally succeeded in 1971 when President Richard Nixon signed the repeal of Title II (Okamura 1974).[7]

Meanwhile, increased momentum in the ethnic and civil rights movements raised the political consciousness of Japanese Americans. At the 1970 national JACL convention in Chicago, Edison Uno, a lecturer at San Francisco State University, introduced a resolution calling for redress for internment. He proposed that the JACL petition the American government to admit its mistake in denying the civil and constitutional rights of Japanese Americans during the war. Subsequently, Uno traveled widely, visiting different JACL chapters to promote his idea (Tateishi 1986: 191; Hosokawa 1982: 344). Although he believed that redress should include

---

[7] Another instance of political activism connected to redress was the case of Iva Toguri d'Aquino, more commonly known as "Tokyo Rose." D'Aquino, born in Los Angeles in 1916, was visiting Japan in early 1941 when war broke out, and she was stranded there. She was employed as one of eighteen English-speaking announcers of Radio Tokyo, who were ordered to read exactly as written scripts intended to induce homesickness and to reduce the fighting motivation of Allied troops. After the war, d'Aquino was arrested and imprisoned in Japan under U.S. occupation for years based on the false testimony of bribed witnesses. After she returned to the United States, she lived in shadow, shunned by many of her fellow Nisei and treated as a traitor. Finally, in 1975 a few Nisei JACL leaders in San Francisco learned about her case and encouraged the JACL to establish a committee. After a campaign that won widespread public support, President Gerald Ford pardoned d'Aquino in 1976. See Uyeda 1978; Chuman 1976.

[35]

acknowledgment of legal liability, he proposed no concrete plan at that point.

In 1972, without knowledge of Uno's advocacy and the JACL resolution he introduced, Henry Miyatake, a Nisei working at a major company in the Seattle area independently began to research the possibility of monetary compensation for Japanese Americans. Though he had little legal background, with the aid of a book titled *How to Find the Law* (Cohen 1965), he looked for precedents. After spending considerable time in libraries, he discovered several cases that might be applicable. For example, he learned that a few German trading companies whose property had been confiscated by the U.S. government during World War II, had recovered some of the property through lawsuits in U.S. courts. He also discovered a case involving an Indiana man, Lambdin P. Milligan, who was arrested in 1864 and imprisoned for refusing induction into the Union army in the Civil War. Milligan later sued the American government for the misappropriation of property and the loss of civil liberty, and he recouped his property (ten Broek, Barnhart, and Matson 1954: 227–33). These cases suggested to Miyatake that there might be legal grounds on which to seek compensation. His lawyer friends agreed that the courts might grant monetary compensation but suggested that legislation might be more easily achieved. They pointed out that several previous lawsuits by Japanese Americans had failed.[8]

In 1972, when the president of the Seattle chapter of the JACL described the national JACL resolution and asked for volunteers to look into the reparation matter, Miyatake volunteered. He had little support in the local chapter, however, and even his friends discouraged him. The common advice was "Don't rock the boat" and "Don't agitate the public." Following a regular chapter meeting in late 1973, he gave a talk on the redress issue, and only three people were willing to stay and listen: Shosuke Sasaki, Ken Nakano, and Chuck Kato. Two of them were friends of his from previous political activities. Eventually, this group persuaded several other Nisei to join them in organizing the Evacuation Redress Committee

[8] For example, the Hirabayashi case (1943), the Yasui case (1943), the Korematsu case (1944), and the Endo case (1944). For details, see Chuman 1976 and Weglyn 1976.

within the Seattle JACL. They were frequently discouraged, for at this stage even chapter leaders were not ready for the redress movement.

In 1974 the president of the Seattle JACL authorized the development of a plan of action. The "Seattle Plan," as it later came to be known, proposed individual payment to all people who were evacuated or interned during World War II, including Latin American Japanese deported to the United States for internment and the Native American Aleuts who were evacuated from their residents.[9] The plan proposed that each former internee be paid five thousand dollars for psychological injury and ten dollars for every day of incarceration as reparation for the loss of personal liberty and income from wages, salaries, businesses, and farms. They estimated the total loss of normal wage and salary incomes to be in excess of $400 million (Seattle Evacuation Redress Committee 1975: 4). The plan also proposed that payment be made through a special trust fund of the Internal Revenue Service, in which federal income tax paid by persons of Japanese ancestry would be accumulated, so that redress would be less vulnerable to opposition by the larger society.

Meanwhile, at the 1972 JACL national convention, a resolution similar to the one introduced in 1970 was passed, and at the 1974 convention redress was made the top-priority issue (JACL-LEC 1987: 2). Nonetheless, little progress was made during these years at the national level. By mid-1974 the Seattle redress group had garnered enough support that the local JACL chapter brought the Seattle Plan to the Pacific Northwest District JACL, where it was accepted. The Seattle chapter then made a presentation at the national board meeting in San Francisco in November 1974. At that time, redress was still controversial, and no definite consensus was reached on whether to pursue it. At last it was agreed to establish a

[9] A total of 2,264 Japanese enemy aliens in Latin American countries, particularly Peru, where there was a great deal of cultural prejudice and antagonism against them because of economic competition, were deported to the United States for internment. Their deportation and internment was totally unrelated to the internment of Japanese Americans by the War Relocation Authority. The Latin American Japanese were held as hostages to be exchanged for American citizens in Japanese territories. About 300 Aleuts were forcibly evacuated from the Aleutian and Pribilof islands to southeastern Alaska and the Seattle area primarily because of fear of Japanese attack on the region. See CWRIC 1981: 305, 323–59; and Gardiner 1981.

political action committee. The *Pacific Citizen,* the national JACL newspaper, reported Miyatake's presentation on November 15, 1974:

> A unique evacuee reparations concept without massive appropria-
> tions was described by Seattle JACLer Henry Miyatake to the Japa-
> nese American Citizens League national board and staff meeting here
> this past weekend (Nov. 7–10). . . . The concept, developed by the
> Seattle JACL reparations study committee, would provide $5 a day to
> all evacuees interned without due cause, at least $114.30 (the wages
> paid German and Italian POWs working in U.S. POW camps during
> WW2) per month to recover lost wages, $1 per day per internee
> payable to community service organizations for cultural activities to
> compensate for cultural deprivation, and a flat sum of $600 per adult
> and $400 for each child to those who voluntary relocated to the so-
> called free zones. . . .
>
> The concept suggests applications from evacuees be processed so
> that those age 65 or older as of Jan. 1, 1974 be compensated first;
> those age 50 or over as of Jan. 1974, next; and then all others includ-
> ing direct heirs of deceased.[10]

Many national JACL leaders still opposed redress, however. Because a majority of its members were hostile or indifferent to the
idea, the leaders were afraid that the issue would divide the organization. Many believed, as Bill Hosokawa points out, that "a demand
for monetary compensation would not only cheapen the sacrifice
Japanese Americans had made in response to their government's
wartime mandate, but well might provoke such a widespread public
backlash that the educational objective would be negated" (1982:
344). Many felt that though the Japanese Evacuation Claims Act of
1948 had provided woefully inadequate compensation for losses, at
least it was a government admission of wrongdoing. They feared
that the kind of campaign needed to achieve legislative redress
would be prolonged and expensive, taking too many resources from

[10] The figures were later increased in the Seattle plan to $10,000, plus $15 a day
for each day of internment. The first redress bill introduced by Representative
Mike Lowry of Washington adopted these figures (National Council for Japanese
American Redress 1979: 4).

other projects. Another prevalent idea was that "it would be more meaningful if, instead of seeking compensation, JACL sought reversal of the Supreme Court decision in the Korematsu and Endo cases, which put the stamp of legality on the Evacuation" (Hosokawa 1982: 345).

Disappointed with the ambivalent reaction of the national JACL, the Seattle group tried to make redress a community issue instead. In late 1975 they made a tape and transcript titled "An Appeal for Action to Obtain Redress for the World War II Evacuation and Imprisonment of Japanese Americans" and sent it to various Japanese American organizations. "An Appeal for Action" emphasized the violation of human rights and the constitutional right to petition the government for redress as well as the need to refute false accusations of espionage and disloyalty during World War II.

> Passive submission or self-abasement when confronted by government tyranny or injustice was alien to the beliefs held by the founders of this nation. If, in the face of British government tyranny, they had acted like the Nisei have in the face of American government tyranny, there would be no 200th Anniversary of the founding of our country to celebrate. In commemorating the birth of our nation, therefore, it is time that Americans of Japanese ancestry repudiate the pseudo-American doctrine, promoted by white racists and apparently believed in by some former Nisei leaders, that there is one kind of Americanism for whites and another kind for non-whites. If Japanese Americans are as American as the J.A.C.L. has often claimed, then they should act like Americans and make every effort to seek redress through legislation and the courts for the rape of almost all their "unalienable rights" by the United States Government over thirty years ago. (Seattle Evacuation Redress Committee 1975: 2)

Some had the misconception that the Seattle redress group at that time was made up of radical militant youth (see, e.g., Hayakawa in the *Seattle Times*, Feb. 3, 1976); on the contrary, Shosuke Sasaki, the primary author of "An Appeal for Action," and a key figure in the movement, was an Issei in his sixties.

The group raised funds for their activity from the Seattle JACL

[39]

chapter, churches, the Nikkeijin-kai (Seattle Japanese Community Service),[11] *kenjin-kai* (prefectural associations), the Nisei Veterans Committee, and other community organizations. The group also received donations from individuals who supported the cause.

The redress group made over two hundred tapes, and sent them to all the JACL chapters and other major Japanese American organizations across the country. With the tape, they also sent a survey, but only forty of the hundred JACL chapters responded. Concerned about the low rate of response, the group started calling some of the presidents of JACL chapters. A former leader recalls one phone conversation: "We meet only twice a year. We have a picnic in the summertime, and a Christmas holiday dance. We don't discuss nothing like that." Such responses gave evidence of the long struggle that would be needed to achieve a national consensus.

In 1976 a survey conducted among 778 JACL board members throughout the nation in conjunction with the distribution of the tape showed that 94.4 percent of them were willing to support the passage of legislation to permit payment of reparation to each person affected by the 1942 evacuation order (Evacuation Redress Committee 1976). In the same bicentennial year the Seattle group won another small battle. Early the previous year the Seattle Evacuation Redress Committee had sought revocation of Executive Order 9066, which they found out had never been rescinded. They contacted Governor Daniel Evans's office, and the governor's office brought the issue to the attention of the White House.[12] On February 19, 1976, exactly thirty-four years after President Franklin D. Roosevelt issued Executive Order 9066, President Gerald Ford signed Proclamation 2714, titled "An American Promise," expunging it at last. "In this Bicentennial Year," the proclamation noted, "we are commemorating the anniversary dates of many of the great

[11] The Nikkeijin-kai, consisting mostly of Japanese-speaking people, was founded after World War II to take the place of the Nihonjin-kai, or Japanese Association in Seattle.

[12] The Seattle group proposed a draft of the repeal, and the White House tried to weaken the language. After a couple of exchanges, somehow the materials were turned over to the JACL office in Washington, D.C. (see also Quan 1988: 7). The Washington representative of the JACL then started a letter-writing campaign, encouraging people to write to the president to urge repeal (Hosokawa 1982: 339).

events in American history. An honest reckoning, however, must include a recognition of our national mistakes as well as our national achievements. . . . We now know that we should have known then—not only was that evacuation wrong, but Japanese-Americans were and are loyal Americans." The order was significant as the first federal acknowledgment of error. Not many Japanese Americans, however, and probably almost no ordinary Americans in the larger society know about this "American Promise." The Japanese Americans who do know of it generally do not attach much importance to it. Monetary payment proved far better able to attract public attention, and it offered a far more potent symbol of contrition.

At the 1976 national council meeting in Sacramento, California, the Seattle chapter again made a presentation, and this time the Seattle Plan passed unanimously. Prior to that, around 1974, Edison Uno had formulated a resolution, called the "Favor of the Ideal of Reparations," but it contained no specific plan with regard to individual payment.[13] The Seattle group's proposal, approved in 1976, was the first national council resolution in favor of a specific plan of individual payments. It was not developed, however. Many national JACL leaders supported the idea of a trust fund from which Japanese American community organizations could draw. Mike Masaoka, one of the most influential leaders of the JACL in its history, later enthusiastically supported the redress campaign with the individual payment plan, but he had held a different opinion until then. He recalled his position in 1976: "I felt JACL's insistence on individual monetary redress was futile, not only because most of the individuals who suffered financial loss would be dead and gone by the time Congress acted, but also because the demand might frustrate realization of the movement's other goals. I believed that the evacuation was a collective crime against a group, and that compensation should primarily benefit the group through community projects, homes for the elderly, and the like" (Masaoka and Hosokawa 1987: 322).

The Seattle chapter was firmly committed to individual payment,

[13] Edison Uno presented, in a January 1975 issue of the *Pacific Citizen,* his position in favor of trust funds for community organizations rather than individual payments.

[41]

contending that evacuation and internment had violated individual liberty and civil rights. In "Case for Individual Reparations Payments," they stated their position:

> In effect, reparations are the same as damages, from the party who caused the injury, being paid to the persons who suffered the injury. . . . The suggested payment of such money to a third party instead would be equivalent in essence to the unauthorized misappropriation of funds which properly should be going directly to each victim of the evacuation. Even if the money from block payments were spent for such things as community recreation centers or community old age homes, many former evacuees and especially those living remote from large Japanese American population centers would receive no benefit whatsoever. (Seattle Evacuation Redress Committee 1977: 1–2)

The conflict between the Seattle chapter and the national JACL became intense. Chuck Kato, a Nisei redress leader in Seattle said, "It got to a point when the Seattle chapter was ready to pull out of the National. It really was a traumatic affair for Seattle. . . . We really thought about pulling out and forming our own chapter or national organization" (Quan 1988: 8).

The Breakthrough (1978–1983)

Frustration over conflict with the national JACL and over the lack of significant progress toward redress was increasing among the leaders of the Seattle group. Then, a significant breakthrough came in late 1978. In the middle of that year, Frank Chin, a Chinese American playwright, and Frank Abe, a Sansei former actor, who had a keen interest in the camp experience and redress, approached the Seattle Evacuation Redress Committee with an idea. These creative young individuals proposed a reenactment of evacuation as part of a Day of Remembrance. Thus, on Thanksgiving weekend, November 25, 1978, participants gathered, just as Japanese Americans had been forced to gather in 1942.

[42]

Re-creation of the evacuation at the Day of Remembrance, 1978. Photo courtesy of Margaret Yanagimachi.

Camp Harmony re-created at Puyallup Fairgrounds, 1978. Photo courtesy of Margaret Yanagimachi.

[43]

Figure 1. Logo for Redress

The reenactment proved profoundly effective. For the old it brought back long-repressed memories of shame and injustice. The young were made to realize just what their parents and grandparents had experienced. The logo for the event, developed by Frank Fujii, a Nisei artist in Seattle, well expressed the intergenerational unity fostered by the Day of Remembrance (see Figure 1). From the Japanese characters for one, two, and three, Fujii devised a symbol to represent the union of all three generations, bound by the barbed wire that separated the Japanese Americans from others during World War II. Subsequently, the logo became a symbol for the redress movement in Seattle.

This event left a strong impression not only on the more than two thousand participants but throughout the local Japanese American community and in other such communities across the nation. It received extraordinarily wide coverage in the media, including all local television stations and newspapers, the Associated Press, and the *Pacific Citizen*, the national JACL newspaper. The publicity and the direct persuasion of the Seattle redress committee inspired Portland, San Francisco, and Los Angeles to hold similar Days of Remembrance the following year, on February 19, anniversary of the issuance of Executive Order 9066.

Later that year the Seattle group planned another Day of Remembrance, to be held at the site of Minidoka Relocation Center in Idaho, where the people from the Seattle area were interned. The plan was to construct and burn a twenty-five-foot-tall guard tower identical to those in which armed soldiers had stood during the detention years. The tower burning was meant to be a symbolic immolation of bad memories, a purging of injustice. The plan was canceled, however, because of opposition by Japanese Americans in Idaho, who feared a white backlash against them (*Times-News*, Sept. 28, 1979; *Rafu Shimpo*, Oct. 25, 1979.)

The first Day of Remembrance was also significant in obtaining the official support of local government. In November 1978 Mayor Charles Royer of Seattle signed a resolution in support of the Day of Remembrance which states: "The City of Seattle acknowledges and condemns the constitutional and moral violations perpetrated against persons of Japanese descent during World War II." This was the first such acknowledgment by a city office in the nation. In 1979 Governor Dixie Lee Ray proclaimed February 19 a statewide Day of Remembrance in Washington. She acknowledged that the evacuation of Japanese Americans was done without any prior hearing or determination of guilt on their part. In July the Conference of Western Attorneys General passed a resolution that declared Executive Order 9066 a violation of the Bill of Rights and supported the redress campaign. In November 1979 the Commission on Asian American Affairs for the state of Washington proclaimed its support of the redress bill that had been introduced in Congress and the establishment of a commission to work for passage.

Meanwhile, as support grew among Japanese Americans, the national JACL at the Salt Lake City convention in 1978 again unanimously adopted redress as a priority issue. They approved the redress guidelines that included a plan for a flat rate of $25,000 individual payment, on the recommendation of the JACL National Committee for Redress (Tateishi 1986: 192). The plan also proposed the creation of a Japanese American Foundation, a hundred-million-dollar trust fund to be used for the benefit of Japanese American community organizations. Prior to the convention, Clifford Uyeda of San Francisco, an interim chairman of the National Committee for Redress and the national president of the JACL, wrote thirty-five articles for the *Pacific Citizen* to promote the redress campaign, taking over from Edison Uno, who died in 1977 (Hosokawa 1982: 345). Together with Uyeda, John Tateishi, appointed as the first chairman of the National Committee for Redress at the 1978 convention, started a public media campaign as part of the effort to educate the general public (Tateishi 1986: 191–92). The idea of individual monetary payment was still controversial, however, and some of the top leaders refused to support it. Many of them felt, as one national leader recalls, that attaching "a price tag" would demean the idea of freedom and liberty (*Pacific Citizen,* Dec. 20–27, 1990).

Senator S. I. Hayakawa was one prominent Nisei who opposed the plan. Attending the 1978 Salt Lake City convention, he commented in an interview with the local press that the demand for individual payments of twenty-five thousand dollars was "absurd and ridiculous." The evacuation had been "perfectly understandable" in a time of national crisis. He insisted that there had been "nothing prison-like" in the "relocation centers," as he preferred to call them (*Sunday Star* [Chicago], May 13, 1979; *San Jose Mercury,* May 10, 1979).[14] The Seattle group responded in May the following year with a full-page ad in the *Washington Post,* an open letter signed by over three hundred prominent people who contested Hayakawa's view.

In early 1979, a small delegation from the national JACL met with four Japanese American congressmen—Representatives Nor-

[14] Hayakawa, a Canadian-born Nisei, served as acting president of San Francisco State College during the student protest movement and later as a Republican senator from California. He himself was not interned and spent the war years teaching in Chicago.

man Mineta and Robert Matsui, both of California, and Senators Daniel Inouye and Spark Matsunaga, both of Hawaii[15]—to consult about the redress issue. The congressmen suggested that to convince the American public and the members of Congress of the injustice it was necessary to establish an official determination of wrong action by the government before advancing reparation legislation. The JACL got the same advice from professional lobbyists and civil rights advocates (Tateishi 1986: 192). As a result, in August 1979 Senator Inouye introduced into the Senate a bill to create a federal commission to investigate the facts surrounding the evacuation order and its effects on Japanese Americans; it passed on May 22, 1980. Jim Wright, House majority leader, introduced a similar bill into the House of Representatives in September 1979, and the House approved it on July 21, 1980.[16] After the Senate and House agreed to send the Senate version to the White House, President Jimmy Carter on July 31, 1980, signed the bill that created the Commission on Wartime Relocation and Internment of Civilians, which started hearings across the nation in 1981.

The Seattle redress group was deeply disappointed at the national JACL's decision to seek the establishment of the commission instead of directly pursuing redress legislation. In May 1979 William Hohri, a Nisei from Chicago who shared the disappointment, came to Seattle to meet with the Seattle Evacuation Redress Committee. As a result of this meeting, the National Council for Japanese American Redress was formed that same month. Hohri was chosen to lead the new group, partly because he had not previously

[15] Congressmen Mineta and Matsui were interned as small children. Senator Inouye served in the 442d Regimental Combat Team, and Senator Matsunaga in the 100th Battalion. In Hawaii, where one and a quarter times as many Japanese resided as on the mainland, no mass evacuation took place, although suspected community leaders were sent to Justice Department detention camps on the mainland.

[16] Congressman Wright of Texas, who had been a pilot during the war, was a young student in law school when he first learned about internment of Japanese Americans. He was outraged. He remembered, as did many others, the heroic rescue of the Lost Battalion by Nisei soldiers. Prompted by personal experience and by the demands of individuals who had been in the Lost Battalion, when Japanese American congressmen approached him, he immediately agreed to sponsor the redress bill.

been associated with the Seattle redress group, which had such negative relations with the national JACL at that time (Hohri 1988: 48). The NCJAR intended to pursue redress directly, through their own congressional sponsor, Representative Mike Lowry.

Lowry had promised at the first Day of Remembrance in 1978 that if he were elected to the House of Representatives he would introduce a bill for redress. In November 1979 he kept his word. He introduced H.R. 5977, a bill to provide fifteen thousand dollars, plus fifteen dollars per day of internment and a formal government apology to each internee. Except for the funding method—congressional appropriation instead of an Internal Revenue Service–administered trust fund—the bill was based on the Seattle Plan. It was referred to the Judiciary Committee and assigned to the subcommittee on Administrative Law and Governmental Relations. There it died.

The NCJAR soon found its base in Chicago, and ties with the Seattle Evacuation Redress Committee loosened. Nevertheless, many of the leaders and members of the Seattle Japanese American community, along with seven hundred contributors from around the nation, continued to support the group (Hohri 1986: 196–99; 1988: 47–50). The NCJAR filed a class action against the U.S. government in an attempt to win redress through the courts. In October 1988, however, the Supreme Court denied certiorari, maintaining that the statute of limitations barred the claims under the takings clause of the Fifth Amendment. After that, the NCJAR campaigned for congressional redress and for an increase in appropriations.

Meanwhile, the relationship between the Seattle Evacuation Redress Committee and the national JACL worsened. Around 1979, the Seattle committee started to dissolve. Members were disappointed at the lack of progress and their loss of voice at the national level, and illness, family tragedy, and divorce among members also played a part. The faces of the redress committee in Seattle changed around this time. Most of the key leaders left the group, but Chuck Kato, Ken Nakano, and several others remained active. They were joined by Cherry Kinoshita, a Nisei who later chaired the redress committee of the national JACL and served as vice-president of public affairs, Chiz Omori, a Nisei who also later represented the Northwest in the lawsuits pursued by the NCJAR, Wayne Kimura, a Sansei who would later chair the redress committee within the Seattle JACL chapter, and several other Nisei. These new leaders, the most important of whom was Cherry Kinoshita, made new efforts during the subsequent decade to educate the public. They spoke before Japanese American gatherings and organizations, wrote letters to politicians, lobbied the entire Washington state congressional delegation in face-to-face meetings, and established networks with other civil rights organizations and governmental entities.

This work began in the fall of 1980 when Kinoshita organized the Washington Coalition on Redress (originally, the Japanese American Community Committee on Redress/Reparation) by calling together representatives of all major Japanese American organizations in the area around Puget Sound. Sixteen of them joined the coalition. Kinoshita asked Gordon Hirabayashi, who was then a visiting professor at the University of Washington, to serve as honorary chair of the coalition in a public relations capacity, while she served as working chair. Later, when Hirabayashi completed his teaching assignment and returned to Canada, Chuck Kato became co-chair. The initial aim of the coalition was to prepare for the congressional commission hearings by seeking out witnesses and encouraging them to testify.

Early in 1980 Karen Seriguchi and Frank Abe, both Sansei involved in the redress movement, organized a conference on internment at which various speakers, including Nisei, Sansei, and other Americans, presented legal, literary, historical, psychological, and personal points of view on internment and its effects (Seriguchi and Abe 1980).

In 1981 the Washington Coalition on Redress conducted a survey on the effects of evacuation and internment. Of the 851 respondents in Seattle (not all of whom were evacuees), 40 percent spent as many as three to four years in camp. The vast majority (84.6 percent) named economic losses such as home, belongings, property lost or damaged as the main problem resulting from the evacuation order (see Table 3) (Japanese American Community Committee on Redress/Reparation, CWRIC 1981).

In July 1981, hearings by the Commission on Wartime Relocation and Internment of Civilians started in Washington, D.C., followed by hearings in Los Angeles, San Francisco, Seattle, Anchorage,

Table 3. Survey on the Effects of Executive Order 9066, Seattle, Washington, February–March 1981

Problem resulting from EO 9066	Number	Percentage
home, belongings, property lost/damaged; economic losses	720	84.61
unable to return to prewar residence	408	47.94
verbal abuse, threats, harassment	502	58.99
acts of violence or terrorism	105	12.34
job discrimination	379	44.54
death, debilitation of family breadwinner	120	14.10
inadequate health or dental care	267	31.41
other physical problems	58	6.82
disruption of education	340	39.95
family disruption, loss of friends	386	43.36
emotional or psychological problems	167	19.62
cultural loss	23	2.70
other problems	65	7.64
Positive effects of EO 9066	**Number**	**Percentage**
strengthened character, etc.	9	1.06

Source: Japanese American Community on Redress/Reparations, CWRIC 1981.
Notes: Total number of respondents to survey was 851. The survey did not target specific generation, and the respondents consist of Issei (10.56 percent), Nisei (71.29 percent), Kibei Nisei (8.9 percent), and Sansei (9.25 percent). Therefore, the percentage numbers do not represent the effects reported by evacuees but include those marked by Sansei who were not born during the war. Nevertheless the numbers reflect most of the negative aspects of the evacuation and internment.

Unalaska, Chicago, Washington, D.C., again, New York, and then Boston (Hosokawa 1982: 354). Over 750 people, including Japanese American and Aleut victims, former government officials, interested non-Japanese Americans, and scholars testified before the commission (CWRIC 1982: vii). In late spring, the Washington Coalition on Redress sponsored a "mock hearing" to familiarize the community with the format of the hearings and the limited five-minute presentations. About two hundred people attended the mock hearing. The coalition also worked with the commission's Washington, D.C., office to help coordinate the three-day hearing that was held in September 1981 at the Seattle Central Community College auditorium. Over 150 people from the Northwest, Hawaii, and Alaska, testified. About 80 of them were Japanese Americans residing in King County, Washington. Those who volunteered were allowed to testify without being screened. Each witness was given five minutes to speak, and topics varied from economic loss, evacuation and camp experience, and psychological damage, to the wartime positions of the government, veterans' experiences, War Relocation Authority policies, the redress plan, and the effects on the Sansei. Throughout the three days the auditorium was filled to capacity.

The commission hearings were not uncontroversial. Japanese American congressmen and the national JACL considered them an indispensable means of educating the general public. Others, such as the NCJAR and the original Seattle Evacuation Redress Committee, opposed them, claiming that the actions taken by the government were self-evidently wrong and that the commission hearings were a waste of time and would only delay the payment to the victims, the oldest of whom were dying day by day. The commission, noted William Hohri, "resulted from the JACL's unwillingness to demand redress directly from the United States Congress. The commission was to do a study, arrive at the obvious conclusion that an injustice had occurred, and then state the victims' demands for them" (Hohri 1988: 87). Many Japanese Americans, including some of the former opponents of the commission, although not the original key leaders of the Seattle Evacuation Redress Committee, now believe that the establishment of the commission was the right choice in educating members of Congress and the public, consequently making the passage of the redress bill possible.

Growth of the Redress Movement (1983–1988)

The redress movement, so slow to show results, began to gain momentum when the Commission on Wartime Relocation and Internment of Civilians issued its formal report in February, 1983, two years after the hearings took place. The report, titled *Personal Justice Denied*, concluded that internment was based on "race prejudice, war hysteria and a failure of political leadership" (1983: 24). In June 1983 the commission recommended individual payments of twenty thousand dollars, a formal government apology, and an education fund.

Another big step toward redress was made by reopening the case of Gordon Hirabayashi. In 1942 three Japanese American men had challenged the evacuation order: Min Yasui of Portland, Fred Korematsu of San Francisco, and Gordon Hirabayashi of Seattle, then a senior at the University of Washington. Hirabayashi, who believed in the American Constitution, deliberately broke the curfew order that applied only to people of Japanese ancestry and then turned himself in to the Seattle FBI office. As the result of his challenge, Hirabayashi was convicted of violating the evacuation and curfew orders in 1942. He appealed his conviction all the way to the Supreme Court, but the Court ruled in 1943 that the evacuation was a military necessity. He spent a total of twenty-four months in jail.

In 1981 volunteer lawyers, in cooperation with a similar team in San Francisco which was appealing Fred Korematsu's conviction, started a legal team to do research on the Hirabayashi case. Hirabayashi, Korematsu, and Yasui were granted a new trial in May 1984 under a writ of coram nobis after Aiko Yoshinaga-Herzig, a paid researcher for the Commission on Wartime Relocation and Internment of Citizens, and Peter Irons, a historian, discovered some crucial government documents. These two had found the original report of General John L. DeWitt of the Western Defense Command, which had been transmitted to the War Department in April 1943. According to this report, no military necessity required evacuation of Japanese Americans. DeWitt's report said: "It was impossible to establish the identity of the loyal and the disloyal with any degree of safety. It was not that there was insufficient time in which to make such a determination; it was simply a matter of facing the realities that a positive determination could not be made, that an exact separation of the 'sheep from the goats' was unfeasible." The War Department changed the report to read: "To complicate the situation, no ready means existed for determining the loyal and the disloyal with any degree of safety. It was necessary to face the realities—a positive determination could not have been made." The War Department then tried to destroy all copies of the original report, concealing evidence from Hirabayashi and from the Justice

Department during his trial (Irons 1989: 393–96). Hirabayashi's attorneys were able to show that racism, not military necessity, was the reason for evacuation.

The hearings took place June 17–27, 1985, and Hirabayashi was finally vindicated in February 1986. Twelve to thirteen lawyers—half of them Sansei, two white, three Chinese American, and the others members of other minorities—had worked for five years on the case. Had they been paid at the usual rate, the bill would have been $400,000. Together with the $100,000 raised for court costs and expenses, the equivalent of a half million dollars was donated.

Meanwhile, the Days of Remembrance continued, together with other cultural events. On February 19, 1983, the Day of Remembrance was observed as a "Fun-Run" at a local park. The participants ran 9,066 feet, the number standing for Executive Order 9066. Those who could not run walked 9,066 inches at the organizers' suggestion. All participants, after completing the run, were awarded a T-shirt emblazoned on the back, "I survived 9066," with a design of barbed wire. In August of the same year, a crowd of seven hundred to eight hundred people gathered at the Puyallup Fairgrounds for the unveiling of a memorial sculpture created by George Tsutakawa, an internationally recognized Nisei artist from Seattle. The sculpture fulfilled the need for a permanent memorial at the site, expressed by some participants at the 1978 Day of Remembrance (*Seattle Post Intelligence*, Aug. 22, 1983). According to Tsutakawa, the silicon bronze sculpture, in which the young and the old of all races hold their hands peacefully, in the form of a column, represents "a feeling of friendship, of more harmonious relationships for a better world to live in." He said he was more concerned about future generations than about commemorating the hardness and misery of the evacuation. At the event, a state historical plaque was also erected, close by the sculpture. In the program, the Seattle *Taiko* (drum) group, whose members are mostly Sansei, played a traditional Japanese percussion piece representing "struggle in warfare" (*Seattle Times*, Aug. 22, 1983).

Evacuation and internment have also been the subjects of several plays produced by local artists of the Northwest Asian American Theater, directed by a Sansei. The most important was *Breaking the Silence,* written by Nikki Nojima Louis and first performed in May 1986 at the University of Washington auditorium as a fund-raising event for Hirabayashi court cases. *Breaking the Silence* depicts the history of Japanese Americans in Seattle and the voices and views of three generations. Other shows dealt with people's lives in internment camps. *Miss Minidoka* was a comedy about camp life and the events surrounding a beauty contest. *Nisei: A Love Story* was a one-woman show in which Tomo Shoji dramatized her own experiences.

The 1986 Day of Remembrance took place in an Asian community hall in Seattle. The program started with the viewing of a videotape titled *Voices Long Silent,* a documentary describing the evacuation and camp life. The highlight of the evening was a candle-light ceremony involving readings by a Nisei minister and audience responses. The first part of the reading described the evacuation and internment and ended with the statement, "We could not find the voice within ourselves to tell others, often even our own children, about what happened to us personally. And so we the victims exiled ourselves to a silence that lasted forty years." The candles were extinguished during a moment of silence. Then the reading resumed with a statement emphasizing the duty to underscore the human experience. It continued, "Underlying all of the accounts is a sense of personal tragedy for having encountered our nation's betrayal of our loyalty and faith. Until a little while ago, painful memories have kept us as Americans unwilling and unable to talk." After a pause when all the candles were relighted, the reading closed with, "But now we shall be silent no more!"

In 1988 the tenth Seattle Day of Remembrance was observed at the same Asian community hall as two years before. The master of ceremonies was one of the Sansei involved in the original Day of Remembrance, who spoke about the early redress movement, which was little known in the community. The highlight of the program was a speech by Congressman Norman Mineta of California, who had cosponsored the redress bill that would be passed later that year. After various speakers gave reports updating the progress of the redress bill, the ceremony concluded with a candle-light service led by a Sansei minister. The names of a number of

Japanese Americans who contributed to the redress movement but had since passed away were read, followed by a moment of silence.

In 1983 the Washington Coalition on Redress led a drive to have the Washington state legislature authorize payments of five thousand dollars each to thirty-eight Japanese Americans who had been dismissed from their state jobs in 1942 because of their ancestry. The city of Seattle then followed suit with a city ordinance authorizing similar redress payments to three Japanese American city employees who had been dismissed from their jobs. The Washington Coalition on Redress then persuaded the Seattle School Board to approve redress compensation to twenty-six Japanese American school clerks who had been forced to resign from their positions in early 1942. It was legally questionable, however, whether entities such as the school district had the authority to make monetary redress. The coalition turned to the state legislature, which passed a bill enabling municipalities to pay redress. In April 1986 in a ceremony at the Nippon-kan Theater, Governor Booth Gardner signed the bill, surrounded by the former school clerks who were to receive the five-thousand-dollar payments. Over a hundred people were in attendance.

Meanwhile, the national movement gradually advanced. The national JACL pursued redress more enthusiastically and actively after the commission report. JACL leaders coordinated lobbying efforts and appeared in court to testify in support of all redress bills. The JACL established the Legislative Education Committee as a lobbying arm in 1982 but continued redress activities under the National JACL Redress Committee until early 1985, when Grayce Uyehara was appointed as the first JACL-LEC executive director. Lobbying efforts intensified, and the LEC set a goal of raising $1.5 million between 1985 and 1988 (JACL-LEC 1987: 6–8). Other organizations, such as the National Coalition for Redress and Reparations, a California-based grassroots organization, also actively lobbied. For example, in July 1987, the NCRR gathered 120 people at the Capitol to lobby Congress.

Immediately after the commission report, in June 1983, Representative Mike Lowry of Washington, along with twenty-four cosponsors, introduced H.R. 3387, the Civil Liberties Act of 1983, which basically incorporated the commission recommendations. Also around June 1983, Senator Alan Cranston introduced the first Senate redress bill; it never left committee. In October, Jim Wright, House majority leader, introduced H.R. 4110; he had seventy-two cosponsors, including forty-two that were transferred from H.R. 3387. In November, Senator Spark Matsunaga of Hawaii introduced S. 2116 with thirteen cosponsors; it died in the Subcommittee on Administrative Law and Governmental Relations. In January 1985, Jim Wright, this time with ninety-nine cosponsors, introduced H.R. 442, taking its number from the all-Nisei 442d Regimental Combat Team, and this bill also died. Spark Matsunaga and twenty-five cosponsors introduced S. 1053 in May 1985. In January 1987, House Majority Leader Thomas Foley of Washington and 125 cosponsors reintroduced H.R. 442. In April, Spark Matsunaga, with seventy-five cosponsors, again introduced S. 1009. In May 1987 H.R. 442 cleared the Administrative Law and Governmental Relations subcommittee, and on September 17, 1987, during the bicentennial of the U.S. Constitution, the House of Representatives approved it by a vote of 243 to 141. In April 1988, the Senate approved S. 1009 by a vote of 69 to 27. On August 3, 1988, the House passed the same conference report and H.R. 442 was sent to the White House for approval (JACL-LEC 1989).

Finally on August 10, 1988, over fifteen years after the movement began, H.R. 442, which provided payments and an apology to Japanese Americans who were interned and the Aleuts who suffered injustices during World War II, was signed into law by President Ronald Reagan. After forty-six years, the injustice was finally beginning to be corrected. The announcement that President Reagan was going to sign the bill the following day was made at a banquet during the national JACL convention in Seattle.

Appropriation and Distribution of Redress (1988–1994)

To celebrate victory in the long struggle the Washington Coalition on Redress held a celebration party at the Nisei Veterans Hall in October 1988, where over three hundred people gathered to share the joy. The ceremony started with the Pledge of Allegiance, followed by a Japanese drum performance by a local *taiko* group, a toast, and the recognition of those who contributed to the redress campaign. The hall was decorated in red, white, and blue, and the balloons read, "Celebrate for Redress—Born in Seattle." Mike Lowry presented an American flag flown over Congress on the day when the bill was signed to the Seattle JACL chapter, which later had it framed and mounted on the wall of the chapter office.

The elation of Japanese Americans, however, did not last long. In January 1989, President Reagan, nearing the end of his last term, proposed a mere $20 million for the redress budget for fiscal year 1990, enough to compensate only a thousand of about eighty thousand surviving victims. Clearly, many more elderly survivors would die before they received payment. The JACL, the NCRR, the NC-JAR, and other organizations urged people to write to politicians who were considered to be influential in appropriations.

Ironically, the Canadian government, which reached its own redress agreement on September 22, 1989, over one month after the U.S. legislation was signed, immediately began issuing a government apology and individual payments of twenty-one thousand Canadian dollars.[17]

The appropriation bill followed a winding path. After $20 million was budgeted at the beginning of the year, in April a House subcommittee recommended the appropriation of $250 million for redress payments as part of an emergency spending bill. This appropriation was deleted in June. In May the Senate and the House had agreed on $150 million for redress payments in fiscal year 1990, but later the amount was reduced to $50 million. In September the House approved $50 million for fiscal year 1990, but later in September the Senate voted to waive the Budget Act to permit the

[17] During and after World War II, 21,700 people of Japanese ancestry, of whom 17,000 were Canadian citizens, were affected by relocation, internment, property seizure, or deportation. The total economic loss to the Japanese Canadian community after 1941 has been estimated at no less than $443 million in 1986 (Canadian) dollars (National Association of Japanese Canadians 1985). In Canada, all people of Japanese ancestry who were British subjects, Canadian citizens, or landed immigrants between December 7, 1941, and March 1949, when the discriminatory law that prohibited their returning to the West Coast was lifted, are eligible for redress.

payments as an entitlement program, while allocating no money for fiscal year 1990. The entitlement program was approved by the House and Senate in late October and finally signed by President George Bush on November 21. Under the terms of the entitlement program, a maximum annual amount of $500 million was allocated to be paid, beginning in October 1990 when fiscal year 1991 started. The entitlement program, which operated like Social Security, automatically funded the amount without the need for yearly appropriation. Japanese Americans considered it a major victory for redress, although it delayed payments for another year.

After the national ceremony in Washington, D.C., the Seattle Japanese American community conducted its own ceremony. At the Nisei Veterans Hall, the five oldest recipients at the Keiro home for the elderly received their apology letters and reparation checks on October 14, 1990.

During the fiscal years 1991 and 1992, those who were born on or before December 31, 1927, approximately 50,000 people (25,000 annually), received letters and checks. There was a budget shortfall in fiscal year 1993 due to underestimation of the number of surviving victims, both because longevity was increasing and because eligibility had been broadened.[18] The Civil Liberties Act Amendments of 1992, which authorized an additional $400 million, however, enabled payment to be made to 25,000 people in 1993 and approximately 5,000 others by March 1994. Consequently, payment has been almost completed, except in the few cases of unsubmitted documents and probation.[19]

Many recipients have donated some portion of their redress pay-

[18] Eventually non-Japanese spouses who went to a relocation center with their Japanese husband or wife; veterans who served during World War II, who were not interned but lost their property because of evacuation; and those who voluntarily evacuated to an area excluded from the military zone designated in early 1942 were also made eligible for redress.

[19] There are a few cases on probation, whose eligibility for redress was being reviewed as of March 1994: those children who relocated to Japan with their parents during World War II; the Peruvians and other Latin Americans of Japanese ancestry who were interned in the United States without permanent resident alien status retroactive to the internment period; those individuals in Glendale, Arizona, just outside the prohibited zone, who claim deprivation of liberty in their daily lives.

ment to community organizations, including an elderly home, churches, and the JACL. The national JACL started its Legacy Fund Campaign in September 1990, to establish a perpetual endowment whose earnings can be used for the organization's activities and programs. By December 1993, the Legacy Fund had received approximately $4.20 million from about 6,300 donors. Many of the individual donations amounted to a thousand dollars.

The fiftieth anniversary of Executive Order 9066, February 19, 1992, was commemorated with two major events in the Seattle community: an exhibit of Japanese American history in the state of Washington, "Executive Order 9066: 50 Years Before and 50 Years After," at the Wing Luke Asian Museum; and a Day of Remembrance seminar, "Legal Remedies: Coram Nobis, Redress through Legislation, and Redress through Civil Action," held at the University of Puget Sound. The exhibit, comprising some 175 pictures, more than 75 artifacts, and a replica of a barracks room in an internment camp, attracted national attention and became the most successful project in the museum's history. Other Japanese American communities across the nation also presented various programs to commemorate the anniversary, such as exhibits, film series, and panel discussions. These events triggered people's emotions, recalled their ethnic history to them, and educated the general public as well as younger Japanese Americans.

The redress movement in the Seattle Japanese American community involved the participation of a great number of people. The media coverage of these activities had profound effects on Japanese Americans, including those who were uninterested in redress. Seventeen years passed from the time Miyatake brought his plan to the local chapter of the JACL to the distribution of an apology letter and monetary redress to surviving victims. Through these years, the opinions of most Japanese Americans were almost completely reversed. In the early 1970s, redress and even camp experiences were taboo subjects. Today, to say "Let's just forget about camp" has become unacceptable. Now one Sansei leader describes it as almost "fashionable" to talk about camp and redress.

[3]

Nisei Experience

Most of the Nisei are now leading comfortable lives after retirement. They have received redress for wartime evacuation and internment. Japanese American communities now celebrate their history of struggles and achievements, and the Nisei, either individually, with family, or more collectively, look back on their lives and experiences more than they did before. In this chapter, I investigate the experiences of the Nisei and their feelings about ethnic identity, racial discrimination, and other aspects of ethnicity, from their childhood up to the beginning of the redress movement. I would like to note that the focus here is placed not on the series of events that befell them but rather on how they interpret their history today. What follows is their emic view of their past experience, and unless otherwise indicated, the ethnography is based on personal interviews.

Prewar Life

About 80 percent of the Nisei in Seattle were born between the latter half of the 1910s and the first half of the 1930s (Yanagisako 1985: 64). By the 1920s, the core of the Japanese community in Seattle had fairly recognizable boundaries. Nihon-machi, or Japan-town, ran from Yesler Way to the north, Dearborn Street to the south, Eighteenth Avenue to the east and Elliot Bay back to the west. The heart of Nihon-machi was at Sixth and Main, the site for community cultural activities.[1] By 1940 there was a good deal of outward movement from this core area.

Nearly all the businesses and organizations in Nihon-machi met the needs of its Japanese residents. Grocery stores, drug stores, laundries, restaurants, banks, insurance agencies, hotels, churches, the Japanese language school, *ofuro* (public baths) were all located within walking distance of where most people lived. Japanese artists in traditional dance, *gidayu* (ballad), and opera, among others, visited the community so often that, as one Issei recalls, the people forgot they were in a place remote from their homeland (Ito 1984: 929).

Many Nisei described Nihon-machi as a little island, an ethnically homogeneous neighborhood. One explained, "The only white persons I ever saw were the mailman, the policeman and the delivery man since we owned a grocery store" (T. R. Goto, quoted in Suguro 1989: 6). Many Nisei called the prewar community a ghetto. The living standard of the Japanese, like that of many other minority groups at that time, was below the national average. Because of their limited English, ineligibility for citizenship, and racial exclusion from unions, mainstream work arenas were largely closed to the Issei. For many Japanese, merely surviving was difficult, especially during the Great Depression. Shigemi Kodaira (real name) said that she ate nothing but rice with soy sauce, unable to afford other food (Ito 1984: 974). The social welfare section of the Japanese Association distributed rice and soy sauce to those who were starving and paid their electricity bills, but the Issei were uncomfortable about the idea of welfare payments from the government. Some Nisei emphasized, however, that they did not feel especially disadvantaged: "We never thought of ourselves as poor," Miki Hayashi told me in an interview, "because in our community we were all poor. And yet, we had a lot of real warmth. Like Christmas, we couldn't afford much, but it was such a happy time. I think when you were all in the same boat—like we didn't have a

---

[1] Cf. Miyamoto 1984: 9. According to Miyamoto, by 1910, Japanese were heavily concentrated in these streets. In the mid-1930s Fifth and Sixth avenues at Main and Jackson streets were the business center of the Nihon-machi (1984: xii, 9).

car. I know a few families did, but we got along. We didn't feel odd because so many of our friends didn't have a car."

The Issei tended to confine their friendships to other Japanese from the same *ken* (prefecture) or the same Japanese church. They took their children to Japanese movies, recitals, family gatherings, *kenjin-kai* picnics, Japanese language school picnics, a Fourth of July baseball game, or *shibai* (plays) at the Nippon-kan Theater.

> We lived in the back of the grocery store. And my folks' friends would come in the back of the store where they had this little table and a heater with a *kotatsu* [that is, a little table with a heater is called a *kotatsu*]. And they'd all gather around and have tea, and the menfolks would play *go* or *shogi* [Japanese chess], and it was a little meeting place. And all these older people are talking, [I] can't help but hear them. Sometimes they were talking about their lives or maybe their marriage problems or something. Their conversation could be pretty serious. (George Saito)

A minority of Nisei grew up in predominantly white neighborhoods away from Japantown but maintained social ties with other Japanese through their parents. The Nisei actively sought and enjoyed adventures in the larger society. For example, S. Frank Miyamoto reports a tendency of the Nisei to shop outside the Japanese community to look for a greater variety of goods and better prices. This practice disturbed the Issei merchants in Japantown, who took for granted the need of mutual support within the Japanese community (1984: 24).

Many decades after they had immigrated, the Issei still preserved many traditional Japanese customs. They and their children ate Japanese food almost every day, wore kimono occasionally, made rice cakes, performed lion dances for New Year's Day, danced *bon-odori* in summer,[2] picked Matsutake mushrooms in autumn, and

---

[2] The Bon Festival, today observed between August 13 and 16 in Japan, is a festival for welcoming ancestral spirits, once believed to return to their families during this period. The *bon-odori* are folk dances. In Japan the festival is not necessarily tied to Buddhism, but in Seattle and in many other Japanese communities in America, it is sponsored by a Buddhist church. In Seattle the festival has some religious nuances: the priest gives a brief prayer and the Shinran *odori* song, which praises the founder of the Jodo Shinshu, the denomination of the Seattle

Girls' Day celebration in the late 1930s. Photo courtesy of Shosuke Sasaki.

observed Girls' Day, Boys' Day, and other annual events. Barbara Yamaguchi recalled:

On March 3, we observed *osekku*, Girls' Day.[3] I still have *ohinasama* [Japanese dolls displayed on Girls' Day], which are very, very old.

Betsuin Buddhist church, is sung. Nevertheless, the *bon-odori* has officially become a part of Seafair, Seattle's summer festival.

[3] *Osekku* in Japanese refers to all the annual celebrations based on folk beliefs, not just Girls' Day. Among Japanese Americans, Girls' Day seems to be one of the most popularly celebrated *osekku*.

When my father went back to Japan in 1927 because his mother was very sick, he brought back the *ohinasama* from my grandmother. Because I was the only girl in the family, she wanted me to have it. When I was little, my mother got me little colored rice, *sakura-mochi* [a bean-paste rice cake wrapped with a cherry leaf], rice cake of three colors, pink, white, and green. We got these at Nihon-machi, and we would display the *ohinasama*.

The Issei had been raised in the Meiji era of Japan, a time when the country strongly emphasized ethics and morals under the leadership of Emperor Meiji. They inculcated national, cultural, and often racial pride in their Nisei children. Bill Fukuda's mother often told him, "You are able to walk the streets because there is a country like Japan behind you." Helen Kageshita's father, like many other Issei, believed in the genetic superiority of the Japanese race. The Issei respected and admired the Japanese emperor, often hanging his picture at home. What Miyamoto calls a "common expression among the Japanese" exemplifies their racial ideology in the prewar period: "We Japanese think of our whole nation as one big family because all of the Japanese families are just a branch of the Emperor's noble line" (Miyamoto 1984: 29). Senator Daniel Inouye gave another such example: "Day after day, the [Buddhist] priest who taught us ethics and Japanese history hammered away at the divine prerogatives of the Emperor. . . . He would . . . solemnly proclaim, 'You must remember that only a trick of fate has brought you so far from your homeland, but there must be no question of your loyalty. When Japan calls, you must know that it is Japanese blood that flows in your veins'" (Inouye and Elliott 1967: 36–37).

The Issei parents emphasized certain traditional Japanese values and behavior patterns: *oya koko* (filial piety), *gaman* (perseverance), *giri* (sense of obligation), *haji* (shame), obedience, honesty, and diligence. *Haji* was an especially pertinent cultural concept in the small, tight-knit community, where "everybody knew each other" and rumors spread rapidly: "All the *Nikkei-jin* [people of Japanese ancestry] were raised up under the shadow of the parents. . . . It was a shame society. 'Don't do this because what your neighbors were going to think.' You can't be different. You have to conform. That attitude has

[64]

certainly prevailed in my life, and in most Nisei's, too," Bill Fukuda told me. *Haji* required that the family's reputation be maintained in the community and the community's reputation be maintained in the larger society: "If you do something wrong, it would be *haji* to the Japanese. The whole Japanese community would be ashamed. Whatever you do would reflect on the community. That was stressed from the time we were young," said Sumi Hashimoto.

The Issei also insisted on respect for elders and emphasized that *kuchigotae* (talking back) to them was unacceptable. Some Nisei link the obedience that was implanted in their childhood to their passive response to the evacuation order in 1942.

The Nisei take pride in the low crime and delinquency rate during their youth.[4] If there was a problem, the community also applied pressure to discipline the child. Barbara Yamaguchi remembers that one nine-year-old boy, rumored to have stolen a car, was sent to Japan, because his family was considered to be unable to control him.

Issei parents placed great importance on education, and expected high achievement at school. Skipping grades was not unusual among the Nisei children; at school, they were often "teachers' pets," performing well and "causing little trouble." Shirley Kobayashi, like other Nisei, thought that Japanese students were smarter: "The valedictorian was Japanese. Every year there was one Japanese who was top, and within the top ten there were always lots of Japanese." Indeed, Miyamoto reports that between 1930 and 1937 there were eight Japanese valedictorians and six Japanese salutatorians in the nine Seattle high schools (1984: 54). Some Issei, believing the Japanese school system was better than the American, sent their children to Japan for schooling. Those children of Issei who were schooled in Japan and then returned to the United States were called Kibei. Sumi Hashimoto refused to go to Japan, but her two brothers were sent there for education and stayed permanently.

---

[4] Miyamoto cites statistics of an "extremely low" rate of juvenile delinquency (1984: 4), and he attributes it to strong group solidarity. Nationally the Japanese arrest rate from 1940 through 1960 was lower than that of whites, African Americans, Chinese, and Native Americans. In 1970 the Chinese rate was lower than the Japanese (Kitano 1976 [1969]: 145).

Such separation of Nisei siblings was not uncommon, and often it was lifelong.

The Issei expectation of high achievement from the Nisei was not limited to school study. Miki Hayashi laughs every time she recalls her father saying, "Just try to be the best of anything. *Dorobo de mo iikara* [Even if you are a thief]."

Although the Nisei acquired these traditional Japanese values and behavior patterns through their parents, their knowledge of Japan was very limited unless they had visited. Most Nisei now regret their ignorance of their parents' background. The primary barrier was linguistic. The Issei in general spoke little English and the Nisei usually spoke only enough Japanese for simple daily conversation, not enough to express complex thoughts or feelings. Bill Fukuda reported:

> We had very little conversation with our parents about what they did at their school, and other things. She never said why she came to the U.S. It's not only me; other Nisei don't know, either. I asked very few questions.
>
> The degree and the level of Japanese was very elementary; so there was a tremendous communication gap. I thought my Japanese was better than many other Nisei's, but still.

The Issei sent their children to the *kokugo gakko*, the Japanese language school, the first of its kind to be established in the nation (Ichioka 1988: 196). Every day after American school, the Nisei hurried to the Japanese language school for an hour and a half of instruction in the summer or an hour in the winter. The school provided classes from the first grade to the eighth, beyond which was a *hoshuka*, or special class, that taught various aspects of Japan besides language, such as its history, geography, and literature. Since the Japanese language was considered to be one of the most important cultural markers, parents were anxious for their children to acquire it. *Nisei Daughter*, an autobiography by Monica Sone from Seattle, opens with a scene in which her mother tells her she must go to Japanese school because she has "Japanese blood" (1953: 4–5). In a speech at a meeting on Nisei education in Seattle in 1908 the Japanese consul exhorted his listeners:

[66]

It is necessary to inspire Japanese thoughts in our children, our inheritors. . . .

It is because Japanese men have a strong spirit that we don't give up in the face of exclusion and other difficulties and we have continued to move forward courageously. Therefore, however assimilated into American customs [our children become], the conception of being Japanese must be maintained.

Inspire the Japanese spirit! Although we follow the American education system in technical details, it is essential to add Japanese ideas in spiritual education. We must establish a new educational organization to this end and should not allow our children to pursue only their own interests in education. (Takeuchi 1929: 417–18; my translation)

Parents wanted their children to attend the Japanese language school because it kept them off the streets, gave them something productive to do, and supervised them while the Issei were busy with work (Kitano 1976 [1969]: 27). But Japanese children were often reluctant to attend. They recognized that the school limited their contact with white Americans and their opportunity to participate in the larger society. "High school," said Setsuko Fukuda, "is when you start to know that you have to go to the Japanese school. High school would have lots of activities after school, but you could never stay to go, because you have to go to the Japanese school. That's why you don't really need to get to know the *hakujins* [lit. white people]."

Many Nisei say they actually learned little Japanese, but they did acquire some Japanese values and behaviors. *Otoban* (persons who take turns doing a particular task), for example, took turns erasing the blackboard and sweeping the classroom—practices alien at American schools, where these responsibilities were left to school janitors. At the Japanese school, different programs were conducted at the Nippon-kan Theater for *Kigensetsu,* or Empire Day. They bowed to the emperor's picture hung at the theater, and celebrated his longevity by shouting *banzai,* in cheers led by the school principal. The Nisei, however, hardly understood the meaning of these programs and felt no loyalty to the emperor. The Kibei, educated in Japan, tended to identify themselves as Japanese and showed more respect for the emperor.

[67]

Like the language school, various clubs and institutions also inculcated Japanese values and behaviors. Bill Fukuda remembered:

I took kendo lessons [at the Seattle Butoku-kai]. The *dojo* [exercise
hall] was at the Seattle Baptist Church up on First Hill. So I used to
walk all the distance once a week. I remember going to *kangeiko*
[midwinter training] in winter at five o'clock in the morning. We used
to go to *keiko* [practice] for two weeks, every morning. It was cold!
The instructors were all ex-soldiers of Japan. In a way they treated us
like they were in a military camp. . . . They taught us a lot of man-
ners, *reigi-tadashii* [be polite]. Certainly they taught you that there
was a pecking order. You know exactly where you are in the pecking
order.

Despite their overall financial difficulty, worsened by the Depression of the 1930s, it was common for the Issei to send their children
to lessons. It seems that they saw culturally and educationally
nourished children who could be accepted by the larger society as
their hope for the future. Miki Hayashi told me:

I was in *odori* [Japanese dancing] automatically because of my mother. . . . It was a big sacrifice for them because we were poor, and the
lessons were not free. But they somehow managed to send me and we
participated in all the community activities. She sewed a lot of costumes. . . . I still have a lot of costumes in a trunk in the basement. I
look at them and I think, "Gee, how so many things were sewn by
hand!" When we were both much older, I asked her, "Why did you
sacrifice so much?" She said—I forgot what exact Japanese words she
used—but she said, "It was the light of my life." I think that it was a
great comfort for her.

Thus, the Nisei acquired their Japanese values, behaviors, norms,
and language at home and in the community. They had, however,
another world to live in: the American school, where they learned
American values and behaviors. Every day, Miyamoto points out,
they pledged allegiance, sang the national anthem, and learned
American history (1984: xv). More important, they learned English,

and at an early age it became their primary language, in spite of limited social contact with non-Japanese. This adoption of English indicates the great impact of the American school on the Americanization of the Nisei. "I don't know what grade I was in when I started thinking in English," Miki Hayashi reported, "but I remember the time one day I thought, 'Oh my gosh! I'm thinking in English!' That kind of thing was a big revelation to me."

Often the practices at the American school came into conflict with what the children were learning at home. Harry H. L. Kitano notes, "It was a rare Nisei who did not feel ashamed and unhappy about his background during some period of his school years" (1976 [1969]: 50). Some Nisei were embarrassed by their parents' poor English. Shirley Kobayashi was one:

> Once when I was in high school, I can't remember where it was, but my mother wouldn't go because she didn't want to be among *hakujins* because she didn't understand the language, and one of the teachers said she'd be my mother for the evening. . . . They didn't understand the Caucasian language, and different meanings and things. She wouldn't go when Caucasian parents would attend. Times like that were a little embarrassing. I think I felt that I was missing out because my family couldn't participate in the activities.

Some Nisei recalled being severely discouraged by white American schoolteachers from speaking Japanese. Barbara Yamaguchi has bitter memories:

> When I was in the first grade, I went to an open house with my mother. I was translating for her, and the teacher said, "You should be ashamed that your mother can speak only Chinese!" I was so embarrassed and humiliated that I didn't correct her that it was Japanese, not Chinese. I never asked her to open house again for a long, long time. This is why Nisei never learned Japanese. We heard that American Indians were beaten if they spoke their own language to each other at school. That is how much *hakujin* looked down on any other language. We were told by teachers that it was shameful to speak our language.

[69]

Some say that they never felt ashamed about their parents or their heritage, but all, consciously or subconsciously, absorbed the message that they must "Americanize." Changing their given names to English ones is a reflection of this pursuit of Americanization. Often they chose names similar in sound or meaning to their Japanese names. For example, Isamu was changed to Sam, Tadashi to Tad, or Shoichi (from *sho* meaning "frankness" or "honesty") became Frank. Women often shortened their names—Miyoko to Miyo or Fumiko to Fumi.

The majority of Nisei went to the Bailey Gatzert, Pacific, Central, or Beacon Hill Elementary school. At Bailey Gatzert, located in the heart of Japantown, 90 percent of the students were Japanese (Miyamoto 1984: 53). At other schools, Japanese represented 10 to 20 percent of the student body.

The majority of the Nisei said all of their five closest friends from preschool to high school or college were Japanese, although a small minority included one or two white or Chinese Americans. For many Nisei, association with non-Japanese was confined to the school playgrounds. A majority of Nisei, who lived in predominantly white neighborhoods in the city, had more contact, but in the prewar era geographical and social segregation of minority groups was the rule. The Issei, moreover, tended to view other ethnic groups negatively and to discourage their children from interacting with non-Japanese, even other Asians. For example, there was animosity between the Japanese and the Chinese deriving from Japan's invasion of China and centuries of enmity between the two countries. Bill Fukuda sensed no outright hostility:

Young Japanese Americans at that time were off by themselves. The Chinese students were also off by themselves. I would call it *shima [-guni] konjo* [insularism]. There was no open conflict, but I think that there was a little bit of that standoffish existence even in the international community. I remember vividly writing an essay [in high school] about the need for all Chinese kids, Jewish kids, black kids, and Japanese kids to get along peacefully. There was no ethnic animosity, but standoffishness. To tell you the truth, you grab this from your parents.

John Ohki, however, described distinct

animosity between Japanese and Chinese. I used to get dirty looks from the Chinese when I walked in Chinatown. You're brought up with the thought that "Chinese are no good," because Japan was at war with China. At the Japanese school, they'd teach you the same thing. So you didn't care for the Chinese at that time. The Japanese looked down upon the Chinese. Not many *kurombos* [lit. black boys] or whites were around. The white shopkeepers were all right.

Shirley Kobayashi commented:

In those days they didn't talk about ethnic backgrounds like we do, like now. I think we kind of tried to forget that we were Japanese, we wanted to be more Americanized. Now they say all the different nationalities, not just Asians but Japanese, Chinese, Vietnamese, Taiwanese or something like that. Back when I was in high school, we didn't have all the different Asians, either. . . . Things were a lot more simple.

Dating, which usually did not begin until after high school, was generally intraethnic, except for a small number of the Nisei who dated white Americans. The Nisei in general felt it was "unthinkable" to marry outside the Japanese community in those days. In fact, statistics show that fewer than 1 percent of the marriages among the Seattle Nisei between 1930 and 1942 were exogamous (Leonetti and Newell-Morris 1982). Sylvia Yanagisako attributes this ethnic endogamy to low geographical mobility, a cultural requirement of parental approval for marriage, and the refusal of Issei parents to accept non-Japanese spouses for their children (1985: 70).[5] In some cases the Issei discouraged even dating of non-Japanese. Their insistence that their children seek marriage partners exclusively among the Japanese may have founded the Nisei preference, although in a much milder form, that their children marry Japanese Americans.

[5] Interestingly, the outmarriage rate right after the war jumped to over 10 percent (Yanagisako 1985: 76).

As long as the Nisei stayed inside the community, they did not encounter explicit discrimination. Some actively avoided possible confrontations by staying within the "comfortable" enclave. Some who went to Japanese-majority schools even felt that they were "kings and queens," as Sumi Hashimoto said. As they became older, however, and their exposure to the larger society increased, the Nisei began facing discrimination and exclusion, although it was not as severe as the bias had been against their Issei parents. Some Nisei recalled no personal experience of discrimination before the war. Others, however, vividly remembered their experiences as children. Helen Kageshita recalled plans for a play when she was in grade school: "They needed [someone to play] a role who had to be small. Classmates said I should, but the teacher said no. She gave some reasons, but I don't remember. I sensed that it was because I was Japanese American." Ed Murakami attended sixth, seventh, and eighth grades at

> a school with mostly *hakujin*. I remember the first day I was there I had to fight four *hakujin* kids. I was sitting on the stairs and they started hitting me on my back. I started to run and they chased me; so I turned around and started to fight them. I punched one in the nose, I tripped the other one, and then I punched the next one in the face, and the other one went away. After that they didn't bother me. That gave me a very bad experience of *hakujins*, for one thing. And then I saw two *hakujin* fellows. . . . They grabbed one student [from Turkey]. And one fellow held him and the other fellow started hitting him in the face. . . . After that I had a very bad feeling about *hakujin*. It never went away, although some *hakujins* are real nice.

Some school activities, such as honor society meetings, were sometimes held at a tennis club and other exclusive places where the Nisei as well as other minorities were not allowed. The social segregation in schools, which derived from both discrimination by the dominant group and self-segregation by the Nisei, led to the formation of Nisei social clubs and organizations in schools. For example, the Fuyo-kai at the University of Washington was a Nisei women's social club.

Miyamoto characterizes the relationship between the Japanese minority and the white majority as castelike (Miyamoto 1984: ix–x). The analogy is more applicable to the experience of the Issei, who were legally relegated to inferior status. They were made ineligible for citizenship and their economic opportunities were restricted by a series of laws, including the Alien Fishing Law of 1914 and the Alien Land Law of 1921 in Washington state.[6] Certainly, however, discrimination also affected the socioeconomic status as well as the ethnic consciousness and orientation of the Nisei.

Employment was probably the area of severest discrimination faced by the Nisei before the war. According to Jerrold Takahashi, employment opportunities were even more limited than in other major cities on the West Coast (1980: 177–78). Minorities were excluded from most labor unions and from most white-collar jobs. Older Nisei, even those with a university degree in chemistry, accounting, biology, or business, worked for Issei gardeners, landscapers, or in the produce market.[7] Ed Murakami, who worked at a gas station owned by an Issei after receiving a degree in economics from the University of Washington, talked about the exclusion practiced against Japanese Americans in employment in those years:

> Nobody got a job. A lot of them were engineers; not one of them got a job. Of course, at that time, it was very *fukeiki* [in a bad recession]— the Depression in the 1930s. A lot of *hakujins* got jobs, but *Nihonjins*, not one got a job. I think quite a few went to Japan. . . . One fellow was a mechanical engineer, he couldn't get a job here. He was in the top ten, and this W—— Company takes the top ten: they hire them. But they took his name out and replaced it with a *hakujin* name.

Employment opportunities were even more restricted for women than for men. Even teaching positions, one of the earliest oppor-

---

[6] Yuji Ichioka describes the significant efforts of the Japanese to protest the Alien Land Law. The Northwest American Japanese Association of Seattle challenged it and appealed to the Supreme Court, only to lose the case (1988: 232).

[7] Even working within the Japanese community was difficult. A survey conducted in 1924 revealed that fifty of fifty-two Nisei felt inconvenienced in their work because they were deficient in Japanese language skills (Takeuchi 1929: 444).

tunities to open for Nisei women college graduates after the war, were closed to Japanese Americans in the prewar period. "The Issei parents couldn't see the value of sending their daughters to college, because there was no job. . . . Especially [for] girls, there was not much incentive to go to college," said Kana Ochiai. The Nisei women in Seattle, however, had more opportunities in small enterprises, if not as professionals, than those in other cities on the West Coast. Evelyn Nakano Glenn reports that nearly one-third of the Nisei women employed in Seattle in 1940 worked as clerical and sales personnel. Other occupations related to small enterprises, such as service workers, proprietors, and managers, also had higher rates than those of San Francisco (1986: 77–78).

Housing was another area of institutional discrimination. "To go outside of the Nikkei ghetto area, so-called ghetto area," Ichiro Matsuda said, "we knew that we could not rent or move into an apartment where it was predominantly white people. Even though there were 'For Rent' signs, as soon as you go in, they'd say, 'Oh it's been rented. Sorry I forgot to put the sign away.' It was common. That was a common experience."

The discrimination that many Nisei experienced even before internment induced them to repress their positive ethnic consciousness. Often they developed low self-esteem and the feeling of being second-class citizens: "You see, everybody in authority was a Caucasian, right?" Miki Hayashi explained. "So right there, you have a kind of attitude that they were better, that their world was a little better than ours. We were never taught that, but you automatically felt like second-class citizens, because we were all poor, because our parents' jobs were not that good. . . . I think that [feeling inferior] was the reason we stuck in our community, because we felt comfortable." Whether or not the Nisei felt inferior, the majority said that they identified themselves ethnically as Japanese and nationally as American. Despite evidence of discrimination, for many it was the outbreak of the war which compelled them to confront their "difference" from other American citizens in terms of race and national origin. In the late 1930s and early 1940s, some Nisei already had a foreboding of the coming war. Harry Tanabe told me:

Well, being in business, you know, and being a foreign trade major, I knew the war was coming when they put the oil embargo and steel embargo on. I knew the war was coming. I could feel the sentiment. Caucasians were really bashing the Japanese. It was about the time they were having the naval conferences. You know Japan, England, and America would meet and limit the number of battleships, and Japan always got the short end of the stick.

The newspapers ran increasingly sensational articles about "the Japs." Many Nisei, however, were still too young to recognize the deteriorating political relationship between the United States and Japan.

Evacuation and Internment

By the morning after the attack on Pearl Harbor, FBI agents, drawing from the custodial detention list prepared years before the war, had arrested over one hundred community leaders in Seattle alone. These Issei were mostly organization leaders, Japanese schoolteachers, Buddhist priests, and judo instructors (Residents of Minidoka Relocation Center 1943). Some were released after interrogation before enemy alien hearing boards; the others were separated from their families and sent to Department of Justice detention camps to be interned as "enemy aliens" (see Map 1). The sudden arrests were terrifying. William Kawata (real name) testified before the Commission on Wartime Relocation and Internment of Civilians:

It wasn't long that after the war started that the town sheriff came armed to the house we were staying at and took Dad to jail at gunpoint like a common criminal. There was no announcement of this act. . . . I remember trembling with rage and feeling helpless and scared. There was no difference between this and the Gestapo. How could we be treated like this in America? I began to resent giving my pledge [of] allegiance to the flag. . . . No it wasn't fair, no there was no liberty, no freedom, we were not equal, there was no justice for all. I was depressed on how Americans could lie about their pledge of allegiance. (CWRIC 1981)

Shizue Peterson, whose father was also arrested, said that the family's belongings were confiscated and never returned. Her mother was left traumatized: "She was scared because she didn't know what they would do to her, and then she was left alone with three kids. No money, no income, no nothing. It was a very trying period."

The Nisei, whose average age was nineteen, were shocked by the outbreak of the war. The sudden loss of a large number of community leaders left them confused and apprehensive. Ichiro Matsuda, who was then a student at the University of Washington, described his despair over the outbreak of the war:

The next day, I debated Monday whether I should go to class at the university. I felt some—I don't know how to explain it. I guess I was stunned, that I felt a little bit inhibited, a little bit embarrassed, maybe. Maybe I felt a little bit of guilt, but I felt very strange.

So when I went back to university, I went to the library—Suzzallo Library—it seemed much more quiet, stone silent. I think all the students must have been thinking about the war. . . . And I was . . . so self-conscious, because I'm a Nikkei. . . . Next day I told my parents, maybe I should quit the university because I just didn't have the interest to continue my studies. I thought to myself, I couldn't see much future, especially after Pearl Harbor. Because . . . prior to Pearl Harbor, life was difficult for Issei and Nisei, and the war was not going to make it any easier, as we soon found out when we were sent to concentration camps. So I thought that was the end of my personal part, as [far as] life was concerned, that I had no future in America.

The Issei started burning Japanese things out of fear that possession of anything connected to Japan would place them in a dangerous position. Family pictures, letters, Japanese books, guest books, and other sentimental articles the Issei had cherished for many decades turned to ashes. Shirley Kobayashi set the scene for me:

Heika [(the emperor's) picture] was way, way up there. When the war broke out and they said if you had anything that was Japanese, they might hold it against you, so we had to burn pictures and letters and things like that. And I remember my mother saying that she had to burn that picture, too, and I thought she had. But not too long ago, my older sister said, "Oh, Mom didn't burn the *Heika no* picture. She hid it someplace.

To Shirley Kobayashi's mother, the Japanese emperor was the symbol of Japan and one of the strongest ties to her home country. Some Sansei today regret the loss of many valuable Japanese objects and family mementos during this time, which made tracing their family history more difficult.

Assets in Japanese banks were frozen. Shortwave radios, cameras, and any objects considered to be weapons, including swords, were confiscated. Because the dominant society tended to lump all Asians together, unable to distinguish them, Chinese started wearing "I'm Chinese" buttons to identify themselves. Kana Ochiai said, "Some of my friends saw 'I'm Chinese' buttons the very next day [after Pearl Harbor]. One of my friends, she used to go to school with a Chinese girl. After Pearl Harbor, she no longer walked with her. They wanted to disassociate from us. . . . That hurt us. From December 8th, we were made to feel guilty."

In early 1942 all Nisei employees of the Seattle public schools were forced to resign because of strong pressure from the Parent-Teacher Association. "I felt very rejected," recalls Shizue Peterson. "I mean, the fact that I was an American just like anybody else, why would they pick on us?"

Executive Order 9066 authorized the establishment of military zones on the West Coast and the exclusion of anyone, whether citizen or not, from these zones. Since it made no direct reference to them, the Japanese Americans did not at first realize that it would be applied to them. On March 2 the voluntary evacuation order was announced, and those of Japanese descent residing on the west side of the Pacific coast states and a portion of Arizona, the area designated as Military Zone 1, were told to evacuate "voluntarily" inland. In mid-March a curfew was imposed on the Japanese from 8:00 P.M. to 6:00 A.M., and travel more than five miles from their residences was prohibited. On March 31, people of Japanese ancestry on Bainbridge Island were evacuated after receiving a few days' notice. They were the first in the nation to be evacuated under the provisions of Executive Order 9066. Rumors that similar evacuation was planned for Seattle intensified. Shirley Kobayashi said:

There were rumors. People on the Bainbridge Island had to evacuate in April [March], and it must have been before then that they said voluntary evacuation. . . . My dad had a cousin that had . . . a truck. So he says, "If we have to move, let's go together." Then Dad said, "Where will we go?" At that time nothing was specific. . . . How far inland you had to go, they didn't say. If we left, how about work, money? 'Cause everything we had in the Japanese banks was already frozen.

The next thing was that American citizens can stay here, but those who are not citizens have to leave. That would mean my mother and dad, and my sister also was born in Japan. So that would mean three would stay here and three would have to leave. My dad kept saying, "Girls are *abunai* [It's too dangerous for you girls]. Somebody might rape you." Well, what can you do, staying at home? My brother was fifteen at that time and he says, well, if my mother and dad and sister had to leave, and the three of us stayed here . . . he would go to work. Well, what can a fifteen-year-old do? So my mother says, "No, if we're going to have to leave, we'll all leave together. Until they say so, we won't do anything." Then the evacuation orders came through.

In the Seattle area, the orders specifying dates and assembly areas were posted about one month prior to the evacuation. The Issei and older Nisei were busy selling businesses and disposing of belongings. Miki Hayashi remembered:

See, I was 21, I think it was very—you know when you're going through something, you don't think, "This is traumatic or this is"— but I remember confusion. You had no time to think, "Is this right or wrong?" You were all busy packing. My dad was busy because he had to get rid of all the stuff at the store, my mother was busy because she was packing everything and we were trying to sell things like our furniture and deciding what to take. We didn't know what kind of place we were going to, or how long we were going to be gone. And nobody could tell us. Actually no one knew what was going to happen to us, really. And no one knew how long the war was going to last. It was just total confusion.

The Issei and older Nisei, in many cases, had to sell their businesses, equipment, stock, furniture, appliances, and other personal belongings for next to nothing. Kaz Miata's father sold his grocery store in Seattle for four hundred dollars. In the urgent situation, bargain hunters and dealers took advantage of many people. Mutsu Homma (real name) lived in Los Angeles at the time of evacuation.

After the army ordered to evacuate the Japanese, other people poured into West Los Angeles to buy the Japanese people's houses and household goods. I never sold anything. I was scared of them. They walked into the house and said, "I want this piano. How much?" I repeatedly said that I do not want to sell the piano because the piano is my life. I studied piano since I was six years old and went to the Southern California College of Music. They said, "You can't take the piano with you; so I will buy it." They put the piano on the truck and they left twenty-five dollars for the piano, a Baldwin piano. Another time I found a person loading the washing machine on the truck. So I begged them not to take it since I had three little children I had to wash for every day. They finally unloaded the washing machine, but by that time the dining room set was gone. (CWRIC 1981)

Others asked their friends to take care of the property, but in many cases, that course turned out to be disastrous, as well. "My husband had a terrible time," said Miki Hayashi.

He had two stores. I didn't know him at that time. [After the curfew] he had to close the store at a certain time. When the evacuation order came, he consolidated the stock into one store. Then he put the fixtures in storage. He asked some people living there to watch it; then we were evacuated. When we were in Puyallup, after two

[79]

months, they brought only $18, and said, "This is the only profit I have." But you know that it can't be true. In other words, they were selling everything and keeping all the money. He asked if he could go to town to put up everything, and he was denied permission. So he got in touch with a lawyer, and asked the lawyer to sell everything. There was almost no stock hardly left, but the equipment. Everything he had at his store, he sold for fifteen hundred dollars.

Pregnant women about to give birth had labor induced before being evacuated, because of the lack of a hospital in the Puyallup Assembly Center.

Like many other Nisei in the community, Toshi Akimoto, who did not have American citizenship at that time, criticized the JACL, which encouraged people to "quietly cooperate" with the evacuation in order to show their loyalty to the United States:

> But at that time I even thought about—if I was a citizen, I would have probably made a big plaque and printed in big letters "I'm an American" and marched down the street, or marched down to Puyallup with that, while they're putting me into Puyallup. And I think that would have had some effect, or at least the newspaper would take a picture of that for our record, because it actually would show the American government imprisoning American citizens into camps. But they didn't do that, the Japanese [American] Citizens League said, "Obey the law, and if the president says so, just quietly go to the camps without raising a fuss," which I was very much against. But I couldn't say anything, being a Japanese citizen myself.

In fact, on February 28, 1942, Jimmy Sakamoto of the Seattle JACL, perhaps the most influential leader in the Seattle Japanese community at that time, stated, "We will be only too happy to be evacuated if the Government orders us, because we feel that the basic loyalty at a time such as this is to obey the order of the Government to which we owe true allegiance" (Daniels 1988: 220). This opinion was consistent with that of the national JACL leadership.[8] Criticism

---

[8] According to Roger Daniels, Mike Masaoka, then-JACL national secretary, issued a bulletin to all JACL chapters in early April of 1942, after its pledge of

against the JACL for the position it took over evacuation, as if representing the entire Japanese American population, often rises in the community even today. Jerrold Takahashi (1980), in his analysis of the diverse political styles among the Nisei, however, points out structural limits within the particular historical context of that time. In other words, such factors as the denial of citizenship to the Issei, their exclusion from or limited access to labor unions, the prevailing ideology of Anglo-conformity (cf. Gordon 1964) and constrained ethnic consciousness, and the reliance on the courts to protect their rights influenced the leadership in the JACL and helped to determine their conservative response. At the time, the organization had the full support of the Buddhist and Christian churches, and its leadership was recognized by other segments and organizations of the Japanese community (Takahashi 1980: 183–84).

While most Japanese Americans followed the evacuation order "quietly," Gordon Hirabayashi (real name) and two other Nisei men resisted the curfew or the order. He was influenced, Hirabayashi said, by his white American associates but mostly by his mother.

> My mother was a very, very strong antagonist against injustice and she was a generation—two generations—early. She was born two generations early to be a feminist. . . . And she used to say, "If something happened and somebody was discriminated against"—we were discussing what happened to somebody—she would say, . . . "He should have stood up a little stronger." And we're getting that sort of thing, so I've got little more urgings in that sort of thing; and foundation for a viewpoint that wouldn't occur to some people.

Hirabayashi recalled the time he discussed with his mother his position on the curfew and evacuation order.

> Neither my father nor my mother opposed. . . . However, they said, "However, this is war and we're all about to be moved someplace. We don't know where we're going or how long. . . . Then if you do this

---

cooperation to FDR, urging them not to support Minoru Yasui of Portland, Oregon, who deliberately violated the curfew. See Daniels 1988: 222–24 for details.

against the government, we don't know what's going to happen to you. You might be strung up, you might be killed by firing squad, we don't know anything. Now, we're proud of what you're doing, but put it on ice and keep the family together because we don't know what's going to happen." And that was a real, true concern. They really didn't know what was going to happen to them. . . . It was quite devastating. She even used tears; she broke down and wept and said she didn't want the family to be separated now.

But I couldn't hold it. If I went with them, I'd have to give up something to make myself go, and what I'd have to give up was what made me an objector to what I considered injustice. And if I went along, that meant defeating myself, and it would affect me. I wouldn't be the same person she's got beside her. And later she realized this. . . . I received one letter after she moved . . . to Tule Lake. During her first few days there, somebody knocked on the door, and it was two women who said they were so-and-so from southern California and they said they heard . . . that there was the mother of the fellow who was in Seattle fighting the case and here all our leaders are kowtowing and so on. "It's so frustrating, we're losing everything and nobody is raising a voice. I just want to come and meet you and say thank you for what your son is doing." She wrote that to me and she said . . . she got a real big lift. When I read that, I realized that—I was carrying a little bit of guilt feeling for not going with the family, regretting it— . . . but when I got that letter, I realized that, you know, that that weight left, because I knew by being with her, I couldn't give her that kind of lift. She got that lift because I stayed behind. (Personal interview, November 8, 1989)

The case generated a good deal of interest. Some knew Gordon Hirabayashi. Barbara Yamaguchi was one:

My boyfriend at that time was a very good friend of Gordon Hirabayashi. I remember that we spent hours talking about the evacuation order. Gordon said, "I'm not going to obey the order." Then my boyfriend said, "I wish I had the courage to do that. But I don't think I could do that." . . . We spent a lot of hours discussing it. "This is against the constitution because we didn't commit any crime."

"They haven't taken us to the court to test anything." Yes, we spent a lot of time discussing and soul-searching. But at the same time, you are powerless, helpless. What can you do—except for those individuals like Gordon who refused to go to be evacuated?

Many Sansei have questioned why the Nisei, except for the three, did not resist the evacuation order. It is impossible to provide a simple answer. The Nisei, first of all, felt that they had no choice, having been placed under the control of the U.S. Army. As Harry Tanabe remarked, "What can you do? Soldiers got a rifle. Why get killed over something like that? We were helpless. . . . When the army says, 'Go,' you've got to go." Many were so preoccupied with selling and disposing of property that they had no time to question the issue. Besides, they were young then, and after the community leaders were arrested, they were suddenly placed in decision-making positions. Although it may not be a popular opinion, some Nisei partially attribute acquiescence to the Japanese cultural norm that instills unquestioned obedience and prohibits questioning the orders of any authority or superior. "We were very unsophisticated. . . . We more or less waited for the instructions," said Helen Kageshita. "I have a feeling that we let the authorities decide. The power of the authority was so instilled that we didn't question what the government did. For most of us in that age group, we didn't ask." Elmer Tazuma (real name) testified about traditional Japanese values, especially perseverance, forbearance, and obedience to authority, which he claims bound the Nisei at the time of evacuation:

To the Japanese, complaining is like breaking a Samurai code. Ever since we were very small, we were drummed with *"shimbo"* and *"gaman."* The meaning of those two words is forebear, no matter what happens. . . . When the American Government says you can't have citizenship, we said, "That's okay." When they said, "You cannot own real estate," we say, "That's okay." When they said, "Now we are going to take you to camp as a prisoner," we said, "That's okay." Now I sometimes wonder if they said, "We have a fiery oven," and told us to walk in, how many of us would have said, "Okay." (CWRIC 1981)

[83]

Government officials and military officers were debating various issues involving military safety and how to handle Nisei who were American citizens. Some racial slurs used at the time still resonate in the memories of the Nisei. General DeWitt, for example, head of the Western Defense Command, remarked: "A Jap's a Jap. . . . There is no way to determine their loyalty. . . . It makes no difference whether he is an American; theoretically he is still a Japanese and you can't change him" (*San Francisco Chronicle*, April 14, 1943). Many Nisei and Issei still cite the phrase "A Jap is a Jap" when referring to the racism of the government at that time.

By early May 1942, nearly seventy-four hundred people of Japanese ancestry in the Seattle area had been uprooted from their residences and taken to Camp Harmony, a temporary "assembly center" in Puyallup, western Washington. Many, including John Ohki, felt that they were betrayed by their own government.

"All the people of Japanese ancestry"—that really puzzled me. Gee! Am I a United States citizen? I was born in the United States. I pledged allegiance every day at school. How come they treated me like I was a foreigner? I don't even know Japan other than what I read about Japan. So it really upset me. I remember when we were about ready to be evacuated, I sat down on the sidewalk and said to myself, "Gee, what does this pledge of allegiance mean?" I said, "'Liberty and justice for all'—Is that only for whites?" It just didn't hit me right. And you know, you become ashamed of being Japanese. "Gee, how come I have to go? How comes whites don't have to go, Chinese don't have to go?" And all of a sudden you start saying, "Gosh! I wish I was something else."

Many youngsters, however, found the evacuation, even riding on a train, an exciting new experience. Michi Walter, who was in California at that time, was ten years old: "It was like an adventure, like 'I wonder where we are going?' I don't remember feeling particularly scared or anything. . . . Getting on a train—that was very unusual. I hadn't even been on a train once before in my whole life, and so it was like an adventure. . . . We went as a group; so it didn't seem so bad.

Children on a train heading for camp, 1942. Photo courtesy of Executive Order 9066 Project.

On evacuation days, Japanese Americans congregated at designated areas to board guarded buses. They were allowed to bring only what they could carry, and they had to wear numbered name tags. Peggy Mitchell (real name) testified at the commission hearings:

The old and the aged and the sickly ones were really pitiful to watch. The atmosphere was tense and intolerable. I was really concerned about my father, for he was not feeling too well. En-route, I asked the driver if he could please stop someplace convenient for my father to go to the restroom and I was completely ignored. I just prayed that he would be all right until we reached our destination. That was the "longest" ride that I had ever experienced! (CWRIC 1981)

Matsuzo Watanabe told me:

The buses came a half-hour late. . . . Many people had to go to the bathroom and got off the buses to use the bathroom at a gasoline

[85]

station. . . . However, one of the men at the gas station locked the door of the bathroom and refused to let the Japanese use the bathroom. . . .

When we were getting to the newly built prison camp awaiting us, I saw the barbed wire. I said, "Barbed wire!" A man sitting next to me said, "No," but I was right.

Miki Hayashi remembered the "dead silence" in the bus on the way to Puyallup. Nobody talked. She saw tears drop from her mother's eyes.

Camp Harmony was a small compound surrounded by a barbed-wire fence with guard posts. It consisted of four areas, where long rows of wooden barracks, resembling chicken coops, had been hurriedly built. People were not allowed to visit friends in another area. Barbara Yamaguchi, who served as a volunteer nurse's aide while interned in Puyallup, remembers being escorted by military police across the street from gate to gate every day. Until they were permitted to move to other barracks, some two hundred internees were assigned to barracks that had been converted from horse stables, where the odor was sickening (cf. Kodaira 1980: 106–11). Except in some newly built barracks, the board floors were laid directly on the damp earth; grass grew through the cracks. Each room had cots with straw mattresses and a light bulb hanging from the ceiling. The partitions between each family were only six to seven feet high, and were open to the ceiling. All lights were extinguished at nine o'clock at night since the curfew order was still in effect. Roll call was taken at certain times every day.

In a film the government presented to the public during the war to explain the relocation and internment of Japanese Americans, the narrator states, "The army provided housing and plenty of healthful, nourishing food for all."[9] Actually, expenditures for food averaged only 38.19 cents per person per day in assembly centers (Daniels 1988: 231), and many Nisei remember its poor quality. Especially at the beginning, the same food was served day after day. Toshi Akimoto described it:

[9] The Office of War Information, Bureau of Motion Pictures, *Japanese Relocation*, n.d.

I just couldn't stand that food. That food was terrible. I tell you exactly what it was: Vienna sausage . . . small sausage in cans. And they served me that for breakfast, and then I had to stand in line and with a plate, and the Japanese kids . . . slap a ladle full of mashed potato, and then gave me about two or three Vienna sausage—that was all for my breakfast. And . . . [he] says you can only have one utensil. . . . The spoons and forks were all gone so I had to take a knife, and I was eating with my knife. Then for lunch I went back and I had the same thing for lunch: Vienna sausage and mashed potatoes! And then for supper I had the same thing again! Then I thought, "Damn it! I'm going to complain about this."

The food was so poor that Akimoto finally volunteered to move to Tule Lake Relocation Center, where for only the first three weeks better food was served to the volunteers who moved there from other camps. Once when spoiled Vienna sausage was served at Puyallup people had severe diarrhea. The limited bathroom facilities, which were located outside at some distance away, aggravated the situation. It was especially hard for the old, the sick, and pregnant women. In addition, the American-style diet, which included cheese and hominy, was unfamiliar to the Issei and Nisei.

Some Nisei recall how their parents deplored the free meals saying, "Kojiki mitai ni" ("This is like a beggar"). Nor was it Japanese custom to line up to be served, cafeteria style. Theresa Hitoru Matsudaira (real name), an Issei woman, testified:

We would go and be fed at a signal bell. Such a beggar-like life continued. I remember crying every time I was given food. . . . For three years, we ate and lived at the signal bell. That is against the Japanese spirit at all. We, Japanese, live on with the money we earn no matter how poor we may be. But we were fed—that hurt very much. I think, our children felt the humiliation, too, thinking why we have to live like this. (CWRIC 1981)

"I was worried," she continued, "about nothing but my children. What would be the future of these children who grew up in the

[87]

U.S.? We came from Japan, so we would bear any wretched life, but all I was thinking about was the future of my children."[10]

Because the partitions were only partial, conversation, baby cries, and other noises carried throughout the barracks. There was no privacy, said Miki Hayashi. "The next room was a young couple. And you could hear everything at night. It was embarrassing. You know how embarrassing that would be for a young person. I would every night go like [covers her ears with hands]. Because it's not sealed to the ceiling. I was old enough to know what was going on." Moreover, all family members, typically Issei parents and their unmarried Nisei children, shared one room. In the women's communal bathrooms, no doors were installed, and in the men's bathroom even partitions were not furnished.

The distrust of the guards and other authorities was humiliating. Matsuzo Watanabe recalled that when he left his barracks to use a centrally located bathroom at night, a search light beam followed him the whole way. Nobuko Suzuki (real name) testified that once a homemade chocolate cake her friends had made, which was delivered through the central office, was split in several places and checked for contraband (CWRIC 1981). Kana Ochiai told of similar experiences:

And an interesting story—when we went to Puyallup, we looked for the restrooms because they were separated. They had these bathrooms, outhouses. They were wooden structures just like our barracks. But we looked, we didn't know if this was for men or this is for women, but that kind of thing is a shock, you know. You don't have facilities in your barrack. So because we had such a change of diet, lot of us had come down with diarrhea and so we all had to go to the bathroom in the middle of the night. And we had to leave our barracks to go to these latrines; so everybody was going with flashlights because it was dark, and so we had these sentries watching—all of a sudden in the middle of the night, they see flashlights, here and there. They thought, "Is there going to be an uprising or what?"

[10] This is an English translation of oral testimony given in Japanese. This portion is not included in the record of the commission hearings; it is taken from videotapes of the commission hearings in Seattle made by a Nisei there.

. . . And then our Caucasian friends would come see us and they would bring us like cakes or some goodies from their home. And they thought there were weapons or something concealed, so like cakes, I remember they cut into it because some knife or something—I don't know what they were thinking, but there was no trust in what these people might do.

Internees were allowed to see visitors only in certain places along the fence and were required to maintain a distance of about five feet from them. Some white Americans visited their interned friends while they were in Puyallup, often bringing food and other necessary goods. Helen Kageshita, however, received no visits and her disappointment was deep: "During the time in Puyallup, none of my friends came. That hurt. There was no support from Caucasian friends. Deep down, these things might have been preventing me from going back to a relationship with Caucasians." Others remembered the humiliation of being watched by curiosity seekers. Sumi Hashimoto reported: "I remember when I first went to the camp in Puyallup—see we were inside the barbed wire fence. On Sundays these *hakujin* people would come and look at us from the outside as if we were people in the zoo. They walked around and looked at us. I remember resenting that. So I wouldn't go near the fence."

The majority of the Nisei named the lack of privacy as one of the hardest things to bear in camps, though the situation was a little better in Minidoka, the permanent camp to which most were later transferred. Setsuko Fukuda said the worst thing in Camp Harmony in Puyallup was "everything—living there. One room, straw mattress, not being able to go anywhere. Eating together, using bathroom together—no privacy, I think that was the biggest thing." George Saito, too, cited

lack of privacy. We hung blankets. It was harder for my sister and my mother, I guess it's harder on the women. The food wasn't great, a lot of people got sick. Maybe I got sick once or twice. Lack of privacy in the men's bathroom. There was like one long bench in there, with no partitions. That kind of got me. And I remember people that lived under the grandstands, they had to live where the cows and horses

[89]

were at one time . . . just smell that manure and all that. . . . Those kinds of indignities mount up. If you're a male and a young teenager, you take a lot—your resiliency is pretty great, I think.

Miki Hayashi also felt "the lack of privacy, and to watch my parents. In two months his hair turned white. I really felt sorry for him because there was nothing for him to do. So he always lay down on the couch. Finally somebody gave him some seeds, and he planted some sweet pea flowers in front of the barrack. I was kind of touched because he never did any gardening until then." Camp life was even more difficult for those who were pregnant or who had small children or a sick family member. Sumi Hashimoto recalled her life as a young mother in camp:

> We had no cooking facilities so that babies' formula— We had to sterilize bottles. We had no way to launder diapers. So I would have a bucket full of diapers, a scrub board, soap, and you had to stand in line because the laundry room would have hot water at six o'clock in the morning. So they were there at five o'clock in the morning. All these mothers would rush into the big laundry. After five minutes, no more hot water.
>
> Taking care of a baby was hard, because the barracks, the wall was only six feet high, and up above that was open. So when the baby was crying, we were at the end of the barrack, the whole place could hear the cry. You couldn't let him cry, so you have to hold him all the time, no crib. . . . I was so busy taking care of the baby and my four-year-old son. How would I have time to sit down and cry about things or get mad at things? Physically you just wore out.

From August to September 1942, people of Japanese descent in Puyallup were transferred to more permanent camps. Nearly 90 percent went to Minidoka, Idaho (Leonetti 1976: 22). After a day-long train ride, during which the blinds were closed and people were not allowed to look out until they had passed a military-related industrial area, they finally stopped in the middle of the desert. From there they rode buses to Minidoka Camp, dozens of miles away from the railroad stop. "The train was old. It was shuttered. It

Moving into a camp barracks, 1942. Photo courtesy of Executive Order 9066 Project.

was a miserable experience," said Helen Kageshita. "After we got there . . . *gakkarishita* [deeply disappointed]. All I could see was dust and dirt in this barren desert. The dust was fine soot. That was more traumatic to see than Puyallup, because it was a permanent camp and we had no idea of the place."

[91]

It was not easy for people accustomed to the mild climate of the Northwest to bear the harsh extremes of the desert. Temperatures could exceed 110 degrees in summer and 20 degrees below zero in winter, and the wind was full of dust. About 10,140 internees, 7,300 of them from Washington and the remaining 2,840 from Oregon, lived in this 68,000-acre camp (*Minidoka Irrigator*, Sept. 10, 1942). Dust was one of their strongest memories. "We would have terrible dust storms. The barracks were never insulated. You have these windows where you could see the dust coming under the window, even if the window was closed. If you go to the mess hall to eat. Oh! the cups and dishes are on the table and you pick up the cup and there is a mark! That is something you never forget," said Setsuko Fukuda. People covered their faces with kerchiefs or caps to keep the sand out of their noses and mouths. Shirley Kobayashi slept with a wet towel on her face to keep out the smell of dust. The flourlike dust turned to deep mud when it rained, and the first goods inter-nees bought when mail order became available were boots. The harsh environment of Minidoka was one of the hardest things in the lives of the residents there. Jane Tachibana directed her anger to-ward the government, which she believed had purposely chosen harsh environments for the camps: "Well, I think the government really knew what areas they wanted to put the camps: in very desolate, dusty, windy, cold areas, or places that would get real hot."

The camp was still under construction when the people arrived from Puyallup. Miki Hayashi recalled hanging blankets between families in a long barracks without any partitions, until her family moved to a completed barracks. Each family again shared a single room. They ranged from about 10 feet by 15 feet to 20 feet by 24 feet, depending on the family size, and this time they had complete partitions. Again, they were furnished with military cots and blan-kets. People over sixty years old were provided with beds. Since there were no closets, occupants hung their clothes on a rope. A potbellied stove in the corner, with foraged scraps of wood for fuel, provided heat. The annoyance from dust diminished as the con-struction progressed and as trees and lawns were planted. Until flush toilets were installed in February 1943, the people went to outhouses, which were only sheltered holes in the ground. When the temperature was nearly twenty below zero, it was especially hard for the old people. Hot water, even drinking water, was in short supply in the beginning.

Although the rooms were not furnished, the people started to make furniture by themselves, using the materials provided by the War Relocation Authority. Facilities were better equipped, and there was a hospital and a fire department in the camp. Elementary, junior high, and high schools started in camp at the end of 1942.

The internees organized a system of self-government, and in September 1942, after the transfer of evacuees was completed, Jimmy Sakamoto (real name) was elected mayor. The camp was organized into forty-four blocks of six barracks each and an average population of three hundred people. At the center of each block was a mess hall, a communal bathroom, and a laundry room. Each block had its own manager (Kodaira 1980: 126).

There were various kinds of jobs in camp, ranging from dishwasher, cook, and carpenter, to truck driver, nurse, and newspaper editor. As of January 1943, 2,910 males and 1,640 females were employed in the camp, about half the entire number of internees (*Minidoka Irrigator*, Jan. 27, 1943). The salaries were set at $12, $16, and $19 a month, depending on the skills required. Professionals, such as doctors, were paid $19. Schoolteachers were paid $16, even though white teachers working in the camps were paid hundreds of dollars a month. Jane Tachibana, who was then a registered nurse, discussed the employment discrimination.

I felt a lot of prejudice in Minidoka, working with the Caucasian nurses. . . . These nurses I worked with were Caucasian and they were getting their civil service salary and half of the time they'd be sitting around drinking coffee, smoking cigarettes, and it irritated me so much. And I was always in charge of the labor in the delivery room. . . . I had to get up in the morning, even though I had been up three hours during the night. . . . They wanted me to do everything, like cleaning up after a delivery. After a delivery they would just go off; you wouldn't even find them any place. . . . [Later] we were able to apply for different kinds of jobs outside of the camp. . . . We didn't have to stay in camp and work with this nineteen-dollar-a-month salary when all these nurses that I was working with were getting something like four hundred dollars.

Tachibana reported that because of the lack of good medication, euthanasia was sometimes practiced at Tule Lake, where she was interned before moving to Minidoka:

I had this cardiac patient who was having a hard time breathing all the time during her whole pregnancy. . . . There was nothing available to ease the pain or take care of her discomfort during her pregnancy whereas I'm sure if we were out of camp, there would have been a lot of different facilities that would have been available to a patient in her condition. . . . Her husband came to me one day and said, "Will you ask the doctor to take care of her because she's so uncomfortable" and he's getting to a point where he couldn't stand to watch his wife any longer. . . . And Dr. T—— said, "Well there's nothing I can do for her here, as long as we're in camp. There's nothing available, and so if those are his wishes, we'll have to abide by it." . . . [She] was under the oxygen tent; that's the only way she could breathe. So then he called all of his children. . . . Each of the children took a spoonful of water and gave it to the mother and then the father nodded to me and I was the one that had to give the morphine shot. A quarter of the morphine and the heart condition like that, they just die right away. Within three or four minutes, she stopped breathing.

Camp life also destroyed family relationships. All of a sudden, the father lost his breadwinner role and, in many cases, lost his authority and control of the family as well. Children ate with their peer group at a mess hall and stayed late away from the barracks. They did not receive *kozukai*, or pocket money, from their parents as they would before internment, nor did their parents feed them. Kaz Miata said that he often argued with his father, though he never had before the war. Young women would gather at a laundry room, where they talked to each other while washing. In camp, both parents often worked in order to save money, even though the salary was nominal. As a result, the family members rarely saw each other. Helen Kageshita recalled one Thanksgiving: "My father was a dishwasher, and my mother worked as a waitress in the mess hall, and my brother was usually somewhere else eating with friends. On Thanksgiving Day when you think of the family eating together, everyone was off somewhere else. I sat down to eat by myself and thought, 'What kind of a Thanksgiving is this?'" Camp life was also destructive for some young couples. Sumi Hashimoto explained: "The bad thing I know camp did was to destroy your family life. It destroyed it for me forever. See, the husband didn't have to work hard any more: room and board were supplied. He didn't have time to eat with us, because he had so many other activities. The family life was just destroyed, I feel."

Minidoka was one of the quietest and most harmonious of all the Japanese American internment camps. There were conflicts, however. People tended to coalesce into regional groups, and animosity often rose among these groups—between the Seattlites and Oregonians, for example, and between Seattlites and Hawaiians. "In the camp," said Bill Fukuda, "a lot of things happened. There was a lot of animosity between groups. Again, if you want to call it *shima* [-*guni*] *konjo* [insularism], it is. The Seattlites, 'That guy is from Portland.' 'That guy is from California.' . . . Fight all the time. Over nothing. There is nothing to do in camp. . . . Simply because they were from Hawaii, *gaijin* [foreigners, outsiders]. Nothing to do is the whole thing."

Probably, the most serious emotional conflict between parents and children surfaced when the government sought volunteers for the 442d Regimental Combat Team. The camp newsletter published a letter by President Roosevelt to the secretary of war, endorsing the recruitment:

The proposal of the War Department to organize a combat team consisting of loyal American citizens of Japanese descent has my full approval. . . .

No loyal citizens of the United States should be denied the democratic right to exercise the responsibilities of his citizenship, regardless of his ancestry. The principle on which this country was founded and by which it has always been governed is that Americanism is a matter

[95]

of the mind and heart, *Americanism is not and never was, a matter of race or ancestry.* (*Minidoka Irrigator*, Feb. 8, 1943, my emphasis)

It was, as Helen Kageshita said, ironic for the government to ask Nisei men from the concentration camps to volunteer for the army. Nevertheless, the men who volunteered felt that this was their only country and wanted to show their loyalty. Peggy Mitchell summarized their feelings in her testimony before the commission: "A Nisei's brother-in-law volunteered for the U.S. Army. Asked by his mother why give your life for a country that treated him and his family so cruelly, he replied, 'Mother, this is my country and the only country I know. I want to prove that I am a loyal citizen. Some day everyone will know and understand. You'll see'" (CWRIC 1981). Jimmy Sakamoto (real name), longtime leader of the Seattle chapter of the JACL, urged the Nisei to volunteer, writing in the camp newsletter:

> This is a challenge to the niseis and the opportunity to show our loyalty. Up to now we have been expressing our allegiance, and the day has come when we can actually demonstrate it.
>
> There are millions of boys in the armed services today, fighting inspiringly. I would like to see as many nisei as possible join them in the fight. (*Minidoka Irrigator*, Feb. 3, 1943)

Bill Fukuda, who volunteered for the army after the war when he reached the qualifying age, described his feeling: "I know mother wasn't too happy. You felt that there was a great injustice. But you have to go there and prove something and to say, 'Hey, you are really wrong.' How can you do that unless you do something? There is nobody who really wants to be a soldier. They went there simply because they had to show somebody what they were."

Most volunteered primarily to prove their loyalty. Volunteering for the army when their families were living behind barbed wire may also reflect the traditional Japanese value of loyalty to one's lord, not mere patriotism, whether or not the Nisei were aware of this cultural tradition. Feudal loyalty often conflicted with filial piety and other familial values. Hoichi Kubo (real name) of San Jose, a former military intelligence service officer in the Pacific, spoke of this "loyalty" norm in a documentary film about the service, made in 1987. Once he was trying to persuade Japanese soldiers in caves on Saipan to surrender.

I took off my helmet so that I look like a Japanese, which I am. [A Japanese soldier asked,] "How come you Japanese? How come you are fighting for the United States?" I said, "Well, if you remember the saying"—I spoke in Japanese, using the history of Japan—there was a son fighting his father. The father was at war with the emperor, and he wanted his son to side with him. So I said, "Chu naran to hossureba Ko narazu. Ko naran to hossureba Chu narazu." This means in English, "If I want to be good to my parents, I cannot be loyal to my country. If I want to be loyal to my country, I cannot be good to filial piety or good to my parents."

So, when I said that, all of them stood up and took a deep bow. In fact, the leader of the group . . . he bowed his head and said, "We are sorry we mentioned that." (Hoichi Kubo, in *The Color of Honor*, 1987 documentary film)

Ichiro Matsuda, a Nisei soldier drafted after Pearl Harbor, described his apprehension about his parents left in camp.

All during that time when I was in army training, I was—naturally deeply, we were all deeply concerned about our family . . . because I was in the army, thousands of miles away, and I couldn't help my family. So my army life was not a very happy one. . . . If they were home, I would feel hopeful that I would see them, I would like to come back, but . . . they were unlawfully detained. They were under very unusual circumstances. I didn't know what was going to happen to them. . . . So, the Nisei, Nisei soldiers, it was not a very easy life. We had a double burden compared to the white soldiers. Our parents were in camp, the white soldiers, their parents were home so they didn't really—they felt lonely I'm sure, they missed their family, but we not only missed the family but we were worried about their welfare.

The 442d's bloodiest single battle occurred when it was assigned to rescue the "Lost Battalion," a Texas division of the 141st Infantry

Regiment. The 442d successfully rescued 211 men, all that remained of the battalion, but at a cost of 814 casualties, including 140 dead, in the twenty-five days of continuous action. Together with those injured or killed in earlier actions, the casualties of the 442d totaled two thousand (Hosokawa 1969: 405–6).

Another major conflict arose over the "No-No Boys," as they were called, those men who answered "no" to both question 27 and 28 of the so-called loyalty questionnaires titled "Statement of United States Citizenship of Japanese Ancestry," which Japanese Americans were required to fill out early in 1943. These two questions read:

> Q. 27. Are you willing to serve in the armed forces of the United States on combat duty wherever ordered?
> Q. 28. Will you swear unqualified allegiance to the United States of America and faithfully defend the United States from any or all attack by foreign or domestic forces, and forswear any form of allegiance or obedience to the Japanese emperor, to any other foreign government, power or organization?[11]

These questions caused much mental anguish and contention between alien Issei parents and Nisei children, as well as between the Nisei and the Kibei. "Yes" to question 27 meant that they could be drafted and possibly required to fight against their cousins, relatives, or even brothers left in Japan. Question 28 was especially threatening for the Issei, whose right to seek American citizenship had been denied. They feared that an affirmative answer could possibly lead to deprivation of the only citizenship they had, making them people of no country. Many Nisei found the question confusing. Their answer was not no, but it was not yes, either, since

[11] Question 28 to the Issei was later rephrased as follows: "Are you sympathetic to the United States of America and do you agree faithfully to defend to the United States from any or all attack by foreign or domestic forces?" On a similar questionnaire, titled "War Relocation Authority Application for Leave Clearance," women were asked similar questions: "Q. 27. If the opportunity presents itself and you are found qualified, would you be willing to volunteer for the Army Nurse Corps of the WAAC?" and "Q. 28. Will you swear unqualified allegiance to the United States of America and forswear any form of allegiance or obedience to the Japanese emperor, or any other foreign government, power, or organization?"

they had never had any "allegiance or obedience to the Japanese emperor" in the first place.

Furthermore, each answer of the questionnaire that the War Relocation Authority used to determine one's qualification for leave was carefully graded. For example:

Q. 14. If subject travelled to Japan 3 or more times. (Reject)

Q. 16. If subject is Shintoist. (Reject)
If subject is Buddhist or has other oriental religion. (1-minus)
If subject is Christian. (2-plus)

Q. 17. If [subject is] member or officer of Kibei Organization.
(3-minus)
If member of K of C, Masons, Rotarian or other American Fraternal Society. (2-plus)

Q. 18. If subject reads, writes, and speaks Japanese good [*sic*].
(2-minus)

[Compare]
Q. 21. If subject has been convicted of any crime. (1-minus)[12]

Subjects then were classified as "white," "brown," and "black," according to their degree of eligibility for leave.

It is reported that nearly 78,000 persons were required to complete the questionnaire, and 75,000 did so. More than 65,000 answered yes to both questions; 6,700 answered no to both questions. Those individuals in many other camps who gave "no-no" answers to questions 27 and 28 were later transferred to Tule Lake Camp, segregated from "loyal" Japanese and Japanese Americans, but the No-No Boys in Minidoka were not sent there. Nevertheless, there was a threat of separation if parents and children gave different answers, forcing many Issei and Nisei into a quandary. In some

[12] A copy of this document came into my possession from Aiko Yoshinaga-Herzig's personal collection. It is dated July 22, 1943.

families, father and son did not reconcile until long after the war. It is reported that some thirty-three thousand Nisei served in World War II, more than half of them from the mainland. About twenty thousand had been incarcerated at one time or another (Masaoka and Hosokawa 1987: 179). Camp Minidoka raised more volunteers than any other camp. At the same time, a total of 267 (from all camps) refused induction. The issue often generated hostility between No-No Boys and their families and Nisei soldiers and their families. Shirley Kobayashi told me:

A lot of things you don't want to remember, so you block it out. Maybe the hardest thing was when they asked the boys to volunteer to join the army, because my brother was of age. He was eighteen. That was a real bad time for the family because he was the youngest, he was the only boy. He didn't volunteer but then he was one of the first ones to be called. . . . I guess we felt that we had no rights; they made us leave Seattle; we were citizens but we had no rights. . . . There were people in our block that refused to go, so-called "no-no." One of the hardest things for my mother was that this one family had two boys and they both said "no-no." So the father came over to my mother and told her, "Well, your son's going to die. My sons will go to jail but they'll be alive."

Underlying reasons for "no-no" answers varied. Some were motivated by a firm belief in the American Constitution; others, often Kibei and Issei, were more patriotic toward Japan. Douglas Tsujii was in his midtwenties at the outbreak of the war. He had visited Japan only once for a short period and did not actively participate in any community organizations before the war. For him, in retrospect, the No-No Boy issue began when he was forced to resign from the Home Defense force because of his ethnic background, one month after he had volunteered in early 1942. This incident "turned me off," he said. Then the same government that had rejected him started recruiting for the army among Nisei in camp. "It seemed so *wagamama* [selfish] on the government's part." Under heavy pressure while his freedom was circumscribed, he decided to answer "no-no." As a result, he spent the next three years in jail along with other members of his group.

> I got rejected in the Home Defense forces right off the bat, and then classified as an enemy alien, and then put behind barbed wire. It just wasn't right. It wasn't right. I don't know which hurt my parents more—If I went into the army, and they are enemy aliens, I'm fighting against their home country. Or if I didn't go into the army then I become—I go to jail. And that again isn't what they want to happen to me. So I think my parents had a very hard time, too. And we had a very hard decision to make one way or the other. Our future just seemed like there was no future. Just absolutely nothing. We can't go to Japan. Even at that time Niseis, when they went to Japan, were treated like Niseis. And, so we really felt like we didn't have a country anymore.

Asked about Nisei veterans, Tsujii replied, "If you are a citizen of a country, I don't think you have to go out and prove your loyalty, otherwise you lose your citizenship. That attitude is not right." He nonetheless stressed the benefit all Japanese Americans received from the deeds of the Nisei soldiers and how grateful he was to them. Tsujii emphasized the difference between himself and the Japan-oriented No-No Boys, whose concerns did not directly involve U.S. citizenship.

Isao Wada, a Kibei educated in Japan between the late 1920s and the late 1930s, was also a No-No Boy. He was transferred to Tule Lake and deported to Japan after the war, but he returned to the United States and settled in Seattle in the mid-1950s. His feelings were different from Tsujii's:

> A friend of mine said, "If you are going to stay in America it is wise to say yes." "What a stupid idea," I said. They put us in a place like this and still [want us to] pledge for America? . . . We couldn't disobey the emperor. . . . I thought of myself as a Japanese. I didn't see myself as an American citizen yet, not at all. I had Japanese citizenship as well.

More and more guys from the camp . . . those who wanted to join the army . . . they all went. Because they didn't know Japan. As far as I was concerned, I didn't know why they were going. Why the hell should I go? After they threw me in a place like this. It wasn't even a matter of going or not. I was against it—against the U.S. What could I do? From the very beginning, I was told to be loyal to the emperor and fight for him. The emperor was the one back then. . . . What else could I do? I thought I was Japanese. I never felt I was an American at that time. I was thrown into the camp right after I came to the U.S. What do you expect? I didn't know what [it was] to be an American or that sort of thing.[13]

There was prejudice against the Kibei by the Jun-Nisei, Wada said. Some told him, "Your country started the war." Wada remembered:

I had an argument with a Jun-Nisei soldier once. Everybody was watching us. "How come you have to be loyal to the emperor," [the Nisei soldier asked me]. So I asked him back, then why, if we are American, then why did they dump us in such a place? Aren't we American? I was more mad because of his broken Japanese. . . . Because he sounded so rude. . . .

[The reason why I didn't want to join the army was that] I didn't understand English. That's what would trouble me the most. I was scared somewhat. It would be a problem if you were out there and didn't understand English at all.

The conflict among Japanese Americans was more visible and violent in some other camps, most notably at Tule Lake. Wada recalled the ultranationalists marching in the camp every day: "Every morning they'd get up and gather at a certain place, like the unions today—running around like 'demonstration.' . . . They'd shout, facing the east, 'Kyūjō ni mukatte keire!' [salute toward the imperial palace!]. There were No-Nos who were [like the] *yakuza* [Japanese mafia] of nowadays, from outside, like Hawaii and California. Those bad boys were sent to Tule Lake. I wasn't in that sort of a group." Isao Wada belonged to the so-called *kachi-gumi*, the group

---

[13] The interview was conducted in Japanese, Wada's primary language.

that firmly believed in Japan's victory: "No one ever believed Japan would lose. . . . Even when I was heading for Japan, I didn't doubt Japan was winning. 'A ship will come and pick us up from Japan. We will be specially treated,' we thought." He added: "There was even propaganda, saying the [Japanese] army would come and throw those 'yes-yes' into another place [laugh]."

Both Douglas Tsujii and Isao Wada experienced "years of infamy" during and after the war, stigmatized by the label "No-No Boys." Both of them, like almost all other No-No Boys, kept silent and stayed in the background.

Besides the conflicts involving military recruitment and loyalty, various sad incidents have yet to fade from the memories of the internees. A boy playing with a ball was shot to death by one of the guards when he climbed over the fence to retrieve it. A young mother in deep depression killed her baby by bashing its head with a hammer. Although it was not considered to be an illness among Japanese Americans, some suffered mental disorientation due to depression. Nobuko Suzuki (real name) testified before the Commission on Wartime Relocation and Internment of Civilians that in January 1943 at the Minidoka hospital she saw a ward full of disoriented patients who were considered to be too dangerous to be wandering about (CWRIC 1981).

The Nisei often say that everybody has his or her own bitter experience—a mother's suicide, a fiance's death in Europe, a marriage problem created by the camp situation. Shirley Kobayashi recounted one said story:

> I have a friend whose mother committed suicide. There was a river running through the camp and she tied her legs and she just drowned herself. And I think another lady, I think she hung herself. Just couldn't accept the fact that they had to go through a situation like that. . . . [She had] three girls and a son. She didn't come home; nobody knew where she went; then they found her. And I think during that time a lot of the Issei were at the age where they were going through a change of life, and that's bad enough without having to go through evacuation. Everything was kind of compounded.

Jane Tachibana told of traveling to Minidoka from Tule Lake to visit her father-in-law, who was very ill:

We got into Burns, Oregon, when we ran out of formula for my son who had to have a special morning milk. Well, I could see Safeway in the distance from the bus, and I said, "There's Safeway, let's just go over there and see if we can get a can of special morning milk." Well, that was during the war and they had to have these little tokens to buy anything that's canned. Well, we were in camp, we never had tokens given to us and so I thought, well, I can't help it, I have to have this special morning milk. So I went over there and I picked up this can of milk and I went up to the counter, cashier, and I was telling her, I said, "I have to have this milk, we're on our way from one camp to another and I have this little baby who's not even a year old and ran out of milk." And so she looked at me and said, "Well, do you have a token." And I said, "No, that's one thing I'm trying to explain to you, we don't have a token. . . ." Fortunately there was this lady behind me and she says, "Oh, I have an extra red token so you can give it to her to use." So that was the way I got my can of milk, but if it wasn't for that lady—she was a *hakujin* lady. It was really hard times when you have little ones.

For Michi Walter, who was only thirteen years old when she was sent to camp, the most painful experience was her conflict with her now-deceased mother, who had decided to renounce her citizenship.

The hardest thing for me personally was after a certain point in time, they began to allow people to leave. . . . My mother renounced her citizenship, and all of us decided to go to Japan. The hardest thing for me was watching all these people leave, knowing that I couldn't— that I was going to—if I was going to go anywhere, I was going to go to Japan, which I didn't want to do. I did something that I still at this point now, I think it embarrassed my parents. . . . But I started writing letters to . . . editors of magazines and such . . . , telling them that I was in this terrible position, and could they help me, could they help me to stay in the United States.

Tom Yoneda was expelled from high school for writing an essay about the Japanese American internment.

[104]

There was a lot of skipping going on. So they instituted a couple of rules in the camp school: . . . [One of them] was if you fail one class, you fail them all. . . . So our student body tried to get a movement to oppose it. At that time, I was taking an American civics class. . . . I wrote a term paper called, "American Democracy: What It Means to Me." It was a long diatribe of things I disagreed with about the camp. The fact that we had a Constitution of the United States and I'm in camp, have no legal process to get out. I did a lot of research, I even got a *Congressional Record.* I cited all these things. The teacher in the civics class said that she would not accept the paper. . . . It became a very big issue to me, because they teach us the freedom of speech and yet we are not exercising it. So I became more stubborn, "No, I'm not going to rewrite the paper." She said, "If you get an F in this class, that means you will get F in all classes." We were trouble-makers, because we were fighting for this. I was trying to change the school system. So I gave them a good excuse to throw me out. So they threw me out.

After the war, Yoneda was able to go to the University of Washington, after taking a high school equivalency test even though he had no high school diploma and his transcript bore the remark: "Not recommended for further education." He later became one of the key activists in the redress movement in Seattle, motivated in large part, he said, by this school incident.

The evaluation of the teachers in camp varied: some gave them high credit, but others said that their quality was poor. All agreed that the school facilities in camp were dismally inadequate. Kana Ochiai summarized this view:

Mainly I think I resented being deprived of a good education, 'cause that's what your life is about when you're in high school, your schooling. And here we are going to school but it's a makeshift school, we don't have the lab facilities, you don't have the home economic type lab type facilities, you don't have athletic facilities, you don't have any of that. We probably didn't have as high caliber teachers, either. We were really cheated out of our public school education.

[105]

The school-age children received no education at all for almost a year, until schools were established at the end of 1942. The gymnasium was not ready until 1944. Libraries contained mostly outdated donated books. According to the testimony of Shuzo Kato (real name), the teaching staff mostly consisted of people who had worked as teacher-missionaries on Indian reservations, and the majority of them were not highly educated or enthusiastic (CWRIC 1981). Kaz Miata talked about the adverse consequences, the loss of motivation: "Some of the kids who were very talented . . . got caught up with things in camp. 'What is the use of studying? They've thrown us in camp. . . .' A number of them got sidetracked. . . . High school kids, because they were very impressionable, tend to fall victims to the state of depression. Now I'm old enough to understand, but everything seemed to be so chaotic and helpless at that time."

Camp memories are not entirely negative, however. The Nisei almost unanimously declared that they enjoyed the opportunity to meet new people. Lifelong friendships began in camp, and a large number of Nisei met their spouses there.[14] Toshi Akimoto acknowledged that he and his wife would not have met "if it wasn't for the war." The Nisei emphasized that they and their parents tried to make the best out of life. Kaz Miata described his parents:

> My father used to have a different kind of philosophy. He used to say to me, "You should make the best use of your time. They're feeding us in camp, even though the food is lousy, they are giving us some form of clothing that we could survive on. You should study when you can, and you should contribute whatever you can to the society." He was very strong on that. "After you help yourself, help other people."
>
> My mother was the same way. She was applying all the tricks she learned in Japan. She used to get the leftover rice from the kitchen and dried them and crumbled the rice like *mochigome* [sweet rice] and made *senbei* [rice crackers].

[14] Although we have no actual statistics on spouses introduced in camp, 27 percent of the Seattle Nisei marriages occurred during the five-year span between 1941 and 1945 (Yanagisako 1985: 66).

In the first issue of the camp newsletter, a Nisei editor encouraged the internees to do their best to make the limited life happier.

We are not here by choice. But it is not likely that protest will alter the fact that we are here, or dissipate the probability that we will be here until we win the war. We, the ten thousand, then, can have but one resolve: to apply our combined energies and efforts to the grim task of conquering the elements and converting a wasteland into an inhabitable community. Our obligation to ourselves is to wrest the nearest possible approximation of normality out of an abnormal situation.

Our goal is the creation of an oasis. Our great adventure is a "repetition of the frontier struggle of pioneers against the land and the elements."

Our future will be what we make it, and there is no reason to despair. (*Minidoka Irrigator*, Sept. 10, 1942)

Internees, especially the young, organized dances, movies, and various contests in the mess halls: "You had so few things to enjoy; so they made holidays. The mess hall would be decorated for each holiday, and the best decoration would be given prizes," said Setsuko Fukuda. At school, students organized the student council and devised extracurricular activities. There were also weddings, funerals, and other ceremonies and events. John Ohki said that they celebrated *Oshogatsu*, or New Year's Day, Boys' Day, and other holidays. His mother managed to bring boys' dolls for Boys' Day for each of her sons. They pounded *mochi* (sweet rice cakes) on *Oshogatsu*.

In mid-December of 1943, as many as seventeen thousand Christmas gifts donated by hundreds of organizations throughout the nation arrived at the camp. They were sent after the press ran a story about a little boy who stood by the barbed-wire fence and asked his mother how Santa Claus could get inside the camp. Many Nisei still appreciate the warmhearted gesture by other Americans.

Unlike the internees in many other camps, who were never permitted to leave, the people in Minidoka were allowed to go to Twin

Falls, a nearby town, to go to a restaurant, perhaps, or shop at the local stores. Naomichi Kodaira recollects a German American owner of a restaurant who treated Nisei volunteers to whatever they wanted when the 442d was going to war (Kodaira 1980: 125–26).

In the summers, Nisei children would harvest potatoes and other seasonal vegetables on farms in the area, which were experiencing a labor shortage. They worked, said Bill Fukuda, "simply because we wanted to get out. Good chance to get out. Actually there was nothing else to do."

Talented people worked at various crafts, using wood, sagebrush, and other material that could be gathered from the desert. Some enjoyed playing *shogi* (Japanese chess). In fact, *keiko-goto* (cultural lessons), such as tea ceremony, knitting, and samisen (Japanese lute) were popular, particularly among the Issei. It was in camp that *shigin*, or recitation of Japanese poems, became popular among the Issei.

Camp also provided the Nisei with new work experiences. "I was lucky, because I had finished high school," Setsuko Fukuda told me. "You can't say it was a good experience. It was good and bad, too. Because I went to camp, and I got the nursing aide experience, I went down to nursing school, which I probably wouldn't have done otherwise."

Many Nisei, moreover, believe that if evacuation and internment had not happened, Japanese Americans would still live in the self-contained ghettolike community and not as many would have become successful professionals on the East Coast.

Feelings about internment have more than one layer. Although many feel bitter, some Nisei pointed out the "easy" life in camp, especially for many poor Issei, who for the first time in their lives were able to take a rest. The evaluation of camp life in fact varied, especially among the Issei, depending on economic level and living standard prior to internment. Those individuals who were hard pressed to make a living before the war appreciated the worry-free life. Those whose economic level had exceeded subsistence and those used to an urban environment found internment painful indeed. It is not uncommon to hear an old Issei woman say that they "had a good time" in camp, being around only the Japanese, taking many lessons they had never had time for, and not having to worry about food and lodging. Ume Sekine, an Issei, insisted that she enjoyed camp life and recalled, "My husband used to say, 'I wish we could stay in camp till the grave.' They gave us free food and we didn't have to work!" Hisa Gotanda, a Kibei who started her married life by living with her in-laws and was responsible for all the cooking and housework before the war, said that for her the life in camp was a happy one because for the first time she could live with her husband alone, albeit in a camp barracks. As Bill Fukuda observed, "There were all kinds of people, from people who were making a living to people who were quite prosperous. People who were at the bottom would say, 'Oh, *gokuraku* [paradise]!' They say we get three meals a day, 'Oh, *gokuraku*.'" The Nisei often mentioned the danger of the "easy life" in camp, which provided free meals and turned some people "lazy." Setsuko Fukuda explained:

> For old people, it was a nice rest. They didn't have to worry about food; you didn't need anything because you were not doing anything. They worked very hard in Seattle. But for young people, . . . if you didn't go out when you felt like it, you become like a vegetable. If you just linger too long, you don't feel like going out, why go out to strange places, people may not like you. There were a group of people like that in the camp.

If the poor enjoyed the freedom from responsibility and the Nisei enjoyed meeting new people, there were many bitter memories and much resentment of the injustice. Asked what they considered the hardest thing about living in the camp, Helen Kageshita replied: "Psychologically feeling we were caged in. How unfair to do this, and to come to ask the boys to give their lives. My disillusionment with the government started then." Sumi Hashimoto also felt suffocated; she hated "the whole idea of being enclosed, surrounded by the barbed-wire fence and those soldiers on the corner looking down on us. There didn't seem to be much hope. As soon as we got to Minidoka, I began thinking, 'I'm going to get out of here,

I'm going to get out of here.' That was my main thing, to get my children out." Saburo Enomoto saw the damage the "easy life" did to his mother.

> I hate to say, but my mother worked hard all her life and in fact when she went to camp and everything was there, food—you go to mess hall, I think that's what killed her. Life was too easy, so you go away from everyday routine. She would work in the hotel day and night, and in her spare time she was doing gardening, she would grow vegetables and so on, that was her life. And camp, life in camp was too easy for her, the everyday routine, and that new environment, she died from kidney trouble.

Ed Murakami declared:

> I think it was terrible, a terrible experience to be in there. The only benefit I can think of is that you can't be discriminated against—you know, how *hakujins* feel towards you. That's about the only thing. I don't think there was anything good about it. . . . I think our progress was slowed down quite a bit because of it. But I think that people who become successful will become successful anyway. It made me distrust the *hakujin* more than before. I never trusted them to start with. It made it worse.

Toshi Akimoto answered: "Well, what bothered me was I just— everything stopped. I was planning on improving my business and starting a business of my own, and I couldn't do that. I felt as if I was in a jail. I felt that I was losing time. . . . I just lost about three [to] four years of my life, because I was doing what I didn't want to do. I was set back financially. Financially I suffered quite a bit. I had to start all over from scratch." Yet Akimoto hides his bitterness from his children; he tells them, "Camp was not that bad."

In camp Americanization was encouraged at the expense of Japanese heritage and ethnic ties. On the school grounds, speaking Japanese and practicing Japanese martial arts such as judo and kendo were prohibited. The curriculum was geared toward Americanization (cf. Yamada 1989: 8). "We were taking, I don't remember

[110]

which class it was, but . . . I think we were brainwashed, we were fed a lot of this, 'You've just got to make sure you get back into the mainstream, become accepted, prove yourself good citizens,' kind of thing," said Kana Ochiai. In a film called *Invisible Citizens: Japanese Americans,* produced by Keiko Tsuno in 1983, Mo Nishioka says: "When we left camp, basically what they told us was not to come together, not to congregate, not to stick out. In that way, the way they told us was there was something bad about being Japanese."

Some Nisei said that the "message" they received in camp kept echoing in their postwar life, impelling them toward "Americanization." Bill Fukuda, for example, felt a strong need to escape: "Many Nisei were eager to leave camp, and tried all efforts to do so. The whole objective I had when I was at school was 'I've got to get out of here.' I took a tremendous number of courses just to get out. I left camp when I was sixteen years old. I graduated high school not because I was smarter than other kids but I was able to get enough credits to leave." Sumi Hashimoto, too, was obsessed with getting out: "My son was going on five; . . . so I knew we had to look for school somewhere. So . . . as soon as we got to Minidoka, I began thinking, 'I'm going to get out of here, I'm going to get out of here.' . . . I began writing my *hakujin* friends . . . , 'I've got to get out of camp. Please help me.'"

Others, however, were worried about anti-Japanese sentiment and exclusion. A camp newsletter in January 1943 published a survey of public sentiment in the five western states. The results were discouraging. Asked, "Do you think the Japanese who were moved from the Pacific Coast should be allowed to return after the war is over," 29 percent "would allow all to return," 24 percent "would allow only American citizens," and 31 percent "would allow none to return," and two-thirds of this last group thought that all should be sent back to Japan. To another question, 26 percent answered that they would be willing to hire Japanese servants to work in their homes after the war was over, but 69 percent said they would not. George Saito was ambivalent about returning to the outside world: "I wanted to get out if I knew that I could have a job and a secure place. I knew how hated we were. You can't just go anywhere: you'd get killed. I didn't mind going out, but I didn't mind staying in camp for being scared of it [the outside world], too. But then again you can't stay there forever." Young Nisei had more opportunities and were anxious to leave camp. The National Japanese American Student Relocation Council encouraged them to pursue their college education during the war and helped them to enroll in the schools it negotiated with. Young Nisei had more opportunities and were anxious to leave camp. Some, especially the Issei who were already in their fifties and sixties and had lost their homes and businesses, however, were scared of the racism in the outside world and worried about how they would make a living.[15]

The Nisei from Seattle typically lived on the East Coast for a year or two after leaving camp before returning to the West Coast. Those who had Christian religious affiliations are said to have had less difficulty finding jobs or being admitted to schools than those who did not. According to Sumi Hashimoto, most of the people who had no sponsors and so had to stay in camp were Buddhist. Many Nisei settled in the Midwest or East permanently, and only 60 to 70 percent of the prewar residents returned to the Seattle area after the war (Leonetti and Newell-Morris 1982: 23).

Life after the War

After returning to the West Coast, Japanese Americans concentrated on reestablishing their lives. At first, many lived in the Japanese school, churches, trailers, hostels, and at friends' houses until they could find their own places to live. A majority had lost their homes and personal property. According to a postwar survey, 80 percent of goods privately stored were rifled, stolen, or sold during their owners' absence (Weglyn 1976: 77). "We lived in a hotel, and we entrusted our stuff with the owner," said Saburo Enomoto. "Well, when we came back from camp, everything was gone. A story like this is common. I guess only one out of ten people got

---

[15] According to a survey taken in Manzanar in the fall of 1942, only 2 to 3 percent of the internees were eager to go outside the camp (Weglyn 1976: 100).

their things back all right. White people are irresponsible, especially during wartime. When a war comes, they are no longer your friends." Many of the older Nisei as well as the Issei who had owned their houses and rented them out during internment found them pilfered, damaged, or vandalized. Only a few found that their property had been well maintained by friends.

Reestablishment was especially difficult for the Issei, already in their fifties and sixties. Many of them, including those who were successful businessmen in the prewar period, could find only unskilled work. Janitorial work was one of the major occupations among the Issei after the war. Miki Hayashi's father "couldn't find any job. Finally he found a janitorial job. He had no cash to start another store. He thought some kind of job was better than just sitting down. They saved money to buy a home. I felt very sorry for him. Even if it's a small store, if you own a store, you have your pride." Some Issei were able to restart their businesses, and others simply retired. Older Nisei who had been engaged in business in the prewar period and had capital to invest were also able to start over. Toshi Akimoto remembered: "I lost my business. . . . I don't think I had three thousand dollars in my pocket when I came back from Philadelphia. And I found out I needed a minimum of fifty thousand dollars to open up my business again. Then I decided to get into the retail end of it and open a retail shop. And that's what I did. So I really started out with about three thousand dollars. I was renting the property; I had a refrigerator, a truck, and all the office equipment—all that I lost."

For the majority of Nisei, college education was the next goal to pursue after leaving camp. According to Sylvia Yanagisako, the cohort of Nisei who went to college after internment, married with little parental involvement, returned to their home communities, and became financially successful represents the key cohort of that generation (1985: 86–87). The sharp increase in white-collar work between 1940 and 1950 marks the beginning of occupational mobility in the postwar era. According to Evelyn Nakano Glenn, the percentage of Nisei women engaged in the professions throughout the nation doubled, from 4.4 percent in 1940 to 9.2 percent in 1950 (1986: 85).

[113]

Although leaving camp for higher education was encouraged, some Nisei were preoccupied with making a living and never went to college. In general Nisei men had better opportunities than Nisei women primarily because of the benefits of the GI bill. Some Nisei women never finished college or never went at all, often because they married in or right after camp. Other Nisei lost their motivation and dropped college plans because they faced financial difficulty. "I think that camp did a lot of harm in that respect," Kaz Miata told me. "When we got out of camp, there was no money. . . . So kids couldn't go to college; so they went to work. Once they started on the work side, they never continued education. That, to me, is very unfortunate."

Another result of internment and the postwar struggle for a new life was that some Nisei remained single throughout their lives.[16] Nisei informants often explained that single men never learned to socialize with women because they were too busy making a living or didn't marry because they were too poor to support a family. Sumi Hashimoto spoke of her brother, who was a senior in college when he was evacuated: "As soon as he could find a job, he went to St. Louis. There were few Japanese. How could he meet Japanese women? So he slept and worked. He is an example, a fellow who didn't know how to meet Japanese women, never socialized with them, never got married. There are quite a few men like that, and also Nisei women who never married. Their social life was cut off."

Right after the war, the hostility toward Japanese Americans and discrimination against them were even more intense than before the war. Furthermore, the Nisei were more exposed to racism, having lost Japantown, their protective enclave. "No Japs" or "No Japs and Dogs Allowed" signs, name calling, and other explicit forms of discrimination reconfirmed to the Nisei the hatred of them in the larger society. For some, this behavior was shocking mainly because it was their first real taste of it. Before the war they had been too young and naive to realize how discriminatory the larger society was. Now that they were adults, it slapped them in the face.

[16] The proportion of unmarried Nisei in Seattle is reported to be 8.2 percent for men and 9.7 percent for women, as determined by random sample (Leonetti 1983: 6).

Nisei men in uniform, even after their heroic service in Europe, found that they were not yet accepted in American society.

> I stopped in a drug store, which was up on Yesler Way . . . and was run by a white woman and a Chinese girl as a helper. . . . Anyway, I went there to see if I could get an ice cream soda or something like that. "No Japs." I had on my uniform, my ribbons, and this and that. There was a sign outside. I didn't see it, I guess. And that was one time when I—well, I knocked everything off the counter and started throwing things. And then I walked out of there. Then . . . a prowl car caught me, because the woman had called the police. They talked to me, took me down to the station, . . . but they understood how mad I was. (George Saito)

The discrimination and prejudice against Japanese Americans existed in various settings. Again, unemployment and lack of housing were difficult obstacles to face. Some Nisei would go out day after day to look for a job. Even college graduates had difficulty finding employment. Not until around 1948 did the Seattle public schools hire a Nisei for a teaching position.

Although restrictive covenants were illegal, many apartment and home owners refused to rent to Japanese Americans. Finding an apartment north of the ship canal in Seattle was extremely difficult, and even in the central area, where Japanese and other minority populations were concentrated, renting was not easy. "I got married in 1956," Wanda Kawasaki said, "and even at that time I had a hard time finding an apartment because we are Japanese. On the telephone they say yes because they don't recognize you, but if we go there, they say like, 'It's already been rented,' or 'I don't rent to Japs.' So after a while, I checked on the phone first, 'I'm a Japanese American. Would you tell me now whether you will rent to me or not,' because I did not want to waste my time."

As Japanese Americans started settling down and employment opportunities improved, their careers gradually progressed. Older Nisei rebuilt their businesses; younger Nisei went to the university and later worked for corporations. In the postwar period, they were considered "success stories" (Peterson 1966), and they drew admiration from the larger society.

In the 1950s and 1960s American society still embraced the notion of the "melting pot" (cf. Gordon 1964), the total assimilation of other cultures to form a uniquely "American" culture. Japanese Americans were upwardly mobile and assimilated into the mainstream, but did so at the cost of deemphasizing their cultural heritage. Unlike their parents, the Nisei did not teach Japanese to their children, nor did they emphasize Japanese cultural values or being of Japanese descent. Nevertheless, some behavioral patterns were unconsciously passed on to the Sansei, even nonverbally. Barbara Yamaguchi mentioned her husband's philosophy of raising their children in those years: "He thought that the grandparents [Issei] should speak English because we lived in America. He is the one who decided it; so none of my children learned Japanese. I said, 'I think that they would understand grandparents speaking Japanese, and that it would be good for them to learn Japanese.' But he said no. Besides there was so much discrimination, it was more comfortable not to speak Japanese."

Religion was another barometer of "Americanization." The Nisei tended to consider Buddhists more Japanese and less "assimilated." Interestingly, not a few Issei converted or started attending Christian churches around the time when naturalization was finally allowed in 1952. The American social ideology, which was based on Anglo-American experience, discouraged the maintenance of values attached to non-European cultures. John Ohki told me: "One thing I didn't like about high school: they used to say Buddhism was wrong because it worships idols. I was going to a Buddhist church." Later, he started going to a Christian church because he could not understand the Japanese service by the Buddhist priest and found a "good" minister at the Christian church. There seems to be limited evidence to show a linkage between Americanization or naturalization and abandoning Japanese markers among some Issei and Nisei. Helen Kageshita's parents, "when they came back to Seattle, they started going to Blaine [Memorial Methodist Church] and became Christians. It was the same thing that my father did after 1952. When the naturalization bill went through, on his own he went to citizenship classes, and became a citizen. We didn't encourage him or didn't speak about it. So there must have been some feeling of adapting to this country."

[116]

From the late 1950s, some Nisei started moving into predominantly white suburbs. They were motivated by the need for a larger house or a better educational environment for their children, but sometimes the move was also an attempt to assimilate into the mainstream. "We were told this when we left camp," said Kana Ochiai, "we have to assimilate and break away from our ethnic groups, and I felt we could do it, and we were ready to. So that was part of it. Personally we wanted to go to a good school district, but there was that element also. But I never did want to ever lose contact with the Japanese community, and I never have because my contact, my continuous contact, has been my church." On the other hand, there was another type of Nisei who chose the opposite path, living in the racially mixed neighborhoods of the central area or the south end of Seattle. These Nisei expressed discomfort about the idea of living in a predominantly white American neighborhood. Nonetheless, overall, Japanese Americans in Seattle scattered, and as a result, the majority of them substantially decreased their involvement in Japanese American community organizations and activities.

The Sansei say that their parents tried to Americanize. Some Nisei admit that they did and some deny it. Some Nisei say they were "brainwashed" by the War Relocation Authority, which urged "assimilation." The degree of assimilation varies among individuals. Some Nisei ceased speaking any Japanese. Some moved out to a suburban white environment to "assimilate and break away from our ethnic group." Some told their children to follow white behavioral standards. Some started going to a Christian church. A less obvious way to assimilate was to work "superconscientiously, staying late and making sure that everything is all right," as Helen Kageshita said; it was a way to prove that they were good, loyal American citizens. Shizue Peterson said that the Nisei always tried to leave a good impression about Japanese Americans on white Americans, so that they would "not bring *haji,* or shame, to the community." "I think we all felt that we had to really prove ourselves," Shirley Kobayashi noted; "so we made a greater effort to be good citizens and do what was expected of us. . . . At work we all did a little extra, to show that we didn't slack off. We did our very best in whatever we did. A lot of *hakujins,* they goof off. As a whole, the Nisei are very conscientious. I think that was to prove that in whatever we did, they could trust us to do what we could do." Michi Walter said: "I spoke perfectly good Japanese until I was about twenty. I had to because my mother didn't speak English. But I deliberately forgot it all and repressed it all. Now I'm really sorry. I wish I could speak Japanese again."

As they won social mobility and assimilation into American society, Japanese Americans were gradually losing their ethnic identity and the cultural traits that marked them as Japanese. Carol Namiki, an older Sansei, commented: "If you had any ties with Japan it was considered negative so that there was this—in some Niseis there was this thing to be accepted by the white community. If you were accepted by the white community, that erased the discrimination of the war, and so then they felt good. And so there were a lot of families who tended to bring up their children so they would be accepted in the mainstream." Yet despite the tendency to try to become "120 percent American and despite low self-esteem or the feeling of being second-class citizens, some Nisei maintained pride in Japanese culture and sent their Sansei children to the Japanese school, kendo, or *odori* lessons.

The evacuation and internment themselves were the products of racism and war hysteria, the propensity of the government and the public to confuse Japanese Americans and resident aliens with Japanese nationals in Japan. Such an experience profoundly influenced the Nisei's identification. It is important to recognize that Americanization was embraced partly as a means of survival. Toshi Akimoto described a significant encounter after the war:

It was bad then. I had difficulty buying groceries, and also finding good customers. I just couldn't make good contacts with the customers, . . . and one time I remember one fellow came in and looked at me and said, "Are you a Jap or a Chink?" How could I answer that? If I said I'm Japanese, he'd cuss me up and down; if I said I was Chinese, he'd call me a dirty Chink or something. I thought for a while; I had a good answer. I said, "I'm an American, what the hell are you?" And then he said, "Oh, pardon me, pardon me, pal," he says, and he bought groceries from me. . . . Just because I said, "I'm American," I made a sale. So it was my livelihood that I was thinking about. So, I got along pretty good. In fact, I started to make Caucasian friends right away quick after I came back.

In fact, Toshi Akimoto provides an excellent example of the Nisei who believe in assimilation and integration with white Americans. He could speak only Japanese in his early childhood. Later, he became determined to learn English and to give up Japanese, and today he says that he does not speak Japanese at all. He gave all his four children English first and middle names with no Japanese name. All his children married white Americans, and he himself believes outmarriage to be preferable. The Sansei should not keep themselves apart. He told me, "My kids all know how I feel to be American; I'm always waving my American flag. That's the only way I influence them." He has discouraged speaking Japanese: "In our family, we have no Japanese relatives, so we don't want to talk about Japanese too much. In fact, to use the Japanese language in our family—we not only discourage it, but we just don't. In fact, most of my kids can't understand Japanese too well, anyway." Akimoto believes, "You have to mix in with the Caucasian people to get along. And I encourage that, and that's what they all follow, and they're doing fine. I hope more Japanese do that, instead of staying together and limiting themselves." Akimoto deplores the self-segregation he believes many Japanese Americans practice. He favors assimilation into white American society, rather than integration with other minorities. His position, now at the extreme of pro-American sentiment, represents the Nisei orientation particularly in those years when "melting pot" ideology, or more precisely, "Anglo-conformity," dominated American society.[17]

In the postwar period, the Nisei were devoted to reestablishing themselves and raising their children. They tried to forget the un-

[17] Milton M. Gordon (1964) defines "Anglo-conformity" as the demand for complete renunciation of the immigrant's ancestral culture in favor of the behavior and values of the Anglo-Saxon core group. Despite the prominence of the "melting pot" ideology in the early twentieth century, American culture in fact showed little tolerance for absorbing non-European immigrant groups' cultures until the rise of the "cultural pluralism" model in the 1960s.

pleasant past in order to concentrate on building the future. Ichiro
Matsuda remembered:

> The fifties and sixties were difficult days, . . . not so much [in] Seat-
> tle, but in the Kent valley area. . . . Kent was very anti-Japanese.
> But I was going to school at that time and I figured, well, I must
> study. I must project myself to my goal without being bitter about the
> anti-Japanese sentiments in the Kent valley. . . . I felt a little selfish
> concentrating on my own studies, but I thought, "Well I've got to
> take care of my own personal self before I get involved with some
> other anti-Japanese sentiment." So fifties and sixties were still hard
> times.

The Nisei bore scars from the experience of internment. Some
could not shake the feeling that they were second-class citizens.
Among some Nisei, low self-esteem was rooted in the discrimination experience before the war, but it was crystallized by the internment. Although some Nisei deny any feeling of embarrassment or
stigma (as Setsuko Fukuda said, "We didn't do anything wrong, why
should we?"), many Nisei have felt self-hatred, guilt, and shame.
"You feel *hazukashii* [ashamed] because you were sort of being
punished," said John Ohki. "You felt like you did something wrong.
They made you feel like you were guilty, guilty of being of Japanese
ancestry because we were the only ones that were punished." Monica Sone, the author of *Nisei Daughter,* clarifies some of these
feelings:

> My guilt came from the feeling that I was abandoning my parents in
> camp. My other guilt came from . . . an old ongoing guilt of having a
> Japanese face. At that time, looking like a Japanese meant being a
> despicable subhuman.
> My self-hate came from the past. I experienced all that hate which
> had poured out from the public and the government officials as a
> death wish upon us—that message had sunk deeply inside me. (In
> Seriguchi and Abe 1980: 26)

Barbara Yamaguchi, like many other Nisei, equated the camp experience with rape: "When a woman is raped, she does not want to

talk, because she feels ashamed. In the same way, even though we did nothing wrong, there was a feeling of shame. We just assumed let's not talk about it." Even the soldiers of the 442d were not immune to such feelings. Kiyoshi Yabuki (real name) testified: "I was very self-conscious about being Japanese. . . . I found that even after fighting in Europe, I still had that feeling and even [with] the fame the 442nd was receiving, I tried to minimize [it]. The reason for this, I believe, was my poor self-image caused by the events that happened with the internment. Being accused as dangerous, treacherous, can't be trusted, and many other unflattering things" (CWRIC 1981). The hatred and discrimination that reached their culmination in evacuation and internment imprinted a negative value upon their ethnicity. In fact, many Nisei, at some point in their lives, wished they were not Japanese. George Saito said:

After Pearl Harbor, when you start feeling all this hate, I'm sure most of the young people felt that way—I wish I was a *hakujin* or something like that. That's another way of saying, "I sure wish I wasn't hated so much. For why, I don't know. But what did I do to be so hated?" When you're young, you don't understand why people want to hate you so much. A lot of things you just don't understand, but you sure understand that hate. I'm sure we were hated worse than— we were the most hated people on earth during those years.

Kaz Miata explained: "I think during the war it was very difficult to be truly *Nihon-jin* and behave like one. The part of our psychological way of thinking forced us into a mode that says, "We are *Nihon-jin*, but it wasn't the best thing to be born as *Nihon-jin* in this country." We were made to suffer as a cause of it." Michi Walter admitted:

For a long time, I had a dislike for things Japanese and for many Japanese Americans. I feel that the camp experience alienated me from my people. I turned my anger against them rather than the government. When I left the camp, I said, "I don't want to have anything more to do with them." I literally left the Japanese community. I married twice, but both of my husbands had been whites. I had next nothing to do with [Japanese Americans].

[121]

Although these feelings were predominant among the Nisei, others asserted that they never wished they were not Japanese. Helen Kageshita, for example, told me:

> I've never regretted that I'm Japanese American. I attribute it to a grade school teacher who favored us [three of us, an elite group]. . . . I hear people say they wished they were different, but I've never thought that.
>
> As a general rule, we are proud of our race. . . . [We were told,] "The Japanese race is special." In that sense, we are racist [laugh]. Japan is the country of our ancestry, not a foreign country totally. Loyalty, being able to trust one another—although there are exceptions.

The Nisei say they were preoccupied with raising their children and reestablishing their lives and businesses; they say today that they were too busy to think about the past. The great majority did not talk about internment to anyone, except perhaps to mention the friends they met in camp. Their memories of evacuation and internment were so painful that many Nisei shut them out of their minds. They were reluctant to dredge up bitter memories, reluctant to provoke emotional friction by recalling the ideological differences that arose in camp over such sensitive issues as the No-No Boys. "With me," said Miki Hayashi,

> there were no feelings like disagreements or anything about camp, but somehow people asked me later, a lot of outsiders who were doing studies, but I purposefully avoided them. I didn't even want to think about it. So, I always said, "Oh it wasn't so bad," and I would just shake it off. I never wanted to even think about it. And people would ask me questions, and it was just too much for me to even try and remember. So I suppose you would have to say you purposefully kind of pushed it down.

Those who spoke of camp, kept the conversation superficial or dwelled on pleasant memories, mainly of friends they met there. Harry Tanabe and his wife talked about "lots of things about food and people. But we tried to forget it. We didn't talk about it too often. We would make a joke out of it, you know, 'That's just like camp, remember?'" Sumi Hashimoto declared:

> I didn't feel guilty. First of all, I didn't have time to think. There were times I cried. The memories of the past, you tend to hide things that were very painful, you remember only happy parts. When our friends get together, for instance, those who lived in the same block, we would talk about only happy times. We do talk about it now. We would say, "Do you remember that so and so's mother didn't have to go to camp because she was in Montana, would visit her and bring sausages; we thought they tasted so good." . . . I remember things like that.

The Nisei emphasize that they have made the best of life, that they did not allow themselves to be overwhelmed by the internment experience. In fact, not a few believe that the experience made them mature and expanded their world. Sumi Hashimoto, for example, acknowledged that

> because of camp, life for all of us changed. For some people better; for some people worse. People that carry the resentment and hatred for having been put into camp, if they still carry it, they're just destroying their own life. You can't say the camp experience was good for us, but camp opened up new avenues, made us grow up and learn how you advance your future. It didn't matter how much education you had, how rich you were, we all were put into camp equally. We all turned out to be the same type of people. But how you advance your future depends on how you take the camp. Sure, it was a terrible thing, but you've got to do something to get out of it.

Yet if the Nisei felt they had surmounted this great setback in their lives, most did so by suppressing deep psychological wounds. They buried the camp memories, and even between parent and child or husband and wife the real subject remained untouched.

Behind the image of the "success story" even in the 1960s and 1970s, discrimination in employment continued, particularly in promotions. Japanese Americans were paid less than their white American counterparts who had an equal level of education (Kitano 1969: 92). Harry Tanabe related an anecdote:

> The Japanese Americans were probably the highest educated people at [a major company in the greater Seattle area] and the lowest paid in relationship to the others. There used to be John Tanaka, who was a very nice fellow, in fact he was supervisor of the group that was very successful and all the people that worked for him were vice-presidents at ———, and John never got an offer and we thought that's not right, and we started the group. After all our efforts, a Chinese man got [a vice-presidency], and his attitude was, I did it all by myself, I didn't get any help from anybody. [But] at least we got an Asian anyway.

From the late 1960s to the 1970s, as the ethnic movement began to filter into the Japanese American community in Seattle, the Nisei men working at this company began to take some political action. In 1970 the company instituted layoffs, and many of the victims were Asian Americans. According to former and current Nisei employees, Asian engineers, especially the Nisei, were paid less than they were supposed to be paid. They filed suit against the company under the Equal Employment Opportunity law. Required by the company to negotiate through an organization that represented the Japanese American community, these Nisei joined the Seattle chapter of the JACL to ask for support. Around the same time, when the U.S. Department of Commerce began stipulating levels of minority employment on government construction projects, the city hired people from unions, which Asian Americans still had difficulty joining. Some Nisei and other Asian Americans formed an organization that provided employment services. Through these political activities in opposition to discriminatory practices in the work environment and employment opportunities, these Nisei met one another and developed their friendships and political awareness. Later, they would become leaders in the redress movement in Seattle.

Conclusion

Life experiences from the pre–World War II period through the early 1970s constantly affected the way the Nisei perceived and identified themselves. Wartime internment, among other factors, exerted powerful pressure on Japanese American ethnic identity, transforming it profoundly. For the Nisei, says Evelyn Nakano Glenn, internment was equivalent to immigration for the Issei: it was a dividing point, marking the end of youth and the beginning of adulthood, the assumption of responsibility for taking care of the older generation and kinspeople (1986: 58). Likewise, in respect to ethnic identity, internment brought an end to youth, when the basis for the Japanese side of identity was inculcated and nurtured, and initiated the next stage, when Japanese ethnicity became stigmatized. Although internment served as a turning point, ethnic identity in the prewar period was not one-dimensional. Three major factors shaped the ethnic identity of the Nisei before the war: inculcation of "racial" and cultural identity in the home and community environment; the pursuit of "Americanization," primarily at school; and exclusion and discrimination against the Japanese in the larger society. In other words, in their childhood, the Nisei learned Japanese language, behaviors, values, and customs from their parents and the ethnic community. Having been born into the Japanese "race," they were expected to acquire and maintain Japaneseness even in the United States. Simultaneously, their identity as Americans was formed and developed in American school. Meanwhile, racial exclusion by the dominant society reinforced their sense of being of Japanese descent and made them self-conscious about their ethnic background. These three factors interacted with one another to generate specific psychological patterns in the Nisei and differentiated them from the Issei immigrants. "Americanization" ideology, virtually the same as "Ango-conformity" ideology, together with discrimination and exclusion of minorities fostered the notion of white supremacy among many Nisei, and the contrast between the homogeneous community and the prejudice of the outside world strengthened "social solidarity" and increased dependency on the protection of the community.

[125]

Evacuation and internment were the culmination of racial discrimination against Japanese Americans. Unlike the discrimination they experienced before the war, however, this action arbitrarily singled out *only* those of Japanese ancestry. Imprisonment by their own government gave the Nisei the feeling that they had been betrayed, that they were people of no country. Furthermore, during the war, ties with Japan and the maintenance of Japanese cultural traits worked disadvantageously. In reaction to American society's confusion of Japanese Americans with the Japanese in Japan, the Nisei tried to emphasize their American identity and minimize their Japanese. Americanization classes in camp and intense pressure to assimilate into the mainstream, combined with the stigma attached to their ethnicity by internment, oriented the Nisei toward assimilation and discouraged the manifestation of Japanese markers after they left camp.

In the postwar years, the Nisei, with a few exceptions, hardly discussed internment. Tetsuden Kashima calls this phenomenon "social amnesia," defining it as "a group phenomenon in which attempts are made to suppress feelings and memories of particular moments or extended time periods" (1980: 113). The memories were avoided, but many suffered from a sense of guilt and shame, even wishing that they were not of Japanese ancestry. The Nisei, in general, made extra efforts to be accepted by the dominant society and tried to Americanize and assimilate. Consciously or subconsciously, they lost the Japanese language and other cultural traits and absorbed white American cultural standards instead.

Nevertheless, the ethnic pride implanted in them during childhood persisted among the Nisei and was further promoted by their ancestral country's rapid economic growth after the war and America's subsequent acceptance and appreciation of Japanese culture. Despite their perception of stigma, the Nisei, at the subconscious level, retained their ethnic pride. They were ambivalent about their ethnicity in a way their parents had not been.

Nisei ethnic identity and feelings about the dominant society and other ethnic groups have affected the socialization of the Sansei, the next generation. Chapter 4 examines the lives and experiences of the Sansei.

[4]

Sansei Experience

The Sansei, with the exception of a very small group, were born and raised in the postwar era, when social and economic paths to mainstream society became much more open to Japanese Americans and their parents experienced upward social mobility. Although the Sansei, in general, have also formed and maintained their Japanese ethnic identity, as did their parents, their particular experience in the new era has been greatly different from that of the Nisei. In this chapter, I continue to elucidate the nature of the experiences of Japanese Americans in the greater Seattle area, but focusing on the Sansei.

Childhood to Adolescence

The Sansei population on the mainland ranges in age from the midtwenties to the early fifties, but most at the time of research were in their late twenties and thirties. Many of the Sansei I interviewed were born on Beacon Hill or in the surrounding area, where a relatively high number of Japanese Americans reside. Some had moved to suburban areas as small children and were raised in a mainly white environment. Others had moved out to suburban areas more recently, after their careers were established.

The environment where the Sansei spent their childhood differed in many respects from that the Nisei experienced before the war. One of the most important differences was the ethnic diversity of the neighborhoods where the Sansei grew up, unlike the tight-knit ethnic enclave where most of the Nisei were raised. Many Sansei, except for those who lived in predominantly white residential areas, were able to interact from preschool age with people from other ethnic backgrounds—not only white but Chinese, Filipino, and African Americans.

The Sansei's parents associated primarily with other Nisei, although in some cases, especially those residing in white residential areas, they also interacted with white American neighbors. Many Sansei recall that their parents took them to family gatherings, community events, or a Japanese church on weekends in order to keep ties with other Japanese Americans. Church was often the only formal connection to the Japanese American community for some Sansei who lived in suburban areas. The switch between the two worlds, the "ethnic" on weekends and the "nonethnic" on weekdays, created an uneasiness in the minds of some Sansei who lived where there were few other Japanese Americans. Dan Hayashi, son of Miki Hayashi, is an example.

> During the week [playing] was mostly interracial, mostly black kids. On weekends we did community things, mostly with other Sansei kids—homes, picnics, and other social gatherings. . . . I always felt different. I noticed that we always did things separately from other people. I thought it was real strange during weekdays I would do things, and during weekends—I mean, taken away and put into the community and Monday I would be back—it was kind of a double standard. I almost felt something wasn't quite right.

Because of the residential dispersal of Japanese Americans and the substantial movement of blacks and other minorities into the city during and after World War II, the Sansei in central or south Seattle went to ethnically mixed schools, either equally balanced among Asians, blacks, and whites, or slightly overbalanced by blacks or whites. The ethnic backgrounds of playmates in elementary school had no discernibly consistent pattern, at least indepen-

Racially mixed school near Beacon Hill, Seattle, around 1972. Photo courtesy of Sharon S. Aburano.

dent from residential areas, for even those living in suburban areas often played with other Sansei children from church or the children of their parents' friends on weekends. The majority of the Sansei were not conscious of their ethnicity until later, although some say that they knew that they were "different."

The overwhelming majority of the Sansei did not learn Japanese in their childhood, other than basic greetings and certain cultural terms and phrases associated with food and values. Some, however, studied Japanese in school or at the university, since Japanese was offered along with the usual European languages in the language curriculum. It was not uncommon for a Sansei to take a course in Japanese in college, although few pursued it to the advanced level.

Most Nisei did not explicitly teach their children traditional cultural values; nonetheless, some values, such as respect for elders, *enryo* (reservation), *haji* (shame), and diligence, were passed on to the Sansei. As Kathy Hashimoto, Sumi Hashimoto's daughter, said, "They didn't have to tell me. I knew that I had to work a little bit harder than anybody else. I don't think they ever told me: 'You're Japanese and you have to work harder, you're expected to be a little bit better.' I just understood that I needed to work a little bit harder. They never told me or pushed me or anything like that." Most of the Sansei interviewed were able to identify the cultural values they believe were transmitted from their parents, but some had difficulty in distinguishing Japanese values from non-Japanese ones. Nonetheless, all Sansei, including those considered to be more "assimilated," recognized the importance of education and studiousness, which their parents stressed, however covertly. They also felt pride in many high achievements of Japanese Americans.

As expected, the maintenance of Japanese customs and observance of various traditional annual events has declined, although there are many individual differences. Some Sansei observed Boys' Day, Girls' Day, and *Oshogatsu* on New Year's Day, although in much simplified forms; others remember celebrating very few such annual events. The annual *Bon-odori* (dance) of the Bon Festival at the Seattle Buddhist church in mid-July, however, attracted all types of Sansei, since it is one of the best occasions for participation in their cultural heritage. In spite of the somewhat religious connotation of this event in Seattle, the Bon celebration now attracts more people than it did in the prewar years, expanding its popularity into the larger society. The Sansei wear a *happi* coat, eat Japanese food sold at booths, and appreciate ikebana, calligraphy, and other cultural exhibitions at the church.

Few men have taken cultural lessons, but some women have taken *odori* (Japanese dance). Apparently, it is more popular among the Sansei than among women of the same generation in Japan. Even so, Jenni Miyagawa told me, it has been less popular among the Sansei than its Western equivalent, ballet: "Very few people [Sansei] did that kind of thing, took the Japanese dancing and stuff. It was kind of strange. Most people took ballet."

The Sansei's diet generally consisted of half Japanese food and half Western food. Most ate Japanese rice daily instead of potato, bread, or American rice, even with Western-style food. In fact, *ochazuke,* or tea over rice, remains popular among Sansei, eaten even at the end of Western-style dinners. Dan Hayashi reported: "I had *ochazuke* just about every day of my life when I was growing up. I had *tsukemono* [pickled vegetables], *takuwan* [pickled radish], almost every day. That's all we ate." Paul Takei also mentioned Japanese food: "My mom cooked a lot of Japanese foods basically because she was raised on a lot of them. . . . [It] wasn't exclusive. Like, we'd have rice and hamburgers, but the main staple was still rice. . . . There's kind of like variations, . . . like American food blended in with Japanese seasonings, like *shoyu* [soy sauce] wieners." Food seems to be one of the cultural elements prominently retained, even among the "assimilated" Sansei, as is true of many other ethnic groups. In the Japanese case, maintenance can also be attributed to the rise in popularity of Japanese food among the general American population.

The acceptance and admiration of Japanese culture, especially visible, material culture, in the larger society has drastically increased over the past two decades. Most of the Sansei, however, such as Alice Segawa, were born too early to be raised in such an ethnically tolerant environment:

> I remember being a child and associating things Japanese as being bad or shameful, without anyone ever telling me. I knew that was bad, and I wanted to get away from it as much as possible. So as a child I refused to eat Japanese food, and I refused to learn Japanese. I never said why; I simply refused. Then as I got a little older and became a teenager, I thought it would be nice to learn Japanese. I was beginning to understand how wrong that kind of thinking was, but by then I was very self-conscious. And when my grandmother tried to teach me a little bit, I was so bad that we all laughed, and I never pursued it. So now I don't speak Japanese and I regret it.

It is of interest to note, however, that as a child Alice Segawa enjoyed the *Bon-odori* and would go every summer. Steve Kondo also attached negative value to Japanese food in his childhood: "I always felt embarrassed going to school with *omusubi* [rice balls]. In fact, I did once, and after that I didn't want anymore. I felt embarrassed eating Japanese food in front of white, even Chinese people."

The Sansei have suffered far less discrimination and prejudice than their parents. Nevertheless, the majority of those I interviewed recalled some experience of prejudice in their childhood—typically, name-calling and remarks on physical characteristics. When Kathy Hashimoto was in the ninth grade,

> somebody at church said something that hurt, because she was a good friend. She couldn't see how I could see out of my slanted eyes. It really hurt my feelings. You are in such shock, you don't know how to respond. I didn't respond immediately. I'd never looked at the mirror. I started wondering if that's why— I had a crush on a Caucasian boy at church. He wasn't interested in me. So I started wondering if it was because of how I look.

Jenni Miyagawa said:

> I remember year after year hating to go to school because of December 7th. That was real horrible, but I think that's typical for almost all Japanese. That's a real bad time of the year to go out of the house. I think the first time that I noticed was one day walking to grammar school and getting rocks thrown at me and people chasing me and calling me, "Jap, Jap, Jap." But that was pretty common. When we were little, it was real common to be called "Ching, Chang, Chinaman." All these things were real common. They happened so much, you don't think about it. They happened repeatedly, it's not isolated incidents. There's nothing that leaves a time in mind, it's more like a whole image.

Many Sansei were not aware of racial or ethnic difference until they reached adolescence, when they started forming their ethnic identity. "In elementary school and junior high," Gary Tanaka said, "I was too young to realize that there were really differences, although I knew there were some differences. In junior high I started realizing there are cultural differences. What I eat at home is different from what my white friends eat at their homes." Oftentimes, Japanese ethnic identity arose in a specific situation that intensified awareness of difference. In fact, even for those Sansei who remembered being conscious of Japanese ancestry from an early age, exposure to discrimination or prejudice seems to have triggered the formation of their ethnic identity. Nancy Matsuda, daughter of Ichiro Matsuda, lived in a white environment in her childhood. "I grew up thinking I was white," she said. "I didn't realize I was different until I reached maybe about sixth grade, because I was always around other whites. I tried out for a part in a play in which it was for *The Prince and the Pauper.* . . . And I realized when I thought I was qualified to play the part of one of the main characters and I wasn't chosen, I thought about it and knew it was because I looked different."

After they repeatedly experienced racial prejudice, some Sansei, like their parents before them, found themselves wishing to be white. Mike Morita, for example, told me:

There was a time when I wanted to be like a Caucasian. It was the second grade. It was because I wanted to become an actor. It lasted for a year. Then I went to Kimball [Elementary School] at the third grade. You know, all those Asians are exciting. Then maybe about fifth or sixth, it started again and lasted about to the tenth grade. . . . Whenever they talk about Pearl Harbor, I didn't want to be Japanese. I wanted to be white. I always hate that: "The Japanese bombed Pearl Harbor."

Susan Ochiai expressed a similar feeling she once had: "When I was in junior high or high school, I was sort of—I felt that I wish I was white because I wouldn't have to put up with being different and having to suffer the pain or awkwardness of not fitting in, or looking different and standing out. . . . I didn't like being Japanese when I was little, when I was younger."

In sharp contrast are other cases, although rather unusual, in which individuals felt a high pride in their ethnic background. "One thing my father used to do at dinner every night," said Jenni Miyagawa.

[133]

He used to say, almost like a chant, grace, . . . "Japanese are the best, Japanese are the best. You are really lucky because you are Japanese; that means you are better and smarter than everyone else." . . . But it wasn't that I always had them as friends, necessarily, . . . but I was always attracted to them and we did seek each other out.

I was very popular in school and I think the thing that made me very popular was being Japanese in a white school. . . . So I felt that all these people wanted to be friends with me because I was really great, I was Japanese.

How one views one's ethnic background seems to be closely related to one's exposure to the culture and one's parents' attitudes, as Jenni Miyagawa suggests. Dan Hayashi did not take any Japanese cultural lessons, associated with other Japanese Americans only on weekends, and sensed from his parents even as a child that "something was wrong."

My parents rarely talked about Japan or their backgrounds, or their parents' backgrounds, even though they had very fond memories of it. I just think that the war—they just stopped talking about anything that had to do with the war, even though they were real strong, real pro-Japanese. But I think the war came and they just stopped talking about anything. So consequently I really didn't learn more about Japan or my grandparents.

It is of interest that not a few Sansei mention World War II and internment in explaining the behavior of their parents or the Nisei in general. I will come back to this point later in this chapter.

The experience of prejudice (albeit more moderate) and low self-image among some Sansei have parallels with the Nisei experience. One of the significant differences, however, is that the Sansei tend to have more ethnically expanded social circles than the Nisei. The Nisei, too, had more interaction with other groups than their parents and consequently hold certain views towards them. Often they discouraged the Sansei from associating with or dating members of other ethnic groups. Steve Kondo recalled racial prejudice: "For the same reason that the white people have a hard time understanding blacks—since my parents, maybe like typical Nisei, trying to follow the way of whites—you know, the whites don't feel too good about blacks. So I was told, 'Don't be too close to blacks.' I was never scolded for having Chinese friends."

The intervention of the Nisei parents became more serious when a Sansei had a non-Japanese friend of the opposite gender or started dating a non-Japanese. Many Nisei often based their discouragement on stereotypes rather than on an individual's quality. Kathy Hashimoto told me:

> At high school, when some Japanese boys from other high schools visited me almost daily, mother didn't say anything. No restrictions. But I had other friends who were Filipino and black. That was the first time I started to see the prejudice of my parents. I remember screaming, "You are prejudiced!" I wasn't dating any of these. The black boy was a yell leader. I was close to other yell leaders and they would invite me to games and different things. My mother didn't even want me to ride in the same car as this one black. She didn't even know this man. "He would give a bad influence," she said.

The majority of the Nisei preferred Japanese Americans for their children's spouses, and often manifested such favor even for dating partners. This explicit preference of her parents and relatives disturbed Cynthia Ube when she was dating a Sansei.

> I remember I had to go to my grandmother's funeral. He came later. At the reception afterwards, a family friend said she was surprised because he was Japanese. You know, he was OK. She was kind of assuming, "He is Japanese. He must be a good, decent person." Basically he was, but I had a kind of feeling, even now, that a lot of parents' are thinking if that guy is Japanese, or Asian, that automatically makes him a good person. It is a real close community, so if it's black or some other ethnic, not Asian person—. I said he was Japanese; then it was OK. It didn't matter whether he was a jerk or anything, you know [laugh]. To me it is so absurd.

Some Sansei confessed to inheriting from their parents the shadow of prejudice against certain ethnic groups. Scott Iizuka, for example, said that he carried some such feelings toward Chinese Americans, because of his parents' influence.

> My parents weren't really fond of Chinese. It was kind of subtle. Part
> of it goes back to camp, maybe. . . . They would say that when the
> announcement came that the Japanese would have to go to camp,
> then the Chinese were wearing buttons that said, "I'm not a Jap." And
> that upset my parents and their parents. But I think it's more histori-
> cal. . . . I think it's deeper than that one incident, but that's what
> they would say.

It seems, nonetheless, that the Nisei perceptions of other minority groups did not necessarily narrow the ethnic diversity of Sansei
friendships. The majority of the Sansei have had Chinese friends or
dating partners; several of those interviewed have dated African or
Filipino Americans some time in their lives. The difference in perception and understanding of other ethnic groups has often pro-
voked arguments between parents and children and reinforced
their feelings of a generation gap between them. Kathy Hashimoto
also says that after coming back from her stay in Japan, she corrected the Japanese words her parents used to refer to Chinese and
blacks, such as *shina-jin* (Chinaman) and *kurombo* (black boy), the
terms now considered to be derogatory in Japan, to *chugoku-jin* (lit.
people of China) and *kokujin* (lit. black people). The Sansei interviewed have rarely had substantive discussion, whether positive or
negative, with their parents about other minorities except for African, Chinese, and Filipino Americans.

The image of white Americans which the Sansei learned from
their parents is complex. It is white Americans who have dominated
the society that excluded Japanese Americans, discriminated
against them, incarcerated them during the war. Yet it is white
Americans who are regarded as "true Americans" and, therefore,
the model to follow for assimilation. It is for this reason that the
Nisei formed somewhat ambivalent feelings toward them. Some
Sansei who were raised among white Americans, have close white
friends, and would be considered more "assimilated" in the Japanese American community, said that their parents sometimes ex-

pressed mistrust of white Americans. Alice Segawa, for example, told me:

> My parents believed that people are equal, and my father in particu-
> lar believes that it's important to know people of all different back-
> grounds . . . , and yet there was strong encouragement for me to
> form friendships within the Japanese community. When we moved
> out to Redmond, . . . I ended up having mostly white friends. And I
> remember my parents, particularly my father, warning me in subtle
> ways that you can never fully trust somebody who is not in your
> community. And that puzzled me at the time. I resented it. . . . And
> it wasn't until I learned about the camps that I understood why he
> meant that, and it wasn't until I understood racism better that I
> understood why he was trying to protect me from becoming just very
> vulnerable and trusting only to be very disappointed. So there was a
> subtle discouragement, but it was a contradictory message.

Susan Ochiai, Kana Ochiai's daughter, had similar recollections of her parents:

> I think they still may have some feeling that they're not quite good
> enough, because if they were good enough, they wouldn't have been
> shipped away and put in the camps. . . . I think going through that
> experience must have wounded them in some way, in a real kind of
> unconscious way, perhaps. My mom and dad have both said, "You
> might have a really good friend who's white, but you never know.
> They might say something that shows that they still see that you're
> different, that you're not white."

The Sansei, in general, see the Nisei as having tried to Americanize "200 percent," and they attribute this effort to the war and camp experience. Both Dan Hayashi's and Steve Kondo's parents now live on Beacon Hill and associate primarily with other Nisei, but they, too, followed the "Americanization" path, while maintaining ethnic ties within the community. Hayashi reported:

> I think they felt very strongly that in order to get ahead . . . , they
> really needed to become Americanized. I mean, they felt strongly

[137]

about going to college and becoming educated, and kind of knowing how American business ran and the American way. . . . A lot of it is associated with the war. They [whites] would discriminate against us, and we needed to beat them; we needed to be better than them. We needed to be competitive, and we needed to be better educated; we needed to be more aggressive—we just needed to be better than them. . . . But when it came too far, like when it came to dating or associating with people socially, they were very clear that they preferred to have us stay within the community.

Kondo told me:

Niseis have this wonderful way of comparing everything to *hakujins*. *Hakujins* don't do this way; *hakujins* do this—da, da, da, da. So I really think the Niseis, they really wanted to be American, but they still wanted to remember their culture, too. But in order to imagine what is to be an American, they watch how *hakujins* act or behave or whatever they do. . . . When you see what they are trying to do, that's no different than what Americans are trying to do, but they are trying to do with Japanese American identity. It's actually a subculture in the main culture, but actually it's the mirror image of the main culture.

Bruce Akimoto's father, Toshi Akimoto, encouraged him to integrate himself into the white American community. Bruce discarded his original belief that an Asian American partner was the optimum after his parents told him that ethnicity did not matter. The mingling his father encouraged, however, was virtually exclusive to white Americans: "Blacks, my parents understood that the blacks were struggling, and they could empathize with them, but they never encouraged me to interact with them. The white people, Caucasians, my father would stress that this is America and that it's basically Caucasians, and if you want to get anywhere, you have to associate with them and not oppose them and assimilate in their society, their culture, and not create a separate identity." Bruce Akimoto stopped dating Japanese Americans after the first two years of college and began dating white Americans mostly because of his involvement in an athletic club. He is now married to a white American.

Kathy Hashimoto had a contrasting experience in which the ethnic background of her white boyfriend distressed her. She discontinued the relationship partly because she was aware of her parents' preference for Japanese Americans and partly because of her strong sense of *haji* (shame) relating to the family and the community.

> He was the first Caucasian that I had ever gone out with, and it was just real strange, but I know it was only because he was white, because in every other way, I felt comfortable with him. . . . If you were in the same situation, I would be the first one saying, who cares about everybody else. I can give that kind of advice, but not to myself. . . . He was very gentle. It was just my problem with what everybody in the community would say, as well as my close-knit friends accepting. . . . Even though I'm not in an organization in the community, I like to go to certain community events about once a month or something, and I couldn't see me bringing him to those events. . . . And I don't even know that because I never tried to bring him out. He would be like a closet boyfriend.

Hashimoto's reservations concerning community reaction to her white boyfriend seem to be uncommon among single Sansei today. Generally, however, the Sansei recognize their parents' preference for Japanese American marriage partners, but they have difficulty finding spouses in such a small pool of Japanese Americans, especially now that they have slowed residential and institutional integration.

The Sansei raised with close ties to the community, especially those who grew up on Beacon Hill, reported different experiences and attitudes from those raised among white Americans. The sensitivity of the Sansei in suburban areas about those "in the community" became intense as they grew older and reached high school age. Some who grew up among white Americans reported feeling some envy of the Sansei in the Seattle Japanese American community. Susan Ochiai even voluntarily transferred to Franklin High School near Beacon Hill for her senior year, and Marianne Nomura would skip school to go to Franklin to "hang around" with Asian Americans and other minorities.

For both Susan Ochiai and Marianne Nomura going to Franklin

[139]

and meeting other Sansei and Asian Americans were positive experiences, but they also tended to confirm their difference from the
Sansei raised in the Japanese American community. They characterized these Sansei as cliquish, associating only with other Asian
Americans and having a limited world view. A number of other
subjects, mostly those who found themselves marginal in or alienated from Sansei or Asian American social circles, also mentioned
the same characteristics. According to them, cliques or peer groups
were often already formed in childhood and were entrenched by
high school, so that the outsiders or newcomers had difficulty in
being accepted. Gary Tanaka and Mike Morita may represent the
Sansei who were members of such groups. Tanaka explained to me:

> In high school, as my thinking matured, I realized I was more com-
> fortable being around Sanseis and other Asian Americans than being
> around blacks and whites. In high school, students start breaking into
> groups. For a nonmember to break into [a clique] unless you are from
> the same ethnic background, it is very difficult. So I found it much
> easier to be a member of an Asian clique. By high school I realized
> that I had to associate with other Asians. Within each clique, there
> were subcliques. The smallest clique we formed was four or five
> people.

Morita confirmed this point: "At Kimball [Elementary School], I
played mostly with Chinese. Within the clique, there were myself,
three Chinese, and one Filipino. I met these people and started
hanging out with them. At Asa Mercer [Middle School], I didn't
play with anybody. I hung around the same friends I did at elementary school."

The interaction with other Sansei and the realization of their
differences created a dilemma for those raised among white Americans, an uncertainty about their identity and their niche. Susan
Ochiai, for example, said:

> I never really felt like I fit in with the Japanese community or the
> Japanese clique, 'cause I didn't feel that I had the same kind of
> background. . . . At the same time I didn't feel like I fit in with the

people in the suburbs, because I knew I had some different ethnic identity. I mean, they saw me, and they said, she's different; she's whatever she is. So I sometimes would feel that I didn't fit in those groups, either, the white culture. . . . So I think there was confusion about who I was, where I fit in. . . . So it was like being between two cultures, not really fitting in either one, not really.

Steve Kondo was raised on Beacon Hill. He received a new perspective about the Sansei when he was transferred to another school:

I didn't feel comfortable being among white people. I mean, I did not feel comfortable socializing with so many white people. I rather felt comfortable mixing with mixed people. But the funny thing about it, too, is I did not feel comfortable socializing with exclusively Japanese Americans, either. . . . Part of it is because [in high school], I had a very hard time being accepted by those Sanseis. So I intentionally tried to find other things to do without Sanseis. So, I'm a very peculiar person who feels uncomfortable in either extreme.

Those who felt distant from what they called "other Sansei" perhaps represent the majority in the greater Seattle area. This generation lacks the solidarity and relative homogeneity observed among the Nisei. Moreover, irrespective of their relation to other Sansei, a number of the subjects said they had had some type of identity dilemma in their adolescence. It is difficult to make any comparison with the Nisei in this respect. The Issei, the Nisei, and the larger society tend to view the Sansei as assimilated and "like the whites." Yet, many of the Sansei themselves have felt as if they belonged nowhere and had to search for their identity. Some have never faced any critical identity problem. Both Paul Takei and Bruce Akimoto could not recall any personal discrimination experience and can be classified as among the more assimilated Sansei.

Like other ethnic groups, Japanese Americans are perceived in terms of some fixed images or stereotypes, including those that other Americans may consider positive (cf. Takezawa 1988). The Sansei, especially the women, are highly sensitive to the stereotypes that portray them as quiet, obedient, docile, and "nice." Jenni Miyagawa said:

> One of the things I always liked was being very big because it seemed like it sort of set me apart, and another thing is that I used to hate when *hakujins* would pat me on the head and say, "You look like a little China doll." People used to do that because they were bigger.
>
> I don't believe in the Japanese being quiet. It's almost terrible: when I'm walking and someone pushes to get through the door, especially if they are white or black, I will push through. I almost think they do that to Japanese. I mean, so many people have done that to Japanese because they know that Japanese won't say anything. I just really don't want them to take advantage in any way.

Susan Ochiai told me: "I used to kind of fool around with the stereotype that other people had of me, because I looked different. I used to be loud just to break that stereotype of being real 'nice.'"

Few Sansei men, however, mentioned stereotypes of Asian men held in the dominant society. That is not to say that fewer stereotypes of Asian men exist or that the stereotypes affect men less than they do women. Even the opposite seems to be the case. Many Sansei women in the community, although not openly, discuss the stereotypes of Asian men held in the larger society, often related to physical characteristics, and their effects on the self-esteem of Sansei men. Men, meanwhile, apprehend how the Sansei women generally view them. The reciprocal portrayal of males and females, still common, created serious tension between the sexes in the 1960s and 1970s. Scott Iizuka reported:

> The Japanese women tended to be real stuck up in the sixties. They tended to ignore Japanese men. I think it was just a phase. The women clearly thought that they were attractive to white men, and the opposite was true as well. I think it was different for Japanese men. The dominant society tends to look at Asian males differently than Asian females. Where an Asian female can be attractive, or a Japanese female can be attractive, Japanese men are generally considered at a lower level. . . . I think that's part of the psyche of being a

[142]

Japanese male. . . . There are a lot of stereotypical images that are perpetuated in the films of those days. And I think the exceptions were the martial arts films, but the rule was the short, skinny, stupid—the stereotype.

Cynthia Ube expressed, on one hand, her ideological preference for Asian American men and, on the other, her characterization of them as "wimpy" and "awkward."

Ideally, I would like to marry a Japanese, but where are these great Asian guys or Japanese guys? I haven't really met one yet. In Seattle, a lot of stereotypes help put them down. They are shy, they are not really aggressive. So after a while, I thought, guys are guys, you don't have to be Asian.

I think Asian men are kind of wimps from my experience. I don't know why. To me they are not confident, because sexually they are categorized as not as being strong in that way. . . . A lot of Asian guys, Japanese guys, Chinese guys, I've talked to say, "Probably that's why we are the way we are," because of the way we, Asian women, treat them. . . . These guys say they are intimidated, and [it's] our fault [laugh]. . . . I'm sure they have a point, but women suffer, too. So we just kind of have to help each other.

The predominant ideological preference for Japanese American marriage partners comes into conflict with stereotypical images of each sex held by the other and has created some ambivalent feelings. Some point out the negative stereotypes of Asian men in the media, especially mainstream films, and many make jokes, but the influence of these images is more deeply rooted than it appears among single Sansei in their thirties or older.

One important difference between the Sansei and the Nisei is the tendency of the younger generation to refer to themselves as Asian, not merely Japanese, Americans. The boundaries of that designation tend to vary among individuals. Some include only Japanese and Chinese Americans; some include Filipino Americans as well; and others, often those active in the community, use the term to embrace every nationality from the Asian continent, including Koreans, Vietnamese, Hmongs, Samoans, and Indians. The Nisei I interviewed did not relate themselves to such terms as "Asian" and "Oriental,"[1] but the majority of the next generation have identified themselves as Asian Americans, sometimes as a primary ethnic identity at least of some point in their life. Karl Beppu noted: "For all of us who grew up here, there are common grounds. You have an Asian American common identity. Usually these people come from a middle-class background. Nisei see the differences between Asian groups. . . . But we are all Asians; we don't say he is Chinese, he is Japanese." Typically, the Sansei assumed this identity in adolescence, in most cases as a result of social interaction with other Asian Americans, especially those of Chinese and sometimes Filipino ancestry. Kathy Hashimoto commented:

> Up until fifteen, I thought I was American even though I told other people I'm Japanese. It was just a word to me. I started identifying myself as Asian American and Japanese American, half and half. When I was with other Asians, I didn't want to be different from others. I wanted to be all the same, because I have not just Japanese but Chinese and Filipino [American friends]. Now I see more differences, but back then we identified together. We were too small to separate. Only if somebody asked me specifically what nationality I was, then I identified myself as Japanese American.

The use of these terms among the Sansei reflects the influence of a major event of their lives, the Asian American movement, which had already taken root by the time most of them reached adolescence.

The Asian American Movement

In the late 1960s, the Asian American movement emerged as part of the rise in ethnic consciousness in American society. Social

---

[1] Today, Asian Americans consider "Oriental" to be a derogatory term, and it is not used among the Sansei. Before the war, however, it was a common expression for the people from East Asia and their descendants.

struggles such as the antiwar movement, the civil rights movement, and the black power movement created a climate in which Asian Americans began to reassess their past and present, especially with regard to the power structure in America and in reference to the problems of Asian people worldwide.[2] The first wave of the movement began with the Third World Strikes of 1968–1969 at San Francisco State University and the University of California, Berkeley.

Campus-based political activists started using the term "Asian American" to replace "Oriental," which had come to seem derogatory, as well as such national categories as Chinese, Japanese, and Filipino. Underlying this movement for unification was the shift from the older generation, which retained hostilities derived from the histories of their ancestral countries, to the younger generation, more concerned with their common status as a racial minority in American society. These young people were intent on breaking their stereotypes as passive, quiet, and obedient. As Larry Kubota put it at the time, the movement "is a rejection of the passive Oriental stereotypes and symbolizes the birth of a new Asian—one who will recognize and deal with injustices. The shout of Yellow Power, symbolic of our new direction, is reverberating in the quiet corridors of the Asian community" (in Uyematsu 1971: 11). The movement soon won victories at San Francisco State and the University of California, Berkeley, where Asian American studies programs were instituted. Other universities and colleges throughout the nation followed suit, especially on the West Coast.

In Seattle, the movement started from the Asian American student organizations at the Seattle Central Community College and the University of Washington. The Asian Student Coalition at the University of Washington was formed during the Kent State–Cambodia antiwar demonstrations during the spring quarter of 1970. By winter quarter of 1971, the coalition's main emphasis

---

[2] Paul Wong points out (1972: 35–36) that in contrast to white Americans in the antiwar movement, who used the slogans "Give peace a chance," and "Bring the G.I.'s home," Asian Americans emphasized the "*racist* nature of the war" with such slogans as "Stop killing *our* Asian brothers and sisters" and "We don't want *your* racist war."

Asian American movement, Seattle, 1971. Photo courtesy of Alan Sugiyama.

became a demand for establishment of an Asian American studies program and for the employment of more Asian American faculty and administrators (Asian Student Coalition 1973: 7–8). The movement occasionally engaged in violent demonstrations and protests.[3] In early 1971 at the Seattle Central Community College, the activists closed a building after a three-month negotiation with the school administration over the student demand for more Asian administrators and instructors. In the demonstration against arbitrary and discriminatory hiring practices, they used the slogan "Asians Now!" The late sixties and early seventies, as Dan Hayashi said, were

> just a very turbulent time in the United States—the civil rights movement and everything. And I became very involved with the civil

[3] One demonstration held in March 2, 1971, at the Seattle Central Community College, for example, resulted in over $1,750 in damage and cleanup costs (Executive Committee, Seattle Community College 1971: 1).

[146]

rights movement and started the Asian Coalition on the University campus and was actually pretty radical. . . . We wanted more instructors, we wanted an Asian Studies Department, we wanted more Asian students, we wanted everything. We felt we were so underrepresented that we wanted gains in every area of academia. We stormed the dean's office and dorms.

These activists and other concerned citizens of all races also strongly opposed the construction of the Kingdome Stadium next to the International District in 1972, for the construction involved closing and tearing down a number of hotels that accommodated many low-income Asian Americans. The protest won a promise from the city to preserve the International District. The city also opened the International District Health Clinic and brought in other service agencies. The "yellow power" movement also spawned a few Asian American community newspapers. One of the most important in the early period was *Asian Family Affair*, begun in 1971 by several University of Washington students of different Asian backgrounds. The goals of the newspaper were to provide information to the Asian community, to unite Asians as a community, to project their concerns beyond the Asian community, and to give the community a political voice (*Asian Family Affair* 1985: 14:2–3).

The influence of the black power movement on the Asian American movement should not be underestimated. In *Beacon Hill Boys*, a film depicting the life of young Sansei men in Seattle, one of the characters copies the speech pattern and dressing style of an African American. Blacks who took new pride in their ethnic heritage and racial background became role models for some militant Sansei. Rie Aoyama, although she was still in her twenties when I interviewed her, mentioned this empathy with African Americans: "We had no role models for finding identity. We followed what blacks did. Within the whole Asian American identity, the part of the black identity came with it. Usually when you say Asian American, you are going to have some aspect of black experience, too." The civil rights and black power movement awoke the desire to fight social injustice and racial oppression in American society. These movements unleashed a good deal of pent-up anger in other ethnic groups. The Asian

[147]

Students Coalition declared: "In the past, Asians have been scared to fight the forces that have oppressed and subjugated to be 'third class citizens.' But Asians can no longer afford to witness the rape and exploitation of themselves. . . . Asians have always had their own cause to struggle, since they have been victims—with visible scars—of American racism and oppression" (1973: 5). Dan Hayashi, who was heavily involved in the student movement and the Asian American movement, also emphasized the influence of the civil rights movement on his political involvement: "If the black movement had not happened, I don't think we would have happened. Clearly that was a point where I became clear about who I was, and began to feel very good about that and also just very aggressive politically and almost militant about letting people know who we were, and that we stood for something, and that we weren't going to take any more."

The black power movement and other ethnic movements also crystallized the sense of being a minority in American society. With the explosion of the yellow power movement, Sansei rejected the pursuit of Americanization as white conformity and abandonment of their own cultural heritage. Amy Uyematsu notes: "In the process of Americanization, Asians have tried to transform themselves into white men—both mentally and physically. Mentally, they have adjusted to the white man's culture by giving up their own languages, customs, histories, and cultural values. They have adopted the 'American way of life' only to discover that this is not enough" (1971: 10). Nancy Matsuda's experience in high school typifies the sudden awakening of ethnic identity many experienced:

> I realized how the blacks were an oppressed people, and I saw how Asians were oppressed, too. So for me, it was a complete turn around from wanting to be associated with the whites to wanting to be associated with the blacks, or just a minority. Building awareness among my white friends, I want you to know that I'm different, that I have my own identity. . . . [In college] I hung around with only Asian friends. It was as if I didn't want to meet any more white people, kind of shutting away that one side of my life, just wanting to totally associate with the Asians. I was very antiwhite. . . . In some ways maybe I felt

betrayed that they tried to make me like them. But see, it's not really their fault. It was a total 180-degree turn where I wanted to reestablish myself as an Asian and so shut myself away from the whites.

The search for identity took other forms as well. The majority of the Sansei interviewed took one or more Asian American studies courses at the university, which triggered their interest in their ethnic roots and pride in their cultural heritage and ethnic history. Some chose to involve themselves in the Asian American community through agencies, a community newspaper, or other voluntary activities.

As ethnic consciousness and interest in their cultural heritage and history grew among the Sansei in the late 1960s and early 1970s, the issues of internment and redress became common topics of conversation. Redress was a perfect rallying point for the Asian American movement, intent as it was on breaking the image of the quiet Asian, on opposing white "Americanization" and challenging racism and social injustice. Not only Japanese Americans but all Asian Americans found they could coalesce around this point, for all had suffered some form of racial exclusion or discrimination.

Seattle Central Community College opened a course on Asian American history after students presented a petition signed by over eleven hundred people. Japanese American internment became a central focus of the new course, presented as an important part of the history of all Asian Americans. Off campus, the Asian American student organization sponsored a series of community forums on the internment issue to raise public consciousness. As early as 1973, about three hundred people participated in one of these forums, and there were guest speakers of Chinese and Filipino backgrounds as well as those from the Japanese American community. In 1977, a small group of Sansei traveled to Minidoka to see the camp site. The organizer, a Sansei named Alan Sugiyama (real name), reported his impressions in an Asian American community newspaper: "I had spoken to many people who had revisited the camp. All of them told me there was nothing there except the old guard house. . . . "They were *all wrong!!* There's a lot there; not only physically but mentally. Just being there, standing where my

The staff of *Asian Family Affair* visits Minidoka, 1974. Photo courtesy of Alan Sugiyama.

parents stood 35 years ago was a very rewarding experience. The feeling was rather ghostly thinking that my parents as well as others were forced to live there" (*Asian Family Affair* 1977: 6:2).

In the social and political mood of the ethnic awakening, the young activists began to develop the idea of redress for Japanese Americans. Jack Sakata recollected the process: "The idea . . . specifically came from a black history class I had. In the black history class, when they freed the slaves, they said that they would get forty acres and a mule as redress for being slaves. And the idea of redress followed that. And a lot of the Asian American movement stemmed from the black movement, because a lot of discrimination and so forth were very similar." These Sansei activists were more concerned with creating awareness of internment among Japanese Americans and other Asian Americans than with pursuing specific monetary compensation. Their primary interest was to increase the awareness of Japanese Americans that the government had never apologized for this gross injustice.

The response of the older generations of Japanese Americans to the demonstration and other political activities of these Sansei was not always positive, however, as Jack Sakata explained:

> They thought we were crazy. . . . I remember going around the different groups and speaking. . . . They were really perplexed as far as why did I do this—bring shame upon Japanese Americans. So we were saying the shame was already brought upon Japanese Americans by internment, by discrimination and so forth, and I'm just calling attention to it to solve the problem that we have. Other groups were very supportive, but I think the general population thought that we were crazy. . . . We knew we were right; so we continued. And I think we made a great impact, continuing doing things.
>
> Redress became an area where you could point out very graphically that there was discrimination in this country, because so many people that aren't Japanese Americans and Asian Americans didn't believe that discrimination actually occurred. . . . Early days when I was talking about just identity—"who am I as a Japanese American?"— the internment was the issue that we always brought up. And a lot of time we spent on talking about what had happened in America. It was America that kept people separate. It was America that did not want competition from its own citizens. So it was always used as one of the biggest examples of racism in America. That's how it helped the Asian movement. That's how the Asian movement helped redress.

This is not a phenomenon unique to the Seattle Sansei. Lillian Nakano (real name), an activist in the California-based National Coalition for Redress and Reparations, had never been involved in the community before the redress movement began.

> Through my involvement, I came to know "J-Town" beyond its glitter of tourist shops and restaurants. . . . I felt proud to be part of this community. . . .
> At the same time, it made me reflect on my own past and how the

[151]

deprivation and alienation caused by the dispersal of Japanese Americans after the camps had affected us all these years. By re-examining the past, all that was in the "Nisei experience"—oppression, fear, alienation, the question "to-assimilate-or-not," and *Gaman* (to accept and endure)—which was forever suppressed came back out of the mire. Slowly the jumbled pieces of the puzzle began to fall into place one by one. (Quoted in Cruz et al. 1982: 27–28)

This kind of ethnic awareness and interest in cultural heritage and history, triggered by the Asian American movement the Sansei students had begun, gradually penetrated into the Japanese American community as well, establishing the social basis for the later redress movement.

Conclusion

The three generations of Japanese Americans, the Issei, the Nisei, and the Sansei, are often placed in a straight-line continuum between the two poles of the Japanese and American cultures. The Sansei, who speak English without an accent and behave in much the same way as white Americans, appear to be assimilated and retain few Japanese cultural markers. There is no doubt as to their high degree of acculturation and assimilation into American society in comparison with the preceding generations.

Nevertheless, it is important to stress that however assimilated the Sansei appear to be, the environment in which they grew up, including the home and the community, and the experiences they have had as members of the ethnic group, differ to a large extent from those of white Americans and other minorities. The Sansei have been exposed to racial discrimination, which, though not as severe as what the Nisei experienced, is substantial enough to make them realize their difference from the dominant cultural model. The Sansei have struggled to find their identity and a niche in society, seeking a way to negotiate the double message they received from their parents and the community with respect to their ethnic heritage and white Americans. Though the Sansei do not speak Japanese, learned little about Japan from their parents, and were encouraged to succeed in schools and professions, they too possess the Japanese American ethnic history of exclusion and discrimination that culminated in evacuation and internment, the same history that encouraged their parents to repress their cultural heritage.

The Sansei differ from their parents in seizing upon an Asian American identity. This phenomenon seems to derive from several factors: close association with other Asian ethnic groups (mostly Chinese and, to some extent, Filipinos as well) in racially mixed schools and neighborhoods; the boundary originally drawn by the dominant society based on racial stereotypes applied indiscriminately to all Asian groups; and the Asian American movement. Asian American identity has been most strongly defined as instrumental ties in political contexts, although the formation of such an identity among many Sansei can also be attributed to a more primordially based, irrational desire. The Sansei know their parents' perceptions about other ethnic groups, but they have escaped being dominated by those views. Instead, they have developed their own association patterns with other ethnic groups, their own perceptions, their own experiences distinct from those of the previous generations and the rest of Americans.

The cry of "Yellow Power" exploded from Asian Americans' self awareness of their pursuit of white-centered "Americanization" and their lack of cultural heritage and knowledge about their ethnic history. Contrary to the stereotypes, they broke silence and demanded a reappraisal of racial oppression and their history as a minority in America. It is this soil that bore and nurtured the redress movement.

In the next chapter, I return to redress to explore how the resurrection of the internment experience and the fight for redress affected Japanese Americans.

[5]

Redefining the Past
and the Present

In the early 1970s, as the social and political milieu changed and redress became an important issue, Japanese Americans began to redefine the past and the present. In this chapter I investigate the responses of the Nisei and Sansei to the redress movement. I describe the intergenerational dialogue on internment and how the different generations reacted to activities related to redress. I also compare and contrast the effects of the movement on the Nisei and the Sansei.

Intergenerational Dialogue on Internment

As discussed in Chapter 3, many Nisei avoided talking about internment or limited their conversation to pleasant memories of friends or to other positive aspects of camp life. Few willingly talked to their children about this traumatic but critical period of their lives. Even those who deny any reluctance to speak believe their children are not interested. George Saito said: "We only talk about it when [our daughter] comes to us and asks us for information. But when the kid doesn't show any interest, you don't try and force it." This is a typical attitude. Surprisingly, even many of the Nisei who were politically active in the redress movement spoke little to their own children of their personal experiences in camp.

[154]

Some Sansei, therefore, heard about internment first from books, films, or relatives, not their parents.[1] Typically, they then approached their parents: "Mom, were you in one of those camps?" "Dad, did you go to camp?" And the parents would admit that they had: "Yeah, we did." Richard Azuma's "younger daughter was watching *Farewell to Manzanar*.[2] She was six or seven at that time. She identified with the girl. She was crying and laughing. When it was all over, she said, 'Were you and mother in one of those camps?'"

Other Sansei had noticed frequent references to "camp" in their parents' daily conversations, but in most cases, the topic appeared only in passing. Many who had heard such references since childhood thought their parents were talking about a summer camp, and they realized the true meaning of internment only later, in school or college. Alice Segawa was familiar with remarks about "Japs" and Pearl Harbor, and her father's plaque from the 442d Regimental Combat Team had familiarized her with internment, but only in high school did she at last understand what was meant: "I remember just being overwhelmed with a sense of horror, just being totally overwhelmed to the point where I couldn't even read it. I'd read a few paragraphs and then I'd have to just shut the book because I was so angry and distraught, upset to realize when they said camp, they meant concentration camp." She described how the conversation about internment began in her family:

My younger sister said, when she decided to do a term paper at high school on the camps, she asked my mother and father to talk about it with her, and this is the first time any of us had done that. And she said my mother went to go and get the yearbook from the camp and she brought it back to show her. And when she opened it, she burst

---

[1] Donna K. Nagata (1990: 55) indicates that if both parents went to camp, 13 percent of the children first learned about internment through books, films, etc., and 39 percent first learned about it by overhearing conversations between parents or relatives. If only one parent was interned the percentages are 23 and 30. If neither parent went to camp, 28 percent learned about internment from conversations overheard.

[2] This film, made in 1976, is based on the novel *Farewell to Manzanar* by Jeanne Wakatsuki Houston and James D. Houston (Boston: Houghton Mifflin, 1973).

[155]

into tears. And this is just very unusual, and my father said nothing. And my sister was very struck about how, first, there had been nothing said, and the first opportunity to say something, that kind of emotion came forth.

Most of the Sansei were shocked by the historical fact, but many were also offended that their parents had never told them the truth. Kathy Hashimoto remembered:

I was about fifteen. I was at a friend's house, looking at his parents' library. I found a book. It was called *Citizen 13*———. . . .[3] I remember coming home very angry about it, angry because of what happened, but also with my parents for never telling me. . . . I said to my mother, how could you just allow 120,000 of you to just go into these camps? Why didn't you tell me before? She said because she thought I couldn't understand what it is like, because the time has changed and it wasn't easy.

The Hayashi family avoided the camp experience as a topic of conversation. In a pattern typical of many other Nisei parents and Sansei children, Miki Hayashi and her son Dan, at separate interviews, revealed their own viewpoints and feelings about the discussion with each other: "I mean, they grew up in a completely white neighborhood and white environment," Miki Hayashi said. "So something ethnic just doesn't seem to interest them at all. I was just busy raising kids. I never talked about camp with my husband. We were just too busy." Later, when the civil rights movement started, her children became indignant when they found out about camps. "They did reports at school, and they became more open about their feelings about evacuation, but I kept away from that, and so did [my husband]." Her children started asking questions, "but I don't think I ever gave them answers. I just cut them off. I really never dealt with it, I never really could deal with it." Dan Hayashi presented a different perception:

[3] Hashimoto refers to *Citizen 13660*, written by Mine Okubo, a collection of sketches and explanations depicting the evacuation and life in an internment camp.

[156]

We never really had a discussion about camp. My father, mother, and I never sat down, and they never said, "Okay, Dan, this is what camp was all about." They never did that. . . .

I think, on one level, I was pretty upset because I felt like they owed it to me to tell me what that experience was, so I could understand them and understand myself better. But I also realized that it was very painful to them. So, while I did ask a question, I really didn't press very hard because I didn't think it was my right.

Shirley Kobayashi witnessed the sudden beginning of the dialogue on camp between her sister and her niece in the early 1980s:

I was over at my sister's house and one of my brother-in-law's sisters says, "Did you know your mother was put in jail in Portland because they were down there for some Buddhist convention the day Pearl Harbor was bombed?" And her daughter says, "Well, Mom, you never talk about the war, you never talk about evacuation, so we thought that was a no-no, so we never asked questions about it."

The children always thought that was something the parents wanted to hide, so they didn't dare ask questions about it.

It is intriguing to observe that while the Nisei interpret the lack of questions about internment as a sign of little interest in the issue, the Sansei say that they refrained from asking questions out of consideration for their parents. Except for a small number of families who openly discussed camp, this was one of the areas in which intergenerational miscommunication and misunderstanding occurred.

Limited knowledge about internment and the silence in the family and the community created in Dan Hayashi feelings of shame about the role of internment in his upbringing: "Until the movement, really, I would say there was a lot of subtle shame about the idea of being treated differently and my parents having been in a concentration camp because they were Japanese. . . . The fact that we had been in camp and that nobody wanted to talk about it gave me a message that there was something to be ashamed about." Gary

[157]

Tanaka also mentioned the stigma internment attached to Japanese American ethnicity:

> It's an embarrassing blotch on the community. It's also true for San-
> sei. White Americans would say, "Were your parents in camp?" Then
> they ask questions, "How was it?" I start feeling this is kind of person-
> al; I don't want to talk about it. Parents being thrown into a prison—it
> is almost as bad as saying, "My parents were in jail: one was for
> robbery and the other one was for murder." It's the same type of
> process you have to go through in explaining why your parents and
> relatives had to go to camp. It is the same kind of stigma. What makes
> this magnified is it wasn't only your parents, but your grandparents,
> uncles, aunts, your friends, everybody was there. And it wasn't just a
> day or two, but it was for years.

Some Sansei shared these feelings of shame which derived from the fact that their parents were turned into inmates. Marianne Nomura said that she openly discussed camp and redress with her white friends, but did not tell them about her father's imprisonment for refusing induction into military service. Although she respects her father's courageous action during the war, she admitted, "I suppose, to be honest, there is some embarrassment in the idea that my dad went to jail."

In contrast, Carol Namiki denied any embarrassment or feeling of stigma. She attributed her lack of shame to the fact that her mother did not go to camp; instead, she left the West Coast for the Midwest in early 1942. She also said that her father, who was drafted into the 442d Regimental Combat Team, is proud of having been a soldier. Namiki explained that her mother did not suffer the low self-esteem common among the Nisei who were interned:

> This is just what I think. For my mother, I think because she didn't go
> to camp, I don't think she felt that stigma of having been to camp, and
> therefore it was not passed down. I think she may have felt she was
> better than others because she didn't go to camp. . . . Maybe it's sort
> of similar to blacks from Africa not having been subjected to slavery
> while American blacks had. So there's this slight feeling of superiority

[158]

for not having been through that experience, or having escaped it. . . . She never admitted to that, but I just got that feeling.

The majority of Sansei, however, felt more anger than embarrassment, anger at the injustice of the government and the racism in American society. "I don't know," said Alice Segawa,

it was a very deep anger, and I'm not sure exactly where it was directed. It was not directed only at the government; it was directed against what I felt was just a white wall of racism. It was generalized anger because I understood suddenly again all of these fragments of what had been said about camps, and my parents telling me you can only trust so far and the distancing, and why it was that I would not get jobs where my white friends would get jobs, and why it was we were blamed for Pearl Harbor and why it was that—and just the whole burial of the subject. My grandparents had lost everything and had to start over. I had all these little fragments of everything, and suddenly it became clear and I was furious.

Bruce Akimoto found his anger diminished after he discussed internment with his father:

I was sort of angry that they put people, Japanese, in camps, whereas they didn't put Germans or whatever in camps, and I talked to my parents. . . . Their attitude about camp was that it happened and there's not much that I, my generation, can do about it. It's just something that happened in history, and there's really no cause for me to get upset or worry about it. They wanted me to concentrate on my life, rather than worry about what happened to them.

His father, Toshi, has mentioned the loss of his business to his son, but Bruce seems to know little more than that: "My children are rather ignorant about the camp experience. We don't talk about it. I don't think they're that curious, either. They don't ask about it. Once in a while they ask why I didn't object to it. . . . But then I couldn't object, being an enemy alien at that time. So we don't really talk about it." According to Bruce, his father stressed the

positive side of internment rather than the negative one, saying that
it was safer than staying in the community and suffering from racial
disturbances. This dialogue between father and son is indicative of
the type of family that has weak feelings about internment and
minimal interest in redress.

One of the subjects frequently brought up in the intergenerational dialogue on internment, especially at the initial stage, was why
the Nisei did not resist the evacuation order. This acquiescence
puzzled the Sansei, whose values and behavior patterns are more
acculturated than those of the Nisei and whose experience as a
minority differs sharply from theirs. Steve Kondo declared: "Since I
was born here, I would have at least tried to protest. I would not
have become violent, but I would have at least tried to say, 'Hey,
there's a book of rules here in the Constitution.' . . . I believe that
they should have acted differently, but knowing what I know now, I
can understand how they acted." Now, more Sansei understand the
historical circumstances in which the Nisei were placed. The Nisei
themselves found the question disturbing, and many alluded to it.
"Young people ask us, 'Why didn't you protest?'" said Richard
Azuma. "But they took our guns and things away, so what can you
do?" Many take the question as an indication that the Sansei cannot
fully understand their feelings about internment.

Many other Nisei, however, appreciated the Sansei efforts to
shed light on internment and pursue redress. In fact, most Nisei
redress leaders, long frustrated by the difficulty in moving the
Nisei, claim that the Sansei have better understanding of the issue.
Frank Narita told me:

> The Nisei are the ones who let these things happen. . . . But the
> majority of the Nisei were still this "Let's bury it. Don't make any
> waves." . . . I think that 10 percent of the Nisei wanted to go after
> redress, but 90 percent didn't. . . . Suddenly, this thing spilled into
> the Sansei, and you've got 50 percent of the Sansei [supporting it].
> That combination of 10 percent Nisei and at least 50 percent of the
> Sansei began to persuade everybody that we should at least struggle,
> we shouldn't just give up. But I would say that the Sansei have
> supplied a lot of muscle for this.

Harry Tanabe echoed this view: "I think they understand better than the Nisei do. I think their thinking is a little better. The Nisei, their heads are so all mixed up. They've been brainwashed so much. So it takes about maybe one generation to clean things up, I guess."

The start of discussions between parents and children concerning the camp experience varied from family to family. Both generations agree, however, that the redress movement created increasing opportunities to talk about it.

Reactions to Events in the Redress Movement

Since the Nisei were attempting to reestablish themselves through hard work, few supported the redress campaign when it started in the early 1970s in Seattle. When the drive succeeded, many Nisei claimed that they had supported the idea from the beginning, but according to the original activists this is not the case. Sayings such as "Don't rock the boat," "Why are you bringing back the bad memories?" and "We should just forget" were most often heard in the community. During the fifteen years that passed between presentation of a concrete plan at the Seattle chapter meeting in 1973 and passage of the redress bill in 1988, Japanese Americans underwent a transformation in their ethnic identity, feelings about camp, intergenerational relationships, and some of their norms and values.

The first Day of Remembrance in 1978 opened an important path leading to the discussion of the internment issue among Japanese Americans. The dramatization of evacuation triggered memories long buried. This event had been organized by a Chinese American playwright and several Sansei, who had approached the redress leaders in Seattle showing a keen interest in camp and redress. Joe Fukiai, one of the key Sansei involved in this program, recalled how a Chinese American playwright approached him with the idea of a reenactment:

> He pitched me and said, "There would be no Japanese American art if we don't say about Japanese American history. If we lose redress, we

lose history. If these people in Seattle fail to win some kind of recognition for the injustice in the camps and to get some token payment for it as a symbol of the recognition that it was wrong, then the myth that camps were justified, that Nisei willingly cooperated with them, would stand. Then, no artist can create plays, books, or stories from the truth, because no one would believe them." Then I thought, "Gee! This is much bigger than me. I have to devote my entire soul to this."

The program planners and activists were surprised and moved by the magnificent response of the community. "When we organized that, it was doubtful how many people would come up," said John Ohki. "We would be lucky if we get a hundred people. When I went down to the stadium and saw all those cars, 'Jesus Christ! That's beautiful!' I thought. 'These guys finally care.' I couldn't believe all those people. That was really an eye-opener."

Several interview subjects, Nisei and Sansei, also mentioned the attendance of many white Americans and other minorities. Shirley Kobayashi told me: "I think I was impressed that there were a lot of Caucasians there to see that. Lots of people, yes. And there were quite a few Caucasian people that gave speeches, too." Harry Tanabe was given a ride to the Puyallup site by one of his white friends, in an ironic twist on the historical evacuation, when the white American authorities who drove him and other Japanese Americans out to the camp had a much different attitude. This change in race relations constitutes one of the critical differences from the Nisei's experience in 1942.

It was an emotional ceremony for the Sansei, as well, exposed to the realistic conditions of camp. Paul Takei commented:

When it really hit me was at the Puyallup Fairgrounds. They had some kind of—it was some display, and they actually showed the living modules. They had set up models, living areas, and stuff like that. And the space that a family had to live in was just like—I couldn't comprehend that: it's like a small, small living area. To hear people talk about it is one thing, but to see some physical display of the thing was kind of unreal. That's when it started to really hit me.

This ritualistic event also created the sense of "togetherness" among the participants, and for the first time since the war as many as two thousand Japanese Americans, with their non-Japanese friends, gathered at one place to share a common experience. At the site, the Issei and the Nisei met old friends from the camp, bringing back more old memories. It was moving for the Sansei to see their parents' response and to stand in the huge crowd of people brought together by the long-buried past. Dan Hayashi told me:

> The mere fact that we had all those people there, I just thought, was wonderful. A lot of people were crying and very taken by it, too, emotionally. But my experience was very different than maybe a lot of other people. It felt very powerful. I felt very good that we were all there. . . .
>
> It definitely motivated me to want to work with people to get it more in the open, to get people to talk about it, to find out more about it. And I knew that it was kind of like catharsis. It's kind of like the Day of Remembrance gave people permission to kind of talk about it. . . . So I think as a community it gave us—it was very therapeutic.

Most of the Sansei interview subjects who participated in the program spoke of their feelings at the event. Nancy Matsuda was conscious of the gulf between her own experience and that of the Nisei:

> I remember being surprised at, "Wow, they were stripped of the niceties and they were left with just the simplest of amenities." And the pictures of camp, the barbed wire—"Gosh, did they need that?" . . . Being a Sansei and not fully understanding and not feeling what they were feeling, because this obviously evoked a lot of memories that maybe had been suppressed for years, and not being able to relate, I felt like an outsider. Even though I was of Japanese descent, I had never been through it. . . . So I felt I was there but I was not there.

Most participants named the Day of Remembrance as one of the most memorable events of the whole redress drive. But many other

Issei and Nisei could not bring themselves to attend, so painful were their memories. Kathy Hashimoto's uncle was visiting at the time of the reenactment: "I wanted him to come, 'Don't you want to go with my mom and me to Puyallup?' He looked at me like I was crazy. 'Are you kidding me? I went to Puyallup once. I never want to see that place again.'"

If the first Day of Remembrance opened the floodgates of memory and emotion, perhaps no other event of the redress movement penetrated so deeply into the wider population of Japanese Americans as the hearings of the Commission on Wartime Relocation and Internment of Civilians held in Seattle in 1981. About 80 of the 150 people who testified were Japanese American residents of King County, including Seattle. The hearings focused the attention of the whole community on the actual experiences of individual people. Many who testified were telling stories that they had kept secret even from their close friends and relatives. After observing the commission hearings, Kana Ochiai's friends and relatives began to speak of what had happened to them and their deep feelings about it:

> Because a lot of the Nisei were testifying and they were telling of their personal experiences, so then among ourselves, like a group of us would be getting together for some reason, . . . and then, while we were having coffee, we started sharing personal experiences or how we felt about things that happened. Like my sister told about her experiences in nursing school and others told about how her father was taken, how her mother reacted, how they felt, how she felt when her Chinese friend wore her Chinese button, things like that, that happened, that hurt us deeply, personally. We started sharing those kinds of things. It became very emotional. Everyone had different experiences, but they were all of the hurting kind.

Ichiro Matsuda, who was drafted by the army before evacuation, debated whether to testify or not. When he eventually did, he felt "born-again," and he vividly described the effect of breaking silence on his self-esteem and ethnic identity.

> Until that time, up until testimony, I was self-conscious of my race, my heritage. . . . But after the testimony, all that self-consciousness

went out the window and I became a new person. Then I was up-lifted, I felt euphoria, exhilaration; I felt newborn. . . . I felt it's great to be living again. . . . I felt so empty inside after all this nearly forty years of mental burden that I've been carrying—prejudice, discrimi-nation, internment. All the stigma, all this anguish, just went out of my body. . . . And so into the vacuum, I think, came my past memo-ries about my life, my family, my heritage. . . . My mind started to fill up with my past memories, pleasant memories. . . . It was stimu-lating; it was refreshing to think about better things after I got rid of all the anger and burden.

The psychological wounds restrained the Nisei from discussing camp with their children beyond a certain level. Yet, as Ichiro Matsuda said, "Even though we did not personally talk about it, publicly it came out."

In the testimony the Sansei, for the first time, were able to hear actual stories and see the emotions of their elders. If the greatest significance of the commission hearings for the Nisei was therapeu-tic catharsis, for the Sansei, it was the enhancement of ethnic pride and a new admiration of the Nisei's courage in speaking out. Susan Ochiai said: "It was part of their catharsis of forgetting about it by talking about it. So I felt kind of like I was taking part in this catharsis and it was kind of an honor to be able to hear people's stories like that, that they were brave enough to get up and talk about it. . . . And it was very painful for them, and it was private, but they still did it. And I was very moved by that experience." David Hayama, too, was moved: "Perhaps it made me appreciate more their courage and strength, that after all these years here they would come forward, step forward in a public forum and say this was wrong."

The commission hearings, held in various locales across the na-tion, made a deep impression on Japanese Americans and were extremely influential in the larger society as well, helping to con-vince Americans of the need for redress. The hearings and the Day of Remembrance were the watershed events that made it possible for the Nisei to speak of the great wrong done to them, but other events related to the redress movement, such as plays, movies, and reparations to former employees of the Seattle school system, also impressed some people.

For Kathy Hashimoto, the play *Breaking the Silence* gave her even greater realization of the damage caused by evacuation: "I never forget the scene where the woman threw nice china one after another when somebody came to buy. . . ."[4] Some of the stories really made an impact on me. It makes me sad to think about things that were destroyed because of the war, family things. That makes me sick, too. That was part of our history. That was permanently destroyed."

Gordon Hirabayashi's court case also attracted great attention in the community. According to Jenni Miyagawa, "It was the main topic of everybody's lives" at that time. Hirabayashi, a former Seattlite, proved an inspirational role model in the redress movement, for in breaking the wartime curfew and challenging the government as an American citizen, he had also broken the stereotype of the docile Japanese American. His renewed appeal was a cause of great ethnic pride, said Dan Hayashi: "I was very proud he was doing what he was doing. It really did give Sansei, certainly myself, a real sense of pride and a sense of real self worth, that it's really okay to stand up and disagree with people openly. I think it was a real significant time for most of us when it happened. Then, from there on, the redress movement built, just kind of picked up steam." Frank Narita told me: "I say we Japanese Americans are the products of Meiji culture. One negative thing is, I would say, that the word *hazukashii* [shameful, embarrassing], comes out so strong— never stick out. . . . When Gordon Hirabayashi did what he did, everybody drew back and left him out there. He was one of the pioneers. I am grateful to him. He was right. What a tremendous thing he did!"

Redress, unlike some other events, took many years to accomplish. Support had to build gradually, not only in the larger society but also among Japanese Americans. Many were at first antipathetic

---

[4] Hashimoto refers to the scene in *Farewell to Manzanar* when a bargain hunter came to the "evacuation sale" and offered only a nominal amount for a nice set of china. The mother then started to throw and break the dishes one after another in front of him.

to the idea, some, to the point of fury. Moreover, the notion of monetary compensation ran directly against Japanese values. Helen Kageshita explained:

> When we first heard about the money, it was sort of, "Do we really want to go in for the money?" That concept was alien to our culture. . . . It was only after exposure to the reasoning of the people in Henry's[5] group that I accepted. Yes, it is the system in our country. Without it, you don't have it. I'd admit that I had to be educated to that, because my initial reaction was typical to those Nisei here.

The overwhelming majority of Japanese Americans, including some Nisei who were opposed at the beginning, eventually came to support redress, but even after the passage of the bill, some balked at the idea of monetary reparation. Toshi Akimoto, in spite of the substantial economic loss he suffered during the war, told me:

> One time in Chicago, I did go to a gathering there. . . . I thought, "Well if we are to get something for this," I was thinking, "the blacks and the Indians would have some rights, too. And if they had the rights, then this country would be in a turmoil and nothing would be settled."
>
> I don't have anything against the United States government, although there are some laws that are unfair and prejudiced, but still we are trying to improve. I feel that I'm part of the United States government. I vote, express my opinion. I feel quite satisfied. I don't want to knock the United States government. The United States is a wonderful country. [Redress is like] I'm taxing myself. I'm really asking for my money back.

Some felt that putting a price tag on internment trivialized their suffering and ignored irreparable damage. Scott Iizuka, a Sansei, was one of these:

> I guess I was not supportive because I don't think that something like that should be. You can't undo what was done with money, to

[5] The reference is to Henry Miyatake, one of the first in Seattle to pursue redress.

me. . . . And I don't like to be critical of the ones who want the money or are willing to take it because it's better than nothing, but I think the issue is far greater than twenty thousand dollars. It's almost like America is trying to buy out, or sell out their guilty conscience, or try to relieve themselves of the guilt by giving money away. It's really cheap. . . . And I know a lot of people don't feel that way, but that's how I feel.

The majority of Japanese Americans in the community, however, have accepted the money as a symbol; it is the American way, they say, to sue and claim monetary compensation for damage. Moreover, it is the most effective way to prevent the government from inflicting the same sort of injustice on other minorities. Sumi Hashimoto commented:

I think it became much more of an issue during the commission hearing. I was listening to all the different testimonies, all sad stories. Then at the same time, *hakujin* people would be writing letters to the newspaper, saying . . . , "They deserved it." The more I read and the more I heard, I got angrier and angrier. By then I knew that just getting an apology was not enough. . . . Because they are saying it, I have become conscious of the fact that it's the only way to let the public know how much we suffered. It isn't the amount of money. It is a principle.

Dan Hayashi said:

This country—this is a very negative thing, but they tend to value things and place meaning on things, based on money . . . , and I think that's a very despicable thing, but that's the only time the people really listen. And until we can translate the wrong that's been done in terms of money, I don't even care where the money—most Isseis don't even care where the money is spent—but it's the mere gesture of turning, saying that, yes we were wrong, and this translates into some symbolic way.

Beyond this general consensus on monetary reparation, individuals have their own ideas. When the legislated redress was not appropriated yet, Carol Namiki, for instance, showed more concern about actual appropriation, not just the legislation. Marianne Nomura hoped that the recipients would make donations to be used for school and social education about the internment and wartime hysteria in general to prevent the same mistake again.[6] David Hayama accentuated what he believes is the next important task assigned to Japanese and Asian Americans, combatting racism.

> I think it was great. It was a great victory. . . . Yes, in terms of its symbolism. Yes, in terms of perhaps closing that chapter on that part of the Japanese American experience. . . . My parents, they can go to their graves, perhaps, satisfied that their honor was restored. . . . But what about here, now, today? This country is still not equal. We're closer to it, but Japanese Americans, other Asian Americans, other minorities, we're still far away from equality of justice. So you cannot rest on that, it is not the last step.

Not all Sansei take such a serious view of redress appropriation, racism, and injustice. Steve Kondo shared Toshi Akimoto's worry about possible demands by other minorities and a potential tax increase, except that he welcomed monetary reparation for the sake of his mother.

> When Reagan signed the bill, it didn't make me feel better because I'm not going to get the money anyway. I looked at it as a totally academic issue, kind of like economics, "Wow, can this country afford to do that. . . . Here we are, taxes are too high, we're all *monku*-ing [complaining] about too-high taxes and now they're going to do this— Oh God! Everybody is going to hate Japanese people from now on. People are going to throw rocks at me." I was thinking that.
>   The other part of me was thinking about the redress for my mother. I think it's great that she would have some extra spending money and that she'll have a chance to do a lot of things which she could never do in the past.

---

[6] The redress bill did provide for a public education fund "to finance efforts to inform the public about the internment of such individuals so as to prevent the occurrence of any similar event" (102 U.S. Statutes at Large 903).

Scott Iizuka and David Hayama mentioned another positive effect of redress in finally "closing the chapter" on the war, which has shadowed Japanese Americans for too long.

Even though the Nisei supported the campaign, few had any hope that redress could actually be achieved. Their pessimism derived from awareness of the national budget deficit and from mistrust of the government. When President Reagan actually signed the bill, they felt great relief, happiness, and pride. Miki Hayashi recounted the moment when the bill signing was announced at a banquet during the JACL national convention in Seattle.

> I didn't think it would come through. I was truly surprised. I thought, "My goodness, it did happen!" It kind of felt like the end of a journey. . . . It's a feeling of pride, initially when I heard it. My only regret, of course, is that [my husband] isn't alive. Also it was announced at the banquet . . . and it was going to be signed the next day. . . . And I'm glad I didn't just pick up the newspaper and read about it. I'm glad I was there with a lot of people my own age.

Around the time the legislation passed, the redress movement reopened probably the most sensitive issue of the war for the Japanese American community: the No-No Boys. At the 1988 national convention in Seattle, the Seattle chapter presented Resolution no. 7, which proposed that the JACL apologize to the No-No Boys for "their injuries, pain and injustice" inflicted by individuals acting on their own and in the name of the JACL. During the war, these men who refused induction into the army as a protest against the injustice of internment were labeled disloyal and sometimes harassed by members of their own ethnic community. Even after the war, draft resisters and other No-No Boys remained silent and kept a low profile in the Japanese American community. At the 1990 national convention, the JACL adopted a resolution that formally acknowledged the loyalty and patriotism of the Nisei draft resisters of the Heart Mountain Fair Play Committee during World War II. Those who resisted had many different motivations and their reactions to redress varied accordingly. Douglas Tsujii, a Nisei who was sent to jail because he refused to join the army while Japanese Americans were being held unconstitutionally, expressed joy and relief.

Finally, legally, realizing that we were not that wrong—that we spent that time in jail which we really shouldn't have and were forced to do it—yeah it was a kind of successful thing. . . . I am very happy, very happy for my children, because what happened to us is past and over and we are comfortably living in this country. We may have lost our rights because we went to jail. But it's our kids that—they are purely American with a Japanese face and at any time it could have happened to them. . . . So, I think it was a very good decision and I'm very happy.

Isao Wada, a Kibei who considered himself a patriotic Japanese during the war, did not expect redress for himself because he felt as if he had a *zenka* (criminal record). When the redress legislation passed, he thought that Kibei who had been loyal to Japan would be the exception.

I didn't think we would get the money because we were the No-Nos. I don't know whether I will get the money. . . . I never go to such things [meetings or events related to the redress], because I hate them. I hate to remember [the time in camp]. . . . I wasn't counting on it at all. If they give it to me, that's O.K., too. . . . I didn't grow up thinking I was an American, not really. I thought I was a Japanese. Because, oh yeah, you know, I was thrown into a camp. I wasn't counting on it at all. If they say, "We cannot give it to you," then I'll say, "OK. Fine."

Hisa Gotanda, a Kibei, seemed to feel that redress was a Nisei project: "The Nisei, they did it to let the American government recognize the injustice so that it won't happen again, I guess. . . . I wasn't particularly excited. We could receive the money, but I felt we didn't have to. We're leading a comfortable life, anyway. . . . I felt a little embarrassed, because it's not the money we earned ourselves." The differences in reactions to redress seem to be highly related to one's national identity. The fact that redress had far greater significance for those who identify themselves as American than for those who see themselves primarily as Japanese affirms that psychological pain caused by internment was rooted in injustice, in the government's refusal to believe in the loyalty of its own citizens.

Those who were in fact loyal to Japan did not have the same sense of having been treated unjustly.

Effects of the Redress Movement

The long campaign for redress has affected Japanese Americans in many ways, beginning with the very possibility of discussing internment and acting to win an apology. One of the most important effects was its restoration of ethnic pride. Although many Nisei say that the feeling of being second-class citizens is hardly erased simply because of redress, others claim that it has indeed made them feel like first-class citizens. Moreover, just as the feelings of guilt and shame were passed on to the Sansei to some degree, redress has enhanced their ethnic pride. The ethnic pride mentioned by members of the two generations, however, is not necessarily of the same character in all respects. The Nisei say that redress acknowledges the past and "cleanses" their wounds, but the Sansei tend to mention a sense of pride gained through the movement. They also express their great admiration for the strength that the Issei and the Nisei retained in spite of the camp and other adversity and for their courage in demanding that American society correct the injustice. In revealing the historical struggle of Japanese Americans, the movement gave the Sansei a new perspective about their ethnic group. Nancy Matsuda commented: "When I learned more about what they went through during the camp times, I grew to have a lot of respect for them, for what they went through, the struggle, and just having lived through it, come out of it, come back into society again, be established as a whole as a hard-working race, and being 'successful' in American society." David Hayama said: "Because they were different, they were excluded, not part of America. Here even after the camp experience, they still come back, they work hard, and they send their children to college and they rebuild their business, whatever, after great financial loss, great psychological pain and suffering. And yet, our parents and grandparents, they still did marvelous things. That's the story that should be told."

The redress movement also helped strengthen intergenerational ties. Because of the movement, the Nisei and Sansei began a true dialogue concerning the family and community history. Gary Tanaka and other Sansei attained a deeper understanding of their parents and the Nisei generation: "The differences between Nisei and Sansei are more subtle in that Nisei are willing to accept and speak out on the issue. . . . On the other hand, the Sanseis, who were not in camp but who were affected by their parents. So it was almost like the case that you have the speakers and the listeners, Nisei as the speakers, Sansei as the listeners."

Many Sansei believe that their families and the whole community would have been more affluent had evacuation and internment not occurred, and the behaviors and orientation of the Nisei and even the Sansei would have been different. "How different Nisei might have been," Kathy Hashimoto exclaimed. "Their personality might have been different. Our relationship with them might have been different. I can't help but think that part of their being the way they are has a lot to do with camp." Gary Tanaka had a similar view:

> There is also a gap formed in our ethnic heritage because of camp. . . . What happened because of the internment, is that we got cut short, and they had to restart, so that you see now where Japanese Americans who once owned land in California and who would have been millionaires today are not, because they lost the land. The same as in the business. . . . That was the other aspect I began to appreciate. What happened to our community was much more than just being forced to go to the camp. It destroyed the whole growth of the particular community.

The Nisei also maintain that they and their families would have been better off financially. A number, however, also said that if there had not been evacuation, they would still be living in a "ghetto," as they did before the war. In exposing them to racism and hardships, the camp experience made them "grow" and "mature." Setsuko Fukuda doubted there would be as many successful professional Japanese Americans as there are on the East Coast today, had evacuation not taken place. John Ohki said, "Probably we would have lived in Chinatown for a long time, and my father would have

[173]

been a successful businessman. After the war, we felt kind of
kinodoku [sorry for him]; so we all went on our own. My brother
would have taken my father's business, and all of us might have
been involved in business." George Saito told me: "Evacuation gave
us more exposure to the outside world. I got kicked around; so that
was a good experience. I became more mature." Steve Kondo, a
Sansei, considers this interpretation of even the hardships as positive experiences typical of the Nisei: "See, that's the thing about
Nisei people. It's the thing about Japanese: you don't dwell too
much on the negatives. They were tough times, but again, *shikata
ga nai* [it can't be helped]. So you just learn from that experience
and try to be—make yourself better."

It is of interest that not a few Nisei and Sansei mention their
gratitude to their parents. Many were amazed by what they learned
of their forebears' struggles and achievements in spite of the crush-
ing economic losses due to evacuation. "One of the reasons why I
went for redress," said John Ohki,

> is to try to reciprocate for all the Isseis for what they did for the
> Japanese community. They started a Japanese language school; they
> started the Nikkeijin-kai [*Nijonjin-kai:* Japanese Association] they
> started *kenjin-kai* . . . things like that—all for the kids. I have to
> admire them. Here, they were struggling for a living and being dis-
> criminated against worse than I ever was, and yet they took time out
> to organize all these things with Niseis. Gee! That's beautiful. How
> can you ever say thank you to them. . . . There is no way you could
> say thank you.

Like John Ohki, when they are asked why they supported redress,
apart from the issue of constitutional rights, most Nisei whose parents were still alive answered that they did so for the Issei, who,
they said, had suffered the most. The surviving Issei said that they
supported redress for their children. Most Sansei, even those uninterested in redress, said they would like to see the payment given
to their parents while they were still alive. Kathy Hashimoto,
whose parents and sisters were interned, described her feelings:

I don't know how many times in the last couple of years when I thought that redress was not going to happen, I kept saying, my only thing I prayed for all the time that if it happened, it would happen while my parents are alive, because it wouldn't mean the same thing. Even if the rest of my family can get the money, it would mean nothing. Really it would mean nothing if my parents couldn't see that something was going to happen. I wouldn't even want it. We weren't the ones that had to suffer.

There was much regret, especially among the Nisei, that when redress finally came, "it was too late" for the Issei, who they think suffered the most and most deserved redress. For the Nisei, the delays seemed intolerable. Henry Tanabe told me:

I was more interested in getting it for the Issei, you know. That was the original idea. Well, my parents are gone, long time ago. . . . I think they [the Issei] suffered the most. You know, the prime of their life, they get pushed into the middle of a desert, dusty, terrible food. . . . They were the ones that stayed in the camps the longest, too. That's why I think the younger people went out, but the older people stayed in camp and I think they suffered more.

Helen Kageshita had vivid memories of her father's suffering:

When I thought about what he experienced and how disillusioning it must have been for him to finally have a business and lose all that and to move and come back to Seattle—he was no longer a businessman; he could only do janitorial work—that loss of dignity and yet he was willing to, on his own, without any encouragement from any of us, to go to citizenship classes and become a citizen. When I think about that, I think I wish he had lived to see this.

The Sansei also wished their grandparents were alive to receive the payment. They took a personal interest in redress because it was their parents, grandparents, relatives, and friends who had spent years in camp, but their emotions were not as strong as those of the Nisei. The pain of the Nisei was rooted in their own bitter experience and exacerbated by the knowledge that death had made it impossible for their parents and friends to see injustice corrected, honor restored. The Sansei, too, were saddened by the deaths of their grandparents, and some believe their lives were cut short by the camp experience.[7] Jenni Miyagawa reported:

> When I see pictures of what people had and what they lost, that's more painful because most of the Issei have learned to cope with it. And they've forgotten it, and they show you real proudly what they had, and they don't *monku* [complain] or anything; they all take it so well. And it's just that they have nothing now. That's real painful for me. . . . Like my father-in-law, when he gets his money, he's too old to do anything with it. I think he would like to go back to Japan, but he's too old to go.

Cynthia Ube also had regrets:

> Personally, the most painful thing about camp is people like my grandmother and uncle who passed away, friends who were active in redress, all those people passed away. They won't get any of this money, and they won't be able to finally see this correction. So many people died, that's the most painful thing.
>
> I don't know if internment has anything to do with it, but all my grandparents passed away when I was very little. I know a lot of my *hakujin* friends, their grandparents were still alive. So when they get together for family dinners, their grandparents are there.

In many cases, redress triggered feelings about identity and enhanced the sense of community among the Sansei. Gary Tanaka, a politically active Sansei, said:

> It reinforced my identity with Nikkei. Up until redress, my ethnic identity was things like the food I ate, people I like to be friends with,

---

[7] I could not find any statistics that show shorter life expectancy for the Issei. The life expectancy of Japanese Americans in general seems to be over eighty (personal communication with Donna Leonetti, Dec. 1, 1989).

interests, things Japanese. With redress, I found a much newer, different, and also very important strong identification with my cultural, historical background, the history of my community. My parents went to camp, that affected me indirectly. Now I became closer to the Japanese American community, whereas originally, before redress, I wouldn't say that I was very close to the community.

Although not all Sansei experienced such an overt identity shift as Gary Tanaka, some said that learning about camp helped them to understand and define who they are. "From that," Steve Kondo told me,

> I learned why it is that I act the way I act. Or I have a better idea of why I behave the way I do. . . . When I was growing up, you always try to act like regular people, regular Americans. . . . I never made any effort to emphasize my difference from everybody else. . . . And now I know why. The way they acted in camp explains to me why I act the way I do oftentimes. You're always kind of hesitant to promote your culture among other people.

Cynthia Ube felt sure that the campaign had strengthened community ties: "I think it brought the Japanese community close nationally, everybody close together. . . . I supported it because it brought people closer. For Sansei there hasn't been an issue like redress that bound us together. . . . This issue is not an emotional issue, but it makes us feel like something we have to fight for, something we get excited about." This seems true for the Nisei as well, and even for other generations. A Yonsei girl whose father is Japanese and mother is white became interested in internment and her Japanese family history because redress was dealt with at school. Setsuko Fukuda, Shizue Peterson, and other Nisei who previously had little association with the Japanese American community, joined the JACL because of redress.

Some Sansei, though they feel that redress was a victory, contend that there are more important issues to be dealt with, such as racial discrimination. Directly or indirectly, redress has made them more aware of discrimination. Susan Ochiai, a Sansei who grew up in a

[177]

white environment and had mostly white American friends throughout her life and little contact with the Japanese American community, explained:

> What happened is early, early on, when I was younger, I was aware of [discrimination]. And then I think when I got older I was less aware of it than when the whole redress issue came up again, I think. I started reading more books, and then I also talked to more people about their experience. I think I realized, okay, it hasn't disappeared; it may have just gone underground. I think there is still a great deal of discrimination and prejudice against Japanese, and Asians, and other minorities. . . . And that has just made me aware that by learning more about redress and what happened during World War II, made me aware that it still does exist.

Ube pointed out that the redress victory has encouraged Japanese Americans to fight against other types of racism existing in the society.

As leaders of the movement anticipated, "Money talks." Attaching $1.25 billion to the redress bill captured public attention and educated the general American populace about the internment.[8] Both Nisei and Sansei remarked that not many Americans previously knew about the internment. Yet very few Nisei voluntarily talked about internment to their white American friends, except to answer direct questions or respond to jokes about the money they received. If they were challenged about the justification for monetary compensation, however, many Nisei would make some rebuttal, despite their cultural preference for avoiding confrontation. Shirley Kobayashi gave an example:

> When we were in Salt Lake two years ago, . . . we went to this real nice hotel and there was this man that had this gift shop there. . . . And my other friend was in there, looking around. And he asked her, "Why do you think you people should get twenty thousand dollars from the government?" So she told him, "If you only had two weeks to

---

[8] The amount eventually increased to $1.65 billion when the additional appropriation was made in fiscal year 1994.

sell your business, you could only carry what you wanted to, and you lost everything, wouldn't you think that twenty thousand dollars wasn't enough but if that's all the government's giving you." So she says, "I would have changed places with you anytime." So that shut him up.

The Sansei bring up the topic more willingly, although some are still reluctant, preferring to avoid potential conflict. Both Paul Takei and Kathy Hashimoto discuss internment when the issue comes up in conversation with their white friends, but the two showed contrasting feelings about mentioning the internment of their own parents. Hashimoto is hesitant about doing so, whereas Takei said he talked about camp with his white friends

> because a lot of them are curious, like, "Did you know anybody who went?" I would say that they're all genuinely interested in it. To me, the more people that know about this, the better for them. I don't feel embarrassed that my parents went to camp. That's a part of history and they have no control over it. To me it's more embarrassing for the American government, that, in my opinion, they could do something so stupid.

Hashimoto, by contrast, said:

> People who work here don't know about camp. When something comes up, I will bring the issue up. People I talked to didn't seem to have any idea. I feel I have to be careful, because there are people who don't understand, partially because I feel almost embarrassed about it, and also because I don't know the appropriate way. . . . Many of us carry that guilt, why don't we say anything, I should be saying even if they are not talking about me. We must be afraid of something, something embarrassing.

For both generations, redress has a double significance: it repairs their own psychological damage and financial loss and it corrects an injustice and a violation of the Constitution. The latter aspect was, in fact, the key message conveyed to all Americans by Japanese American political leaders.

[179]

Both Nisei and Sansei are apprehensive that the same sort of mistake might happen to other minorities, if not to Japanese Americans themselves. Many cited the hostage crisis in 1979, which aroused hostility against Iranians in this country. Bill Fukuda found it "really significant. We got into the Middle Eastern conflict. There was a lot of talk, 'Let's detain all the Iranians.' I said, 'Oh, the same thing is happening all over again.' And it could happen all over again. It could happen very easily." Paul Takei, too, was concerned: "In my opinion, I guess there really isn't enough other than hopefully it won't happen again to anybody, not just the Japanese Americans but anybody, 'cause they came awfully darn close with the Iranians, too. I'd be almost surprised if it didn't happen again in my lifetime. It sounds kind of cynical, but there's nothing a whole lot different now than it was in the forties."

One of the important effects of the redress campaign was to enhance the empathy of Japanese Americans with other ethnic minorities. The movement received political support from many other minority groups as well as white politicians, especially in the legislation process, strengthening the alliances of Japanese American organizations with other minority civil rights groups. Leaders from these organizations, by attending and speaking at a number of redress-related events, confirmed their common experience of racial discrimination in American society. The redress campaign, which emphasized the discrimination experience, has made Japanese Americans aware of sharing a similar history with other minorities. Asian Americans in particular, who share physical and cultural similarities, have been drawn into closer solidarity. Japanese Americans have become especially close to Chinese Americans, another major Asian group that has lived for over three generations in Seattle. As Dan Hayashi noted:

We certainly share a history, certainly in terms of how we've been treated by this country, in terms of exclusionary acts, discrimination, process of migration. We share that broader community base: we're both Asians. And in some ways culturally, I certainly know that the two cultures are very close in terms of where their roots are. Their art forms, their writings. I mean there's a difference. It's kind of like

Chinese, to an extent, are a generation behind in a lot of ways, but I feel very closely akin to what their experiences are.

Although some Nisei see more cultural differences from Chinese Americans than similarities with them, for the Sansei the psychological distance has been diminished, and in fact, many emphasize the similarities between the Sansei and Chinese Americans in their age range. The relationships of Japanese Americans with other Asian Americans are, in general, not as well established as with Chinese Americans. The overwhelming majority of the Nisei feel themselves to be distant from Southeast Asian refugees and immigrants. John Ohki, however, stressed the need for solidarity among all Asian American groups.

All the Asians, we are sort of the same group together. We should stick together and help each other, because we don't have a political voice like blacks or Chicanos, and yet we have problems, especially now Vietnamese. Before, it used to be Chinese immigrants from Hong Kong. You know, whenever the Chinese or Vietnamese or whatever Asian group it is, does something, . . . [it affects] the whole Asian community, because Caucasians, they can't tell the difference between Chinese, Koreans, Vietnamese. They lump all together. In that sense, Asian Americans have to stick together.

Some Sansei, although not a majority, relate the experiences of these recent immigrants to those of the Issei. Susan Ochiai talked about why she decided to do volunteer work at church to help refugees from Southeast Asia:

I had sort of an interest in kind of connecting up with—I could sort of relate to them, like I thought, "Well these people must be like how my grandmother and grandfather were, when they came to this country." It just sort of interested me. Here are these people in a similar situation, first generation. I mean they'd come over under much harder circumstances, because they didn't choose to come. . . . But it's still fascinating to me that they've come from this other culture and they have to learn and adapt to this culture, Western culture. I

[181]

also got involved with the younger kids, these teenagers, and I thought these teenagers are like my parents. You know, second generation. They could speak English and then they could speak Laotian or Cambodian, kind of caught between the two cultures. . . . I just see somebody who's Asian, I kind of think, "Oh, there's something about them I can identify with, even though they come from a very different culture," but still I have an interest in them.

Except for a few Nisei, such as John Ohki, the use of "Asian," or "Asian American" is not as prevalent among the Nisei as among the Sansei. In general, the Nisei have, to a lesser degree than the Sansei, incorporated an Asian American identity. Some Sansei, identifying themselves as a minority and not just as Japanese Americans or Asian Americans, show serious concern about racism and oppression of minorities in American society. More of the Sansei than the Nisei among my interview subjects specifically expressed concerns about other minorities. Alice Segawa was eloquent on the subject.

It matters deeply to me that my parents, my grandparents, my aunts, my uncles, that my friends in some cases were incarcerated unjustly in concentration camps for over three years, and that the losses are great and continue to this day. That goes to the core. And yet, I feel that as harsh and unjust as that treatment was, it is not an aberration. It is something Native Americans have experienced in different ways throughout their history, and as horrible as it is, it is not on the same level as slavery, which blacks endured for hundreds of years. It's not totally different from what happens to many immigrants who come to this country if they are undocumented. . . . This is not by any means to diminish the suffering that went on in our community, and yet again I see it as something that is part and parcel of what people of color in this country have suffered. So, yes, I feel it very deeply that my parents and those close to me experienced this, but I feel it equally deeply that others continue to experience this or also have the heritage of experiencing similar things.

This recognition of sharing the racial discrimination in American society and the strengthened alliance with other ethnic minorities, however, are not directed toward widening the racial distance from white Americans. In fact, the appeal for redress was directed toward all Americans, regardless of their color, because it was solidly based on the American Constitution and doctrines. The issue is intimately associated with how Japanese Americans have perceived and presently perceive American ideals and the American government. Unjust and unconstitutional incarceration by their own government in the first place, the recruitment of Nisei soldiers from concentration camps, the redress movement based on the Constitution, the legislation of the government apology and individual payment, the disappointing nominal appropriation, and the final achievement of redress—all these involve the question of American doctrines. In view of their history, the firm loyalty to the United States which the Nisei exhibit is striking. Though they felt betrayed by evacuation, abandoned in camp by their own government, insulted by the so-called loyalty questionnaires, and disappointed at the first meager appropriation, the Nisei always maintained their allegiance to the country. "We aren't disowning our country," said Helen Kageshita. "We still feel the same amount for our country. Our country betrayed us, but that does not lessen our allegiance. This is our country." Steve Kondo marveled at his parents' loyalty: "Only after I started studying about it, and asking, they'll tell you some of the times that were tough. But it's not like they told you 'Americans are bad people, they sent us to camp and we had to endure all this suffering even though we didn't do anything. And your grandfather lost his business and we blame it on Americans.' They never, never talk like that." Alice Segawa's father lied about his age to enlist in the 442d Combat Team during the war. He feels, according to Alice, obligation and gratitude to his country.

I once asked him, once I began to understand what the camps were about and American racism, why it was that he would volunteer out of the concentration camp to fight in this war. I was totally flabbergasted that he did this. And he explained to me, what many Nisei explained, that he felt that he owed his life to this country, that his family at one point was very poor and he had contracted TB and most of his family died and he had that disease very seriously. And "In any other country in the world, I would have died, but the health care in this country

[183]

allowed me to live. And yes, there are many injustices, and yes, there is racism, and yes, there are all these things, but this is my country and it's your country."

Gary Tanaka said, his heavy involvement in redress was rooted in his keen sense of being an American citizen as well as in personal feelings toward his family and community.

> As an American, I felt it's almost my duty to try to do something. . . . I've always said that I believe the Constitution is one of the greatest documents ever been developed by man. But it is only as good as those who are willing to follow it. I don't want to see something as important as the Constitution have this fatal flaw. That's why I felt almost a patriotic duty, to do something, so that things like this, which is directly against the Constitution, can't happen.
>
> I had a special interest, too. If there was another constitutional issue, probably I wouldn't get involved. Because this particular one affected me more directly and closely through my parents and ethnic community, I felt it would be worth being involved. So it requires two things.

The Nisei in particular have come to magnify their embrace of American ideologies, values, and norms, in comparison to the early *shikata ga nai* [it can't be helped] attitude toward internment and their initial reluctance to seek redress, which many view as a typical Japanese attitude. Bruce Akimoto told me: "Japanese, when the redress act came about, a lot of families thought, 'Oh, forget it, don't even worry about it.' And I thought, it's a very Japanese thing to do, not to bring ourselves back in focus and create trouble." Michi Walter had similar views:

> In this country, Nikkei, by and large, have been very quiet. That's part of their Japanese heritage. . . . The redress movement, what it is doing, is bringing out more American values. That's really the important part. We have this Constitution, we have certain laws, the American democratic ideal, which is an ideal. We haven't reached it. . . . That's the ideal that we all should be working for, because ethnic

identity will kill us all one of these days. . . . It seems important that
we need to rise above ethnicity if we are going to survive as a race.

Ichiro Matsuda said that his sense of being an American citizen
drove him to testify at the commission hearings. He interpreted the
hesitancy of many Nisei veterans to testify as *enryo* (reservation out
of courtesy), a traditional Japanese value.

> There were some Nisei veterans that testified, but the majority did
> not testify. I think that has something to do with the Nikkei syn-
> drome. *Enryo, enryo* to the government. . . . It was not the fact that
> they were all American citizens or they didn't want to say anything
> against the government. I think it's partly, largely, because of their
> heritage. You might say false pride; I call it false pride. . . . And so
> they hesitated; they were modest about testifying. . . . But if a wrong
> was done to any of your family, or any American, regardless of their
> color, white, black, or yellow, injustice was done to your neighboring
> American citizen; if you're a true American, you should stand up to it.

The following case, cited by Shirley Kobayashi, embodies the syn-
drome of *enryo* toward white Americans, an issue that is confusingly
connected to American society and government:

> I guess even in the Japanese community, we have one person who
> says, "I'm not going to ask for any money." He says his daughter is
> married to a Caucasian. But whether his daughter is married to a
> Caucasian or not, still he should get some compensation, or the gov-
> ernment should acknowledge that what they did was a mistake. If
> they have to really pay for something, it means more to them, that
> they really did a wrong.

The fact that the internment of American citizens violated human
rights guaranteed by the American Constitution made redress a
constitutional issue, which accentuated Nisei's sense of being American. The tragedy began when American society lumped together
Japanese nationals in Japan with American citizens of Japanese ancestry and longtime Japanese residents who had been denied access

[185]

to American citizenship, calling them all "Japs." This confusion was one of the things Japanese Americans had to combat again when they began to pursue redress. They repeatedly emphasized that they were Americans, not Japanese (nationals), that it was *as* Americans, protected by the Constitution, that they sought redress. Mike Morita experienced opposition derived from this confusion:

> It makes me mad when people say, "Why should we pay back the Japanese who were interned when my son died at Pearl Harbor." There is no relation. A lot of Caucasians don't differentiate Japanese Americans who have been here for three or four generations and the Japanese in Japan. . . . One time a man called our office and said, "What do you guys think you are doing, trying to get redress for the enemies during the war!" Then I go, "Excuse me, sir, but Japanese Americans were just Americans. . . . Japanese Americans here are not responsible in any way for bombing Pearl Harbor. That was done by the Imperial Government of Japan." But he didn't hear anything I said.

The redress victory reaffirmed belief in the American government. Some Nisei remark that they now feel less like second-class citizens. Min Tashiro (real name) said in a media interview that when Reagan signed the bill he really felt like a full-fledged member of this country for the first time. "I think most of [the Nisei], they've always believed in America, but it reinforced even more their belief," said Cynthia Ube. "I think that for a while a lot of people thought the government does really care about these people."

Just as the dream seemed to approach realization, however, there was another frustrating delay. In spite of President Reagan's promise to "right the wrong," after the redress bill was signed, not a single penny was paid to any former internee for over two years. There was intense disappointment in the Japanese American community until the entitlement program that guaranteed payment was signed into law in November 1989 and payments finally began in the fiscal year of 1991. It was especially galling to realize that the Canadian government, which passed legislation over one month later than the American government, actually began issuing redress to individuals soon after. During this long lag phase between legislation and payment, many were angry. When I interviewed him in September 1988, over a month after the legislation passed, Henry Tanabe was outraged: "Look at even now, we have to wait until 1990 before they even get started. America is supposed to be the greatest country in the world. Come on! Isn't that absurd?! It's a disgrace, really, for America, to string out the payments like that. When you stop and think about it, twenty thousand dollars, you can't even buy a good Acura Legend." I interviewed Ed Murakami in July 1989, after Congress had appropriated only $50 million for fiscal year 1990, enough to compensate only those survivors who were over eighty-six years of age. He revealed his skepticism: "Well, we thought that [Reagan's signing] was just a gesture. We won't get the money. No *shin'yo* [trust]. You can't trust them. Bush has reduced the appropriations. They just do it to make it look good at that time, but they turn it around and change it. I don't think we'll ever get the money. Maybe the last two hundred people that's left will get it. We talk about it, laugh about it. We don't seriously expect to get it. None of us count on it." The redress leaders proclaimed, "Justice delayed is justice denied," and many, especially the Nisei, grew bitter as survivors died without having their honor restored.[9]

The distribution of the apology letter and the money finally began in October 1990, at the start of fiscal year 1991. Sumi Hashimoto and her husband shared their redress money with their grandchildren to make them mindful of this experience.

We were very fortunate that at Christmastime we were able to share, you know, with our grandchildren. Instead of our immediate children we gave it to—we have fourteen grandchildren. So that we were able to give quite a bit at Christmastime. But with each one I wrote a note, saying we are very happy to share our portion of this redress check. . . . And I said, with a portion of the redress check which the government gave to us for days that we spent in camp, and I said in your spare time I want you to go into the history of it and learn more about your grandpa and grandma, who were put into camp.

[9] It is estimated that two hundred former internees die each month.

The gifts did awaken her grandchildren's interest in the internment history.

> So from then on it was so good that the grandchildren have written back or else told me that they're so much more interested now in what happened in camp. Up to then, you know, we had never been talking to them about it. No. No. Let alone my own children. They never asked questions. And . . . we didn't want to talk about it so much. But, now, now that the redress checks came, we are able to talk more freely. It's like a load, you know, that came off of our chests.

Saburo Enomoto talked about the monetary benefits of redress: "The Issei and Nisei community has changed. They became a little richer. Twenty thousand dollars is big money. Besides, it was unexpected. People of my age benefited from this. Those who are older than us are too old to do anything with it. I'm planning to go to Japan this year with this money, although I made a token donation to Keiro [a home for the elderly]."

Matsuzo Watanabe, one of the original leaders of the redress campaign, had mixed feelings about the achievement. He was present at the Nisei Veterans Hall where the first apology letters and checks were given to the oldest victims in Seattle in October 1990. Though he was happy to see the old Issei finally receive redress, he felt bitter about the delay, which he attributed to the decision to hold congressional commission hearings, rather than introduce legislation directly as he and his group had strongly advocated.

> I was totally conscious of the fact that the Issei were old, and they were dying off. And that is why I opposed that so-called congressional investigation committee that went around and wasted three years going to Japanese communities. . . . But because of that three-year delay most of the Issei were dead and gone. . . . I would say, the younger Nisei, they did not really suffer from that evacuation. They were children. . . . But I felt that those Issei that showed up and who were old enough, who were able to get that money—I felt grateful that at least a few token people survived—the Issei. . . . I thank them for having lived long enough to get it.

[188]

Many Nisei recipients donated a portion of their redress money to Japanese American community organizations. Ed Murakami gave part of his to his parents' church, since he feels that their parents deserved redress the most.

Japanese Americans, especially those who are concerned with current racial discrimination and tensions such as the resurgence of white supremacy, anti-Asian sentiment, and so-called Japan bashing and their effects on Japanese and Asian Americans, emphasize the next agenda. "You know," said Jack Sakata, "it's a good feeling that if you stick to it there is justice. At the same time, too, it was an issue that occurred a long time ago and there still are issues that're coming up today that need to be addressed. So we can't relax or rely on past success, but we have to continue to move forward. And that's what makes the world turn, too."

Conclusion

The feelings of the Nisei and the Sansei about internment and redress were in some ways similar, in other ways different. Until the redress issue arose, the subject of internment remained untouched or touched only in passing in most families. The Nisei were restrained, they said, by their children's lack of interest, and the Sansei were reluctant to ask their parents about such a sensitive issue. The absence of serious dialogue on internment is confirmed by Donna Nagata's survey results (1990). According to Nagata, only 30 percent of the Sansei said that their parents had discussed internment as a central topic. The remainder said that camp appeared in discussion with parents only as an incidental topic (e.g., "We knew her from camp") or as a reference point in time (e.g., "That was before camp"). She also states that Sansei with either one or two interned parents had had an average of approximately ten conversations on the subject in their lifetime by the time the research was conducted.

After decades, however, "silence" was broken as the ritual dramatization of the past through Days of Remembrance, the testimony at the commission hearings, and other events culturally reconstructed

[189]

Japanese American history. Here, the ways in which various symbols were used in these events deserve special attention. These symbols played a significant role in generating a feeling of togetherness among Japanese Americans and the sense that they shared a common history, while effectively evoking memories and inducing people to talk about them to each other and to outsiders. S. N. Eisenstadt has described one of the patterns by which modern societies reconstruct traditions: members of the society "make a positive connection between their personal identity and the symbols of the new political, social, and cultural order" and "thus accept the new symbols as the major collective referents of their personal identity" (1973: 23). Although the social and political context in which the symbols emerge in Eisenstadt's theory differs from that of the case under examination here, his point with regard to the role of symbols as a linkage of personal identity to the constitution of collective identity has significant relevance to our understanding of the transformation of ethnic identity, especially that of the Nisei. The barbed wire, the most condensed symbol of internment, sometimes along with other symbols related to camp, evoked long-buried emotions and memories, but because it was presented ritually in public, a positive valuation was attached to the commemoration of internment itself. In this process, the feeling of shared suffering, which had previously constructed the subconscious core of the *individual* identity was transformed into the core of the *collective* identity of Japanese Americans.

In this process, the ethnicity of Japanese Americans was revived. For the Nisei, the redress drive served as catharsis and helped bring about healing. For the Sansei, it educated them about the history of their community and their place in American society. It also made them aware of racial discrimination and helped them to develop interethnic relations and emotional affinities with other minority groups, in particular, other Asian Americans. Through this cultural reconstruction of the past in the redress campaign, both generations came to redefine the past and the present, that is, what it means to be Japanese American and what it means to be a minority in American society.

Redress not only reinforced their ethnic identity as Japanese and their minority consciousness, however; it also served to America-nize them in many respects. Redress is, after all, an American issue, supported in Congress and by many other Americans. That they fought for redress as Americans, working within the American system, appealed to Japanese Americans themselves, as well, and persuaded many Nisei who were originally opposed to the idea. Through the successful campaign, the values, norms, and ideolo-gies of Japanese Americans undoubtedly became more Ameri-canized than before, and their national identity was strengthened. I discuss this issue more extensively in the concluding chapter.

[6]

Transformation of Ethnicity

The ethnicity of Japanese Americans, as we have seen, has gone through different phases, from before World War II, during the war, in the postwar era, during the redress movement, to the present. In this concluding chapter, I will recapture and synthesize my descriptions and analyses to disclose the transformation of ethnicity among Japanese Americans from three different angles: first, from a historical perspective; second, from a comparison and contrast of the experiences and the ways in which the Nisei and the Sansei express their reinterpretation of their ethnic experience; and third, from an examination of the relationship between the revival of ethnicity and Americanization among Japanese Americans.

Historical Transformation of Ethnicity

The changes in Japanese American ethnicity have occurred in response to a unique series of experiences, including internment and the redress movement. I have detected four stages in its transformation. It began with the primordial attachments, most prominent before World War II. There followed a long period of ethnic stigma, superseded, in a third stage, by a sense of shared suffering, and now dominated by ethnic pride.

The Issei who migrated to the United States in the late nineteenth and early twentieth centuries exhibited a high degree of regional variation with regard to food, dialect, and customs. Nevertheless, the Japanese society they left was highly homogeneous compared to the racially and culturally heterogeneous American society. As the Japanese encountered white Americans and other immigrant groups and as they experienced racial discrimination and exclusion, their own differences tended to be minimized and their consciousness of being Japanese crystallized. The formation of an ethnic group is a social response to interactions in a multicultural setting, and it is in this very sense that the Japanese immigrants *became* an ethnic group in their host country. Ethnicity developed as the Issei were forced to recognize that their "given" cultural background differed significantly from that accepted in the new society they had entered. What defined being Japanese among the Issei, then, were the same racial and cultural features that are ascribed, in their common belief, to being born to Japanese parents and the Japanese race. In other words, the ethnicity in this early period of Japanese American history is characterized by primordial affinities and attachments (cf. Geertz 1963; Isaacs 1975).

Probably the most powerful constituent of these primordial bonds was the cultural concept of "blood" (cf. Keyes 1981). In traditional Japanese belief, blood is used to explain identity, personality, and behavior.[1] This sense of common descent was enhanced and sustained by the growing national pride in the Meiji government, which started in 1868, not long before the Issei were born. Remember, the Issei were prohibited from becoming American citizens. They remained Japanese nationals.

With the cultural emphasis on descent, the Issei were eager to pass on Japanese cultural markers to their children, and the Nisei, though they were American citizens by birth, largely retained their parents' primordial attachments. Moreover, the core of the ethnic

---

[1] Thus, a certain personality of *kenjin* is explained by *kenjin* blood. For example, the people from Tosa in Kochi prefecture are said to have quick tempers because of their Tosa blood. Similarly, the imperial family is distinguished by its blood, as are lesser families. Moreover, according to the traditional belief, all members of the *Yamato-minzoku*, or the Japanese race, are thought to be connected by blood, and their common blood is said to be the source of *Yamato-damashii*, or the Japanese spirit.

identity of both generations was forcefully reaffirmed from outside by racial hatred of the "Japs." Whereas some Nisei maintained their ethnic pride, protected against any substantial discrimination by the ethnic enclave, other Nisei consciously or subconsciously came to feel that the larger society considered them second-class citizens.

The Nisei, however, unlike their parents, were born and raised in the United States. At school they developed American identity to add to their Japanese ethnicity, and they learned loyalty to the United States. In some cases, association with white Americans reinforced this American identity, as did generational conflicts with the strongly Japanese Issei.

The ethnicity of Japanese Americans reached a critical turning point when they were evacuated and interned because of their Japanese ancestry and as the culmination of racial discrimination against them. These events, together with the war itself, attached a negative valuation to anything related to Japan and the Japanese. Respected community leaders were arrested and sent to separate detention camps simply because of their cultural connection to Japan or involvement in Japanese community organizations. Fearful of what was to happen, people burned things associated with Japan. Children were forbidden to speak Japanese on school grounds in camp. People were labeled "black," that is, were denied a work release if they had a certain number of Japanese cultural markers or ties to Japan. Internees were told to assimilate and not to congregate with other Japanese when they left camp. As one Nisei said, Japanese ancestry was made into a source of guilt and shame; Japanese ethnicity was stigmatized (cf. Eidheim 1969).[2] As a result, many were self-conscious about being of Japanese descent and suf-

[2] Harold Eidheim describes the somewhat similar case of the Lapps in Norway, whose ethnicity is socially stigmatized: "In very general terms one may say that the basis for their dilemma is that in order to achieve the material and social goods they appreciate, and to share the opportunities available in the society, people have to get rid of, or cover up, those social characteristics which Norwegians take as signs of Lappishness" (1969: 45). Lapps switch cultural codes, most notably language, according to circumstances, behaving differently in each of three spheres, a public sphere, a Lappish closed sphere, and a Norwegian closed sphere. Among Japanese Americans, however, the aspiration for Americanization was strong enough to invade the Japanese closed sphere. In other words, even within the home and community settings, Japanese cultural markers, including language, behavior, and customs, were often restrained and American markers substituted.

Sansei's birthday party, 1971. Photo by Sharon S. Aburano.

fered guilt and shame during and after the war. In the postwar era, the memories of the evacuation and internment were highly suppressed and repressed. As one Nisei said, "It was something you buried under the carpet and hoped the dust would never show up again." This phenomenon, which Tetsuden Kashima calls "social amnesia" (1980), dominated the Nisei for decades after the war.

The stigma attached to Japanese ethnicity was, in implicit and subtle ways, passed on to the Sansei. They received the unspoken but underlying message from their Nisei parents that being of Japanese ancestry was not an advantage in American society. The lesson was further reinforced by the Sansei's own discrimination experiences.

The majority of the Nisei, whether they now admit it or not, identified as American at the expense of their Japanese cultural heritage. They ceased speaking Japanese and didn't encourage their children to learn it. They moved out of the Japanese American community. They worked superconscientiously. The "melting pot" ideology (cf. Gordon 1964) that was still prevalent in American

[195]

society in that era was congruent with this tendency and further accelerated their social and cultural assimilation.

The ethnicity of Japanese Americans reached another major turning point with the redress movement. Although the political movement itself started in Seattle in the early 1970s and became gradually known to the community after the mid-1970s, the event that burst open the tomb of Japanese American history was the Day of Remembrance in 1978. As the campaign progressed, associated events helped to break the reserve of those who had spent the war years in detention and concentration camps, while they provided the Sansei with opportunities to ask questions. In this process, the past has been revived and a transformation of ethnicity has taken place.

The past, however, was not easily or automatically revived, as is shown by the fact that the political movement for redress initially faced tremendous difficulty in being accepted even among Japanese Americans. The large success of the 1978 Day of Remembrance in commemorating evacuation and internment and breaking the "silence" among Japanese Americans is attributed to the cultural reconstruction of the past. Various symbols used in this event, especially barbed wire, the most condensed, most powerful symbol of internment, acted effectively to evoke people's memories and to induce them to talk about the camp experience. As discussed earlier, the role of symbols, which Eisenstadt (1973) has indicated, in connecting individual members of a given society to a newly emerged society has a relevance in the ritualized events among Japanese Americans.

As long as the memories of internment were hidden and buried in individual psyches, they could not be incorporated into a conscious ethnic identity. It was through ritualized reconstruction employing powerful symbols that the memories of the experiences were brought to the surface and then made the basis of collective identity. It is in this process that Japanese Americans were able to realize and confirm that their bitterness and suffering were collective. The sense of suffering, which previously dominated the subconscious core of the individual identity, thus became the core of the Japanese American collective identity.

However little bitterness the Sansei may feel at the conscious level, the sense of shared suffering involves them as well. For them, the redress movement has triggered an appreciation and recognition of their ethnic history and a consciousness of racism in American society, which I discuss more extensively in the next section. At the basis of these changes is their redefinition of the past as centered upon the discrimination experienced by their forebears and their struggles against it. Because they lack the strong bitterness of the Nisei, the Sansei have been more able to develop a positive reinterpretation of the past which enhances their ethnic pride.

Important as the sense of shared suffering was, it would only have worsened the ethnic stigma had the suffering not been repudiated or seen as furthering progress toward a positive goal. The stigma would then have acted on Japanese Americans to weaken their ethnic identity or, at least, to discourage their display of Japanese cultural characteristics and their identification as Japanese Americans. As George De Vos and Lola Romanucci-Ross (1975) have noted, rituals and dramatizations of ancestral suffering and triumph play a strong role in affirming ethnic identity. In this case, however, these methods were enhanced by the political movement that lifted the guilt and shame of the internees and reassigned them to the government. Moreover, the demand that injustice be corrected embodied one of the strongest, most appealing ideologies of American society. Thus, asking for redress was interpreted as "good conduct," and the shared suffering reached its apotheosis in a triumph for the ethnic group.

Many Nisei declare that redress has freed them from shame and endowed them with high ethnic pride. Others maintain that they will always feel like second-class citizens, that the psychological wounds are too deep to heal. Yet even if they perceive that the larger society has not stopped discriminating against them, they do not feel the same shame within themselves. Overall, the transformation of their ethnicity over the generations in the continuing history of Japanese Americans is, I contend, directed from the negative to the positive, from shame to pride.

Erik Erikson has explored the processes by which the valuation of ethnic identity changes from negative to positive and vice versa. In a "negative conversion" previous negative identity elements are totally converted to positive elements while elements previously embraced as positive are totally removed (1968: 313). In the present case, the camp experience, which constructed the core of the negative identity, has been reformulated to provide the most crucial symbolic index of positively valued traits: endurance, effort, achievement, and the courage to speak out. Likewise, the once-taboo subjects of camp and redress are now acceptable, even encouraged, in conversation, whereas forgetting about camp and criticizing redress have become unacceptable, at least in the public sphere.

Revival and celebration of ethnicity tend to reinforce it, and the Japanese American case is no exception. Redress has also strengthened intergenerational relationships and community ties. The sense of community has never been stronger since World War II than over the past fifteen years.

Thus, the recollections of Japanese Americans and generational differences among them show that the major emphasis of ethnicity among Japanese Americans has been transformed over time: from fundamentally primordial attachments before World War II, to stigma during and after the war, to a collective sense of suffering upon the reopening of the past, and finally to ethnic pride derived from a positive reinterpretation of the past. This pattern, however, tracks the primary emphasis of Japanese American ethnicity, that which appears most explicitly at the surface. I must stress that none of these four stages is exclusive, and more than one has often coexisted at one period of time. When ethnicity is transformed by the ethnic group's own evolution, not by artificial external force, the transformation does not take place suddenly.

For example, in the postwar era, although their ethnicity was stigmatized, Japanese Americans did not try to "get rid of" or "cover up" (Eidheim 1969: 45) their social and cultural characteristics all the time. One Sansei who, as a child, refused to eat Japanese food or to learn Japanese and who saw things Japanese as inferior and undesirable nevertheless enjoyed the Bon Festival every year.[3] Ambivalence toward their ethnicity was particularly strongly rooted

[3] Several Sansei said they were embarrassed to bring Japanese food to school for lunch. The picture is perhaps different among the Yonsei today, now that Japanese and other ethnic cuisines are celebrated in American society. The situations and materials to which ethnic pride is attached thus seem to be affected by the valuations of the mainstream society, which are, at least in the case of Japanese Americans, influenced by the image of their ancestral country.

among the Nisei, whose parents inculcated racial and cultural pride, which was strongly opposed by racial discrimination and internment. These blows left long-lasting scars on their self-respect.

I argued at the beginning of this book that especially when ethnicity is socially stigmatized, what George Devereux (1975) calls ethnic personality or what Howard Stein and Robert Hill (1977) call ideological ethnicity determines the form of ethnic identity and the use or abandonment of some cultural behaviors and norms that reside at a surface level. Because their ethnicity was stigmatized, many Japanese Americans pursued Americanization and suppressed the manifestation of Japanese cultural markers. Under this condition, the ideological aspect of ethnicity determined the direction of some of the more superficial aspects of behavioral ethnicity.

It is important to remember, however, that these changes were at the surface level. Underlying at the deeper level was their ethnic identity as Japanese, which is not necessarily of the same nature as the one recognized as stigmatized. G. Carter Bentley (1987) discusses the unconscious dimension of ethnic identity, using the theory of practice (cf. Bourdieu 1977) to explain the formation of ethnic identity in the individual. This identity is founded on common experiences and shared habits, unconsciously maintained by members of the ethnic group and transmitted to their children as part of their socialization. This deeper identification makes it possible for members to manifest Japanese cultural markers on such occasions as the Bon Festival openly and proudly when the mainstream attaches a positive valuation to them.

But if it is clear that the redress movement reconstructed the valuation of Japanese American ethnicity by reviving the past and reinterpreting it, it remains to be asked why the past resurfaced at all. It was not revived merely to supply sentimental recollections; the past is a resource people use to make better sense of present circumstances, and in terms of ethnicity, it is revived to usher in a new phase. Japanese Americans felt the need to search their history as a subconscious response, I believe, to two emerging phenomena. One is the crisis of the declining community caused by social, cultural, geographical, and marital assimilation of younger people and the aging and death of the first and second generation. The other is the escalation of anti-Asian sentiment derived from such factors as

[199]

United States–Japan trade friction[4] and the explosion of Asian population over the past decade in the United States. According to the 1990 census the number of Asians and Pacific Islanders has grown by 107.8 percent, more than twice the next fastest rate—Latinos, at 53.0 percent.[5] Under these circumstances Japanese Americans felt the need to revive their ethnicity and defend it against the larger society. They sought clues from their history to explain why the community is as it is now, why their parents and they themselves behave and think as they do, or what the sources are of violence and discrimination against themselves and other Asian Americans.

At the macro level, therefore, Japanese Americans have experienced a transformation of their ethnicity. In the next section, I turn my attention to the micro level to discuss generational differences within the Japanese American community. Both the second and the third generations have reinterpreted their ethnic history and reconstructed their ethnic identity through the redress movement, but there are differences in how the two generations reacted to internment history and redress and how they express their reinterpretation of the historical experience.

Generational Experiences and Expressions of Ethnicity

Among Japanese Americans, generation is a key factor in understanding their integration into American society. The Nisei and the Sansei have had different experiences, and these brought about different reactions to internment and redress. Although both generations have undergone the reinterpretation of the historical experience and the reformulation of ethnic identity triggered by the redress movement, there are significant differences in the ways in which the two generations express the reinterpretation and draw on this past for the present.

[4] Anti-Asian prejudice and violence have become the next large concern among Asian Americans. The worst tragedy attributable to trade friction was the murder of Vincent Chin in Detroit in 1982. Two white Americans who were involved in the auto industry bludgeoned him to death with a baseball bat, having mistaken the young Chinese American for a Japanese.

[5] Asians and Pacific Islanders now make up 2.9 percent of the total U.S. population.

Ethnic identity is basically formed in the home and community and through interactions with other ethnic groups. The Nisei and Sansei had significantly different experiences in these three arenas. At home, one of the crucial differences was the language spoken with their parents. Because their parents generally did not speak English, the Nisei acquired Japanese as their mother tongue, although English became their primary language after they started school. By contrast, the Sansei generally spoke only English, even with their parents. Since Japanese Americans consider the Japanese language one of the most distinctive cultural markers of Japaneseness, this difference is relevant to their ethnic identity.

It was also primarily in the home environment that the Nisei absorbed Japanese values, norms, and racial pride. These were reinforced by a community environment that included the Japanese school, Japanese cultural lessons, and a general community pressure to conform to Japanese norms. This cultural heritage was also passed on to the Sansei, but in greatly diluted form. Even the Nisei exposure to a picture of the Japanese emperor or the shouting of *banzai* at the emperor's birthday, however little the Nisei may say it meant to them, is an experience alien to the Sansei.

The nature of the Japanese community and the larger environment that surrounded the Nisei in the prewar period differs sharply from that experienced by the Sansei. The majority of the Nisei were raised in a geographically and socially segregated community with limited social contact with other ethnic groups, in sharp contrast to the upbringing of the Sansei in the postwar period. Except when attending American school, many Nisei lived during childhood and adolescence mostly within the boundaries of the Japanese American community. Their Issei parents took them to *kenjin-kai* (prefectural association) picnics, Japanese grocery stores, Japanese banks, *ofuro* or public baths, and so forth, and the Nisei went to the Japanese language school every day, formed their own clubs, and took lessons in such activities as kendo and *odori*. On the other hand, American school played an important role in their Americanization and the construction of their national identity as Americans.

The Sansei ethnic community consisted of the International District, the symbolic community for Asian Americans in Seattle, and

Beacon Hill, an area with a high residential concentration of Japanese Americans and other minorities in the city. Some of the Sansei were raised in white environments, where contact with other Sansei was confined to ethnic churches, family gatherings, and school, although substantially fewer Japanese American students were enrolled in such districts. The Sansei raised on Beacon Hill and in other parts of the Central District had more settings in which to interact with other Sansei, mostly in a neighborhood that usually included several Japanese American families, and a school that had a larger proportion of Japanese Americans than in other districts.

The Sansei, raised in a more heterogeneous environment, failed to develop the strong ethnic solidarity of the Nisei. Instead, the Sansei associated with many other ethnic groups in racially mixed schools and neighborhoods. The Sansei's wide interaction with other ethnic groups and the American social ideology that since the 1970s has celebrated ethnic diversity are responsible for their generally more open views toward other ethnic groups, despite occasional discouragement from associating with members of other groups by some Nisei parents.

The two generations also experienced different degrees and types of racial discrimination. Some Nisei even show surprise upon hearing about the Sansei experience of personal discrimination in their childhood, saying, "What kind of discrimination are they talking about?" Many Sansei have vivid memories of racial remarks during their childhood and adolescence, but none experienced the kind of prejudice the Nisei remembered—segregation, housing discrimination, exclusion from labor unions and hence from the mainstream job market.

Internment during World War II, the culmination of racial hatred, constitutes the most decisive experience separating the Nisei from the Sansei.[6] Among the Sansei, the camp experience of Japanese Americans is a matter of historical record, not something that

[6] It is true that those Nisei who were not living on the West Coast in early 1942 were not affected by the evacuation, and it is also true that a few Sansei, born before that time, were affected. Nevertheless, Japanese Americans themselves identify this as the main difference in generational experience between the Nisei and the Sansei.

directly affected them. Because the internment targeted only people of Japanese descent, many Nisei were made to regret their ancestry. Some Sansei expressed a similar wish to be white, but the factors that created a self-consciousness about their ethnicity were more serious and fundamentally threatening to that ethnic identity among the Nisei.

Unlike the Sansei, the Nisei do not generally identify themselves as Asian Americans. The Japanese American identity of the Nisei of the prewar days was relatively exclusive and did not merge with larger categories such as "Asian American" (or "Oriental" in older terminology). This relative exclusivity can be attributed to the mutual antagonism between Chinese and Japanese, to minimal social contact between the Nisei and Filipinos, and to the small proportion of Asians in the general population. The Asian American movement had much more effect on the Sansei than on any other generation, although its influence on the entire community is undeniable. It was the "yellow power" movement that awakened the consciousness of ethnic heritage and racial oppression as a minority in American society among the Sansei, who had shown a substantial degree of acculturation into mainstream. In addition, increased interaction with other Asian American groups and the tendency of the dominant society to lump all Asian groups together generated Asian American identity among the Sansei.

These different experiences brought about different reactions to the recollection of internment and to the redress movement. The imprisonment of the Nisei during World War II was a traumatic psychological blow to their faith in the United States, nurtured in school and through such patriotic rituals as the Pledge of Allegiance. Internment generated guilt and shame so painful that most buried their memories deeply in their psyches. As Minako Maykovich (1972: 59) says, they aspired to Americanize "120 percent" and be accepted by white Americans. Such an orientation, Marcus L. Hansen (1938) maintains, is common for the second generation of other immigrant groups, as well. It seems, notwithstanding, that the aspiration was more intense among Japanese Americans because of internment and other discrimination experiences. Motivated by the American "melting pot" ideology, self-contempt, the feeling of being second-class citizens, compounded by total economic loss, the dispersal of the community, and the all other factors derived from internment and discrimination, Japanese Americans developed an especially strong need to prove themselves good Americans.

Because of this aspiration to Americanize and to achieve through diligence, the idea of redress for internment initially disturbed the Nisei. Many believed it was best to forget the past. Others felt that demanding redress implied criticism of the government and the country. This political movement, nonetheless, succeeded, and the increased conversation about internment it generated permitted catharsis and healing among the Nisei. The apology of the American government for its misconduct during World War II eased their bitterness, restored some pride to them, and gave them a feeling of being "first-class" citizens.

The Sansei, by contrast, were born and raised in the period when Japanese Americans began to be touted as a "success story."[7] In their childhood and adolescence, they generally enjoyed affluence and advanced educational opportunities, which were made possible by the Nisei's hard work and efforts to be accepted by the larger society. The Sansei, thus, found it easier to take their Americanness for granted and had a weaker identity as ethnic Japanese than did the Nisei.

Precisely because of their increasing economic, institutional, and cultural integration into American society, by the time they reached adolescence the Sansei were shocked and angry to learn about what their parents and grandparents had suffered. Some Sansei directed their anger not only at the government but also at their parents, for acquiescing in the evacuation order and for not telling them an important part of the family and ethnic history. The Asian American movement reopened internment history among some Japanese

---

[7] Peterson 1966. Asian American scholars have criticized this portrayal as a myth and have rejected the other popular label: "model minority." This label, they say, has been used to blame other minorities for their social and economic difficulties, and it conceals racial discrimination, injustice, and other realities that involve minorities in American society. The myth, moreover, ignores the many difficulties faced by diverse Asian American communities, such as poverty, ill health, poor housing, and unemployment in Chinatown, Japantown, and recent refugee communities, as well as discrimination in university admissions and promotions ("glass ceiling"). See, for example, Suzuki 1980; Kim 1973.

Americans, but mainly only among those with keen political and social concerns. It was the redress campaign that brought history and its meanings and effects home to the whole Japanese American community and to the nation at large. The Asian movement made the Sansei aware of their history, and that history interested them in the Asian movement. Together these influences brought them to an understanding of themselves as part of the Asian American minority in the United States.

For the Sansei, evacuation and internment signify appreciation of their family and ethnic history and renewed recognition of racism in American society. The individual Sansei has a significantly less emotional reaction to the idea of camp than the individual Nisei. Nevertheless, it is doubtful how much the Sansei would have appreciated their family and ethnic history and whether they would have developed their present identity as a minority if internment had not happened or if they had remained uninformed about it while still enjoying the social and economic status they now have.

The Nisei desire to forget the past and be accepted by the mainstream society, together with the language barrier between the Sansei and their grandparents and their general lack of interest in the past, to a large degree minimized the Sansei exposure to family and ethnic history. Through the long process of learning about camp and observing or participating in the redress movement, they gained or, in some cases, reinforced their ethnic pride and their appreciation of the significant achievements of their forebears, despite hardship and substantial economic loss.

The other important by-product of this whole process is the Sansei's growing recognition of racism in American society, racism involving themselves. For many, disjointed childhood memories of discrimination came together as a whole once they understood the internment history. Their awareness and reinterpretation of racism was related to the issues of their own time. They identified with African Americans and other oppressed minorities in American society; felt empathy toward the Iranians in the United States who were harrassed during the Iranian crisis in 1979 and the Arabs who, because of their ethnic background, began to be investigated by the FBI during the Gulf War in 1991; perceived their similarities to other Asian Americans.

[205]

Their discovery of the incarceration and its resemblance to discrimination suffered by other Asian Americans inspired the Sansei to raise their voices in political unity with other Asian Americans and start redefining the Asian experience in the United States (Amerasia staff 1971: 70). This pan-Asian identification cannot separate itself from the need for political unity among different Asian groups, but I believe it has more substance than Richard Trottier allows. He calls it "no more than a matter of political expediency" (1981: 300). For many Sansei, their identity as Asian American was formed in junior or senior high school, often through an Asian clique or in association with their Asian American friends. The identification developed in the political context, usually in the college setting, is often more clearly defined than that developed in the associational context.

The boundary of Asian American identity among the Sansei is vague, and there are substantial individual differences in which ethnic groups a Sansei includes in such identification. In most cases, they feel strongest empathy with Chinese Americans, but some feel the same empathy with Filipino Americans, another major Asian American group with a long immigration history. A small group of Sansei even includes Vietnamese and Koreans, whose immigration history is much shorter, finding similarities as targets of racial discrimination against "Asians." The fact that the Sansei use the term "Asian" when discussing stereotypes of the opposite sex indicates that the categorization imposed by the larger society affects the internalization of identification as Asian American among the Sansei. Pan-Asian ethnicity does not require the inclusion of all the groups the U.S. census identifies as Asian. Yet, however vague the boundary may be, if it has meaning in the Sansei consciousness, even as an "imagined community" (Anderson 1983), we must admit its existence.[8]

[8] The development of Asian American identity among the Sansei in Seattle may also be related to the unique International District there, which is rather pan-Asian than ethnicity-specific and where there is demographic equilibrium among the three major Asian ethnic groups. See Espiritu 1992 for the discussion of pan-Asian ethnicity. More recently, however, not a few Asian Americans began to reject the single label and to emphasize diversity within the group. The term "Asian American" was defined and used by Chinese, Japanese, and Filipino Americans during the ethnic movement in the 1960s and 1970s; since then, the population of Asians of

The Asian American and the Japanese American identities do not exclude each other but coexist. One appears stronger than the other, depending on the situation, or takes the place of the other as the primary identity during certain times of a person's life. Some of the Sansei find their niche by identifying with other minorities as well as with other Asian Americans. Thus, their ethnic identity forms, what Ivan Light (1981) calls "ethnic scope," comprising the levels of Japanese American, Asian American, and a minority in the United States, from the smallest unit of the generational Sansei identity to the largest unit of the American national identity. At the beginning of this book, I proposed that a situation involving a relevant cognitive contrast of ethnic groups as social organizations is one of the prerequisites to a selection of the level of identity. The identification with the broader levels of ethnic identity in the hierarchies is more prevalent among the Sansei than the Nisei because the Sansei are less exposed to the elements that construct Japanese American identity. Their identification as Asian American or as a minority is a way of solving the identity crisis they confront after recognizing overt or covert racism, a way that provides them with a psychological niche but requires a less specified or rigid cultural definition of membership than the identification as strictly Japanese American.

Now finally, let us compare the ways in which each generation

---

different nationality backgrounds has increased because of revised immigration laws and the fall of Saigon, and the diversity of the group has also increased. The emphasis on diversity has arisen because serious problems such as poverty and maladjustment are often overshadowed by the successful image of "Asian Americans" and because new members of the community began to challenge the hegemony of the Chinese and Japanese Americans in various community organizations. Nevertheless, this strong emphasis on diversity could be a temporary phenomenon. As Yen Le Espiritu (1992) indicates, regardless of one's political interest, racism against Asian Americans by the larger society leaves them with little choice, affecting all of them. Furthermore, pan-Asian organizations, mass media, and Asian American studies at colleges—all foster a pan-Asian American identity. There is no doubt that Asian groups in the United States are diverse. Nonetheless, it is a matter of degree, and despite a high degree of diversity, such ethnic groups as Jews and Native Americans, have developed common ethnicity. As discussed in the first chapter, ethnicity cannot be understood if we are bound by the concept of cultural and racial commonalities; rather, we should pay more attention to the fact that in spite of such differences and the historical antipathy between the groups, pan-Asian ethnicity has emerged.

relates its Japanese American identity to other forms of identification in American society. I have pointed out the aspiration for "Americanization" and the reaffirmation of their Japanese American ethnic identity among the Nisei, and acculturation, development of Asian American identity, and reinforcement of Japanese American ethnic identity among the Sansei. In other words, the Nisei, because of their limited exposure to other minority groups and the historical situation that enforced a choice between American and Japanese during the war years, made their choices in identification within a single continuum between the two poles of American and Japanese. By contrast, the Sansei have had a wider range of choices, which extends to Asian American and minority identification.[9]

How can it be, we must ask next, that the identity of the Sansei as Japanese Americans has been reinforced at the same time as they have identified as Asian Americans and as a minority? This question is also related to another: Why was the redress movement so successful, enough to persuade the government to spend $1.3 billion, despite a serious national deficit, for a tiny segment of the population, amounting to a mere 0.3 percent of all Americans?

The Revival of Ethnicity and Americanization

In this final section, I want to examine the implications of the reemergence of Japanese American ethnicity within the larger American society. Many sociologists once viewed ethnicity and assimilation as mutually exclusive, assimilation advancing at the expense of ethnicity. The chief debate was whether ethnicity wanes as assimilation progresses or whether it is vestigially retained in the form of cultural attributes. Since then, a number of works have proposed revisions of this classic view, which placed heavy emphasis on cultural characteristics as the basis of ethnic identification (e.g., Yancey et al. 1976; Gans 1979; Reitz 1980; Waters 1990; Fugita and O'Brien 1991). Among others, Jeffrey Reitz (1980) and

[9] Again, the generational designations form categories with exceptions I have no wish to deny. There are Nisei who think of themselves as Asian Americans and Sansei who consider themselves only Americans of Japanese ancestry.

Stephen Fugita and David O'Brien (1991) contend that a group can retain ethnic cohesiveness in spite of structural assimilation into American society, largely through social interaction and ethnic institutions.

I agree that structural assimilation does not preclude the retention of ethnicity. Whereas these scholars attribute the retention of ethnicity largely to the social interaction and institutions within an ethnic group, however, my attention in this book is directed to historical experience of the Japanese American ethnic group in American society, a society in which they transformed themselves from Japanese immigrants to Japanese Americans as an American ethnic group.

What we need to illuminate is the relationship between resurgence of ethnicity and Americanization—Americanization not only in the sense of "structural assimilation" but in terms of cultural values and norms and, most important, identification. The redress movement unquestionably helped to revive ethnicity and just as undeniably pressed the Americanization of Japanese Americans further than ever before. It was as Americans that they were encouraged to seek redress, and a series of activities inspired by the movement reaffirmed their consciousness as Americans.

First, the very idea of redress was possible only because internment had unjustly deprived American citizens of their constitutional rights. It was this injustice that left such deep psychological wounds in the Nisei. Indeed, several Kibei subjects who identified as Japanese expressed much less bitterness about that aspect of internment. The redress campaign, therefore, needed to underscore "true" Americanism. Let us recall, as an example, the appeal the Evacuation Redress Committee of the Seattle JACL chapter made to promote the redress campaign. "*If Japanese Americans are as American as* the J.A.C.L. has often claimed, then *they should act like Americans* and make every effort to seek redress through legislation and the courts for the rape of almost all their 'unalienable rights' by the United States Government over thirty years ago." (Evacuation Redress Committee 1975: 2, emphasis added).

In order to correct such injustice and achieve redress, Japanese Americans employed "American measures." They abandoned the "quiet American" stereotype (Hosokawa 1969) to pursue a class action and coram nobis appeals in the courts, and to introduce and lobby for legislation authorizing formal apology and monetary payment. Further, as the past was reopened and internment history became no more a hidden secret, the movement began to display the American flag more and more—on the cover of the program for the 1986 Day of Remembrance, for instance, and in the red, white, and blue balloons and decorations at the redress celebration in October 1988. Even before the war the Nisei pledged allegiance to the flag; now they used the national emblem to reassure themselves that the pursuit of redress participated in American national ideology. The symbol was a reminder that Japanese Americans are citizens of the nation and have every right to be protected by, and a duty to protect, the American Constitution for the sake of justice and freedom.

Furthermore, the campaign promoted the idea expressed in the National Council for Japanese American Redress slogan, that redress is "an issue for *all* Americans." The movement expanded its base of support into the general population largely by presenting redress as an issue of American justice. It was in recognition of redress as a repair of the Constitution that Representative Norman Mineta arranged for the final vote on H.R. 442 to occur on September 17, 1987, the two hundredth anniversary of the Constitution (*Pacific Citizen*, Dec. 21, 1990). Meanwhile, numbering the bill H.R. 442 to honor the 442d Regimental Combat Team accentuated Japanese Americans' contribution to American society. By joining in coalition with other minority groups and civil rights organizations, Japanese Americans underscored the common experience of American minority groups and the issue of civil rights in American society. Finally, in achieving redress, many Japanese Americans felt that they had at last been granted full citizenship and their belief in their country was reaffirmed.

Clearly, the redress campaign and its victory have strengthened the identification of Japanese Americans as American and has furthered assimilation in behavioral patterns, norms, values, and ideologies. At the same time, it reawoke and enhanced their sense of themselves as Japanese Americans.

Thus Americanization and ethnic identification have grown simultaneously.[10] Similarly, the ethnic movements of the 1960s, which drew upon the concepts of injustice and white racism, elevated the ethnic consciousness of minority members. At the same time, the battle against discrimination and the demand for justice and equality are based on fundamental premises of American society, namely, the idea of civil rights. In other words, the basis of ethnicity in American society shifted from cultural and racial features derived from ancestral countries to something more than that, something that accentuates the social status and experience of each ethnic group in the American social context.

Historically, however, "Americanization" was not considered compatible with retention of ethnicity. After World War II Japanese Americans pursued assimilation at the expense of their ethnic heritage and identification. Two main factors, one external and the other internal, may be responsible for this phenomenon. When the notion of the "melting pot" was the dominant American social ideology, "Americanization" was essentially "Anglo-Americanization." The stigma attached to their Japanese American ethnicity, then, promoted their Americanization defined by Anglo-American culture and experience. The civil rights movement, succeeding ethnic movements, and the concept of cultural pluralism to a large degree liberated Japanese Americans and other minority groups and permitted them to take pride in non-Anglocentric norms and standards.

Another factor is internal. Because of the total economic loss due to evacuation, distrust by the larger society, and their lower social and economic status in the prewar period, many Japanese Americans felt compelled to make extra efforts to be accepted by American society, to prove themselves as "good Americans." The rise of ethnic consciousness in the late 1960s and early 1970s, however, started to make a distinction between Americanization and Anglo-Americanization. On the other hand, Japanese Americans themselves, once they achieved a certain level of upward mobility and social acceptance by American society, had much less need to

---

[10] Richard Alba (1990: 319) also suggests that there is no contradiction between being American and asserting an ethnic identity. I became aware of his argument only after completing my manuscript. My argument, however, is more extensive and is based on an empirical study.

struggle for assimilation. The shift of American core social ideology and their own social advancement combined to permit the reexamination and reinterpretation of their past experience. In the redress movement, Japanese Americans repudiated the stigma attached to their ethnicity and persuaded American society to atone for its un-American conduct during the war.

Japanese American ethnicity, thus, has followed its own course, from an identity tied to Japanese cultural features to one based on an interpretation of ethnic experience in American society. The increased significance of the interpretation of historical experience to the formation of ethnic identity is relevant not only to Japanese Americans but to other minorities, including African Americans, for whom slavery forms their core basis of suffering, and Native Americans, who were deprived of their land and forced to adopt new ways. Seeing ethnic identity as an interpretation of experience rather than the retention of traditional cultural characteristics seems to increase its relevance to actual lives.

The focus of this book on the Japanese American community in Seattle should not jeopardize the wider applicability of my findings. One might question the applicability of my argument about the transformation of ethnicity to Japanese Americans who were not directly affected by evacuation or to Japanese Americans in other parts of the country where the redress movement did not concern their community as strongly as in Seattle. One might also take an interest in speculating on the ethnicity of future generations of Japanese Americans. What matters in constructing ethnicity is how the members of an ethnic group interpret and reinterpret their experiences, collectively and individually. These two levels, the collective and the individual, have been closely tied together among Japanese Americans, at least up to the present, since they, among other groups, practice "quasi kin" social relationships (Fugita and O'Brien 1991: 5) and both internment and redress occurred as collective experiences. For the Yonsei, the Gosei, and succeeding generations of Japanese Americans, these "quasi kin" social relationships will be progressively loosened. As outmarriage increases, ethnic identity will likely become more an individual option (cf. Waters 1990), especially if a person of mixed descent is physically indistinguishable from members of the majority group and hence not forced by racial discrimination to recognize her or his ethnic background. Nevertheless, Japanese American ethnicity as collective ideology will continue to exist as long as a core group of Japanese Americans with discrete Japanese American identity continue to exist.

On the collective level, the reinterpretation of the internment and other discrimination experience, social and economic achievement after the war in spite of these setbacks and obstacles, and success in forcing the government to acknowledge its misconduct— all have become legend among the members of the ethnic group and in the larger society. These are the markers of Japanese American ethnicity, for instance, in the exhibit "A More Perfect Union: Japanese Americans and the U.S. Constitution" at the Smithsonian Institution;[11] in documentary films produced by the Sansei, such as *Days of Waiting*, an Academy Award–winning documentary film about a white American woman who went to an internment camp with her Japanese American husband, directed by Steven Okazaki; in various Japanese American community events including the Seattle exhibit "Executive Order 9066: 50 Years Before and 50 Years After" and the Los Angeles opening of the Japanese American National Museum;[12] and in a number of Japanese American plays and literary works. I believe that Japanese Americans will continue to embrace this legend of suffering and triumph.

In many respects, Japanese Americans are now facing a new critical turning point. They have entered a new era, not only with the resolution of the redress issue, but also as they are affected by both domestic and international factors. Since the beginning of the 1990s, and especially after civil unrest in Los Angeles in 1992, there has been a growing sense that the racial cleavage in American society has again surfaced, more than it had during the previous two decades. That two books dealing with the subject—*Two Nations* by Andrew Hacker and *The Disuniting of America* by Arthur M.

[11] The exhibit at the Museum of American History opened in September 1987, marking the two hundredth anniversary of the Constitution. Roger Kennedy of the Smithsonian remarked: "Japanese Americans had moved all of us a giant step closer to that more perfect union envisioned by the Founding Fathers two centuries ago" (*Pacific Citizen*, Aug. 17–24, 1990).

[12] It opened in May 1992 as part of the fiftieth anniversary of Executive Order 9066 commemorated during the Day of Remembrance.

Schlesinger, Jr.—became best-sellers, attests to this notion. Whether or not the trend merits the label "disuniting" or "two nations," there does seem to be an effort on the part of many African American community leaders to make their ethnic community autonomous and independent, at least in the economic sphere, and possibly in others. Entrepreneurs and small businesses are increasing among African Americans. And as African Americans, a significant minority with a strong political voice, begin to claim institutional independence, Latinos, another important minority group, may follow suit, even though their economic base is different. To what extent this movement may affect Japanese Americans and other Asian Americans depends on the degree of racial discrimination they pereive themselves to suffer.

Another factor affecting Japanese Americans today which we must not underestimate is transnational relations with Japan. Japanese and Asian American communities recognize the impact of the economic and emotional frictions between the two countries, as they are expressed in anti-Asian sentiment and violence. With burgeoning transnational migration, there has been a growing influx of Japanese nationals such as businessmen and students. Japanese American community leaders now take the initiative, politically and in the media, in fighting the discrimination issues that involve the Japanese from Japan. Such has not always been the case, however. For nearly fifty years after World War II, Japanese Americans maintained a distance from Japan as they consciously tried to avoid being confused with Japanese nationals by mainstream society. With the completion of redress, however, the need for this constraint is mitigated. If, as the transnational movement increases, contact with the Japanese and Japanese culture increases, that interchange will inevitably affect the ethnic identity of younger generations of Japanese Americans, if only indirectly.

We should, therefore, watch closely the direction Japanese Americans are heading, so that we may deepen our understanding not only of them but of the diversity of ethnicity in American society.

Bibliography

Alba, Richard D. 1990. *Ethnic Identity: The Transformation of White America*. New Haven: Yale University Press.

Amerasia staff. 1971. An Interview with Warren Furutani, National Community Involvement Coordinator, the Japanese American Citizens League (Los Angeles, California). *Amerasia Journal* 1:70–76.

Anderson, Alan B., and James Frideres. 1981. *Ethnicity in Canada*. Toronto: Butterworth.

Anderson, Benedict R. 1983. *Imagined Communities*. London: Verso.

Asian Student Coalition, University of Washington. 1973. *Asian Student Coalition Handbook*. Seattle: Asian Student Coalition, University of Washington.

Banton, Michael. 1983. *Racial and Ethnic Competition*. Cambridge: Cambridge University Press.

Barth, Fredrik, ed. 1969. *Ethnic Groups and Boundaries*. Boston: Little, Brown.

Baum, Rainer C. 1991. Editor's Introduction: Identity of Descent in Modernity. *Qualitative Sociology* 14:3–12.

Befu, Harumi. 1965. Contrastive Acculturation of California Japanese: Comparative Approach to the Study of Immigrants. *Human Organization* 24:209–16.

Bentley, G. Carter. 1987. Ethnicity and Practice. *Comparative Study in Society and History* 29:24–55.

Bloom, Leonard. 1943. Familial Adjustments of Japanese-Americans to Relocation: First Phase. *American Sociological Review* 8:551–60.

Bloom, Leonard, and Ruth Riemer. 1949. *Removal and Return: The Socioeconomic Effects of the War on Japanese Americans*. Berkeley: University of California Press.

Bonacich, Edna, and John Modell. 1980. *The Economic Basis of Ethnic Solidarity.* Berkeley: University of California Press.

Bosworth, Allan R. 1967. *America's Concentration Camps.* New York: W. W. Norton.

Bourdieu, Pierre. 1977. *Outline of a Theory of Practice.* Cambridge: Cambridge University Press.

Brewer, Marilynn, and Donald Campbell. 1976. *Ethnocentrism and Intergroup Attitudes.* New York: John Wiley and Sons.

Caudill, William. 1952. Japanese-American Personality and Acculturation. *Genetic Psychology Monographs* 45:3–102.

Caudill, William, and George De Vos. 1956. Achievement, Culture, and Personality: The Case of Japanese Americans. *American Anthropologist* 58: 1102–26.

Chin, Frank, Jeffery Paul Chan, Lawson Fusao Inada, and Shawn Wong. 1983. *Aiiieeeee!* Washington, D.C.: Howard University Press.

Chuman, Frank. 1976. *The Bamboo People.* Albany: Del Mar.

Clifford, James, and George E. Marcus, eds. 1986. *Writing Culture: The Poetics and Politics of Ethnography.* Berkeley: University of California Press.

Cohen, Abner. 1969. *Custom and Politics in Urban Africa: Hausa Migrants in Yoruba Towns.* Berkeley: University of California Press.

Cohen, Morris L. 1965 [1931]. *How to Find the Law.* Seventh edition. St. Paul: West.

Cohen, Ronald. 1978. Ethnicity, Problems, and Faces in Anthropology. *Annual Review of Anthropology* 7:379–413.

Cohn, Bernard S. 1983. Representing Authority in Victorian India. In *The Invention of Tradition*, ed. Eric Hobsbawm and Terence Ranger, pp. 165–210. Cambridge: Cambridge University Press.

CWRIC (Commission on Wartime Relocation and Internment of Civilians). 1981. Collected Statements Submitted to the Commission on Wartime Relocation and Internment of Civilians. Unpublished papers in a personal collection.

——. 1982. *Personal Justice Denied.* Washington, D.C.: Commission on Wartime Relocation and Internment of Civilians.

——. 1983. *Personal Justice Denied: Summary and Recommendations of the Commission on Wartime Relocation and Internment of Civilians.* San Francisco: Japanese American Citizens League.

Conrat, Maisie, and Richard Conrat. 1972. *Executive Order 9066.* San Francisco: California Historical Society.

Cruz, Philip Vera, et al. 1982. Personal Reflections on the Asian National Movements. *Eastwind* 1:25–40. Essays by Cruz, Lillian Nakano, Happy Lin, Lori Leong, May Chen, Alan Nishio, and Wes Senzaki.

Daniels, Roger. 1972. *Concentration Camps, U.S.A.: Japanese Americans and World War II.* New York: Holt, Rinehart, and Winston.

———. 1985. Japanese America, 1930–41: An Ethnic Community in the Great Depression. *Journal of the West* 24:35–50.

———. 1988. *Asian America: Chinese and Japanese in the United States since 1850.* Seattle: University of Washington Press.

Daniels, Roger, Sandra C. Taylor, and Harry H. L. Kitano, eds. 1986. *Japanese Americans: From Relocation to Redress.* Salt Lake City: University of Utah Press.

Despres, Leo. 1967. *Cultural Pluralism and Nationalist Politics in British Guiana.* Chicago: Rand McNally.

———. 1975. Ethnicity and Resource Competition in Guyanese Society. In *Ethnicity and Resource Competition,* ed. Despres, pp. 87–117. The Hague: Mouton.

Devereux, George. 1975. Ethnic Identity: Its Logical Foundations and Its Dysfunctions. In *Ethnic Identity: Cultural Continuities and Change,* ed. George De Vos and Lola Romanucci-Ross, pp. 42–70. Berkeley: University of California Press.

De Vos, George. 1955. A Quantitative Rorschach Assessment of Maladjustment and Rigidity in Acculturating Japanese Americans. *Genetic Psychology Monographs* 52:51–87.

———. 1975. Ethnic Pluralism: Conflict and Accommodation. In *Ethnic Identity: Cultural Continuities and Change,* ed. George De Vos and Lola Romanucci-Ross, pp. 5–41. Chicago: University of Chicago Press.

De Vos, George, and Lola Romanucci-Ross. 1975. Ethnicity: Vessel of Meaning and Emblem of Contrast. In *Ethnic Identity: Cultural Continuities and Change,* ed. De Vos and Romanucci-Ross, pp. 363–90. Chicago: University of Chicago Press.

De Vos, George, and Hiroshi Wagatsuma. 1966. *Japan's Invisible Race.* Berkeley: University of California Press.

Dorman, James H. 1980. Ethnic Groups and "Ethnicity": Some Theoretical Considerations. *Journal of Ethnic Studies* 7:23–36.

Drinnon, Richard. 1987. *Keeper of Concentration Camps.* Berkeley: University of California Press.

Duus, Masayo Umezawa. 1987. *Unlikely Liberators: The Men of the 100th and 442nd.* Honolulu: University of Hawaii Press.

Eidheim, Harold. 1969. When Ethnic Identity Is a Social Stigma. In *Ethnic Groups and Boundaries,* ed. Fredrik Barth, pp. 39–57. New York: Little, Brown.

Eisenstadt, S. N. 1972. Intellectuals and Tradition. *Daedalus* 101 (2):1–19.

———. 1973. Post-traditional Societies and the Continuity and Reconstruction of Tradition. *Daedalus* 102 (1):1–27.

Endo, Russell, and William Wei. 1988. On the Development of Asian American Studies Programs. In *Reflections on Shattered Windows,* ed. Gary Y. Okihiro, Shirley Hune, Arthur A. Hansen, and John M. Liu, pp. 5–15. Pullman: Washington State University Press.

Erikson, Erik H. 1968. *Identity: Youth and Crisis.* New York: W. W. Norton.

Espiritu, Yen Le. 1992. *Asian American Panethnicity: Bridging Institutions and Identities.* Philadelphia: Temple University Press.

Evacuation Redress Committee, Seattle Chapter of the JACL. 1975. An Appeal for Action to Obtain Redress for the World War II Evacuation and Imprisonment of Japanese Americans. Unpublished paper.

——. 1976. Provisions Necessary in Any Reparations Plan. Unpublished paper.

——. 1977. Case for Individual Reparations Payments. Unpublished paper.

Executive Committee, Seattle Community College. 1971. Minutes. Executive Committee, Seattle Community College.

Feagin, Joe R. 1972. On the Assimilation of Japanese Americans. *Amerasia Journal* 1:13–30.

Fienup-Riordan, Ann. 1988. Robert Redford, Apanuugpak, and the Invention of Tradition. *American Ethnologist* 15:442–55.

Firth, Raymond. 1973. *Symbols: Public and Private.* Ithaca: Cornell University Press.

Fugita, Stephen S., and David J. O'Brien. 1991. *Japanese American Ethnicity.* Seattle: University of Washington Press.

Fukuda, Miryo. 1957. *Koryu Seikatsu Rokunen.* San Francisco: Konkokyo Kyokai.

Fukuoka, Fumiko. 1937. Mutual Life and Aid among the Japanese in Southern California with Special Reference to Los Angeles. M. A. thesis, University of Southern California, Los Angeles.

Gans, Herbert J. 1979. Symbolic Ethnicity: The Future of Ethnic Groups and Culture in America. *Ethnic and Racial Studies* 2:1–20.

Gardiner, C. Harvey. 1981. *Pawns in a Triangle of Hate.* Seattle: University of Washington Press.

——. 1986. The Latin-American Japanese and World War II. In *Japanese Americans: From Relocation to Redress,* ed. Roger Daniels, Sandra C. Taylor, and Harry H. L. Kitano, pp. 142–46. Salt Lake City: University of Utah Press.

Gee, Emma. 1976. *Counterpoint: Perspectives on Asian America.* Los Angeles: UCLA, Asian American Studies Center.

Geertz, Clifford. 1963. The Integrative Revolution: Primordial Sentiments and Civil Politics in the New States. In *Old Societies and New States,* ed. Geertz, pp. 105–57. New York: Free Press.

Gehrie, Mark Joshua. 1973. Sansei: An Ethnography of Experience. Ph.D. dissertation, Northwestern University.

Girdner, Audrie, and Anne Loftis. 1969. *The Great Betrayal: The Evacuation of the Japanese Americans during World War II.* New York: Macmillan.

Glazer, Nathan, and Daniel Moynihan. 1963. *Beyond the Melting Pot: The Negroes, Puerto Ricans, Jews, Italians, and Irish of New York City.* Cambridge: MIT Press.

Glazer, Nathan, and Daniel Moynihan, eds. 1975. *Ethnicity: Theory and Experience*. Cambridge: Harvard University Press.

Glenn, Evelyn Nakano. 1986. *Issei, Nisei, War Bride*. Philadelphia: Temple University Press.

Gordon, Milton. 1964. *Assimilation in American Life*. New York: Oxford University Press.

Government of Canada. 1988a. Historical Agreement Reached on Japanese Canadian Redress. September 22.

——. 1988b. Redress for Japanese Canadians: Eligibility and Application Information.

Hacker, Andrew. 1992. *Two Nations*. New York: Charles Scribner's Sons.

Handlin, Oscar. 1951. *The Uprooted*. New York: Grosset and Dunlap.

Hansen, Marcus L. 1938. *The Problem of the Third-Generation Immigrant*. Rock Island, Ill.: Augustana Historical Society.

——. 1952. The Third Generation in America. *Commentary* 14:492–500.

Hetcher, Michael. 1978. Group Formation and Cultural Division of Labor. *American Journal of Sociology* 84:293–318.

Hill, Howard C. 1974. The Americanization Movement. In *Race and Ethnicity in Modern America*, ed. Richard J. Meister, pp. 27–40. Lexington, Mass.: D.C. Heath.

Hirabayashi, Gordon. 1985. *Good Times, Bad Times: Idealism Is Realism*. Argenta, British Columbia, Canada: Canadian Quaker Pamphlets.

Hirschman, Charles. 1983. America's Melting Pot Reconsidered. *Annual Review of Sociology* 9:397–423.

Hobsbawm, Eric. 1983a. Introduction: Inventing Traditions. In *The Invention of Tradition*, ed. Hobsbawm and Terence Ranger, pp. 1–14. Cambridge: Cambridge University Press.

——. 1983b. Mass-Producing Traditions: Europe, 1870–1914. In *The Invention of Tradition*, ed. Hobsbawm and Terence Ranger, pp. 263–308. Cambridge: Cambridge University Press.

Hohri, William M. 1986. Redress as a Movement towards Enfranchisement. In *Japanese Americans: From Relocation to Redress*, ed. Roger Daniels, Sandra C. Taylor, and Harry H. L. Kitano, pp. 196–99. Salt Lake City: University of Utah Press.

——. 1988. *Repairing America*. Pullman: Washington State University Press.

Horowitz, Donald. 1975. Ethnic Identity. In *Ethnicity: Theory and Experience*, ed. Nathan Glazer and Daniel Moynihan, pp. 305–49. Cambridge: Harvard University Press.

Hosokawa, Bill. 1969. *Nisei: The Quiet Americans*. New York: William Morrow.

——. 1982. *JACL in Quest of Justice*. New York: William Morrow.

——. 1986. The Uprooting of Seattle. In *Japanese Americans: From Relocation to Redress*, ed. Roger Daniels, Sandra C. Taylor, and Harry H. L. Kitano, pp. 18–20. Salt Lake City: University of Utah Press.

Hosokawa, Fumiko. 1978. *The Sansei: Social Interaction and Ethnic Identi-*

[219]

fication among the Third Generation Japanese. San Francisco: Robert D. Reed and Adam S. Eterovich.

Houston, Jeanne Wakatsuki, and James D. Houston. 1973. *Farewell to Manzanar.* Boston: Houghton Mifflin.

Ichihashi, Yamato. 1932. *Japanese in the United States.* Stanford: Stanford University Press.

Ichioka, Yuji. 1988. *The Issei.* New York: Free Press.

——, ed. 1989. *Views from Within.* Los Angeles: Resource Development and Publications, Asian American Studies Center.

Inouye, Daniel K., and Lawrence Elliott. 1967. *Journey to Washington.* Englewood Cliffs, N.J.: Prentice-Hall.

Irons, Peter, ed. 1989. *Justice Delayed: The Record of the Japanese American Internment Cases.* Middletown, Conn.: Wesleyan University Press.

Isaacs, Harold. 1975. *Idols of Tribe: Group Identity and Political Change.* New York: Harper and Row.

Isajiw, Wsevolod. 1974. Definition of Ethnicity. *Ethnicity* 1:111–24.

Israely, Hilla Kuttenplan. 1976. An Exploration into Ethnic Identity: The Case of Third-Generation Japanese Americans. Ph.D. dissertation, University of California, Los Angeles.

Ito, Kazuo. 1982. *Amerika Shunjuu Hachijuunen.* Tokyo: PMC.

——. 1984 [1973]. *Hokubei Hyakunen Zakura.* Tokyo: PMC.

Iwai, Yasuko. 1985. A Japan Town—the Past and the Present: The Study of Voluntary Associations and Ethnicity of Japanese-Americans in San Francisco. M.A. thesis, University of Washington, Seattle.

Japanese American Citizens League, Legislative Education Committee (JACL-LEC). 1987. Brief History of JACL and JACL-LEC Redress Action. Unpublished paper.

——. 1989. History of Redress Legislation: U.S. House of Representatives. Unpublished paper.

Japanese American Citizens League, Seattle Chapter. 1971. *Pride and Shame.* Seattle: JACL, Seattle Chapter.

Jayawardena, Chandra. 1980. Culture and Ethnicity in Guyana and Fiji. *Man,* n.s., 15:430–50.

Johnson, Colleen. 1972. The Japanese-American Family and Community in Honolulu: Generational Continuities in Ethnic Affiliation. Ph.D. dissertation, Syracuse University.

——. 1974. Gift Giving and Reciprocity among the Japanese Americans in Honolulu. *American Ethnologist* 1:295–308.

Johnson, Frank A., Anthony J. Marsella, and Coleen L. Johnson. 1974. Social and Psychological Aspects of Verbal Behavior in Japanese Americans. *American Journal of Psychiatry* 131:580–83.

Kagiwada, George. 1974. Assimilation of Nisei in Los Angeles. In *East across the Pacific,* ed. Hilary Conroy and T. Scott Miyakawa, pp. 268–78. Santa Barbara, Calif.: ABC-Clio Press.

Kanazawa, Toru J. 1989. *Sushi and Sourdough*. Seattle: University of Washington Press.

Kashima, Tetsuden. 1977. *Buddhism in America*. Westport: Greenwood Press.

——. 1980. Japanese American Internees Return, 1945 to 1955: Readjustment and Social Amnesia. *Phylon* 41 (2): 107–15.

——. 1984. The Japanese Alien Internment Process in America prior to World War II. In *Japanese American: Iju kara Jiritsu eno Ayumi*, ed. Soken Togami, pp. 393–421. Kyoto: Minelva.

Kato, Shin'ichi. 1961. *Beikoku Nikkei-jin Hyakunen-shi*. Los Angeles: New Japanese American News.

Kendis, Kaoru Oguri. 1979. Persistence and Maintenance of Ethnicity among Third-Generation Japanese Americans. Ph.D. dissertation, University of Pittsburgh.

Keyes, Charles F. 1976. Towards a New Formulation of the Concept of Ethnic Group. *Ethnicity* 3:202–13.

——. 1981. The Dialectics of Ethnic Change. In *Ethnic Change*, ed. Keyes, pp. 4–30. Seattle: University of Washington Press.

Kiefer, Christie. 1974. *Changing Cultures, Changing Lives*. San Francisco: Jossey-Bass.

Kikumura, Akemi. 1981. *Through Harsh Winters*. Novato, Calif.: Chandler and Sharp.

Kikumura, Akemi, and Harry H. L. Kitano. 1973. Interracial Marriage: A Picture of the Japanese Americans. *Journal of Social Issues* 29:67–81.

——. 1980. Interracial Marriage: A Picture of Japanese Americans. In *Asian Americans: Social and Psychological Perspectives*, vol. 2, ed. Russell Endo, Stanley Sue, and Nathaniel N. Wagner, pp. 26–35. Palo Alto, Calif.: Science and Behavior Books.

Kim, Bok Lim. 1973. Asian Americans: No Model Minority. *Social Work* 18:44–53.

Kitagawa, Daisuke. 1967. *Issei and Nisei: The Internment Years*. New York: Seabury Press.

Kitano, Harry H. L. 1976 [1969]. *Japanese Americans: The Evolution of a Subculture*. Englewood Cliffs, N.J.: Prentice-Hall.

Kitano, Harry H. L., Wai-Tsang Yeung, Lynn Chai, and Herbert Hatanaka. 1984. Asian-American Interracial Marriage. *Journal of Marriage and the Family* 46:179–90.

Kodaira, Naomichi. 1980. *Amerika Kyosei Shuyosho: Senso to Nikkeijin*. Tokyo: Tamagawa.

Leach, Edmond R. 1954. *Political Systems of Highland Burma*. London: G. Bell and Sons.

Lee, Sharon M., and Keiko Yamanaka. 1990. Patterns of Asian American Intermarriage and Marital Assimilation. *Journal of Comparative Family Studies* 21:287–305.

Leighton, Alexander. 1945. *The Governing of Men*. Princeton: Princeton University Press.

Leonetti, Donna. 1976. Fertility in Transition: An Analysis of the Reproductive Experience of an Urban Japanese-American Population. Ph.D. dissertation, University of Washington, Seattle.

——. 1983. *Nisei Aging Project Report*. Seattle: University of Washington Press.

Leonetti, Donna, and Laura Newell-Morris. 1982. Exogamy and Change in the Bio-social Structure of a Modern Urban Population. *American Anthropologist* 84:19–36.

Light, Ivan. 1972. *Ethnic Enterprise in America*. Berkeley: University of California Press.

——. 1981. Ethnic Succession. In *Ethnic Change*, ed. Charles F. Keyes, pp. 53–86. Seattle: University of Washington Press.

Linnekin, Jocelyn S. 1983. Defining Tradition: Variations on the Hawaiian Identity. *American Ethnologist* 10:241–52.

Lopez, David, and Yen Le Espiritu. 1990. Panethnicity in the United States: A Theoretical Framework. *Ethnic and Racial Studies* 13 (2):198–224.

Lyman, Stanford. 1972. Generation and Character. In *East across the Pacific*, ed. Hilary Conroy and T. Scott Miyakawa, pp. 279–314. Santa Barbara, Calif.: ABC-Clio Press.

McKay, James. 1982. An Exploratory Synthesis of Primordial and Mobilizationist Approaches to Ethnic Phenomena. *Ethnic and Racial Studies* 5:395–420.

McWilliams, Carey. 1945. *Prejudice*. Boston: Little, Brown.

Marcia, J. E. 1966. Development and Validation of Ego-Identity Status. *Journal of Personality and Social Psychology* 50: 143–52.

Masaoka, Mike, and Bill Hosokawa. 1987. *They Call Me Moses Masaoka: An American Saga*. New York: William Morrow.

Mass, Amy Iwasaki. 1986. Psychological Effects of the Camps on Japanese Americans. In *Japanese Americans: From Relocation to Redress*, ed. Roger Daniels, Sandra C. Taylor, and Harry H. L. Kitano, pp. 159–67. Salt Lake City: University of Utah Press.

Matsuoka, Jack. 1974. *Camp II, Block 211*. San Francisco: Japan Publications.

Maykovich, Minako K. 1972. *Japanese American Identity Dilemma*. Tokyo: Waseda University Press.

Mazumdar, Sucheta. 1991. Asian American Studies and Asian Studies: Rethinking Roots. In *Asian Americans: Comparative and Global Perspectives*, ed. Shirley Hune, Hyung-chan Kim, Stephen S. Fugita, and Amy Ling, pp. 29–44. Pullman: Washington State University Press.

Meister, Richard J., ed. 1974. *Race and Ethnicity in Modern America*. Lexington, Mass.: D. C. Health.

Minami, Dale. 1986. Coram Nobis and Redress. In *Japanese Americans: From*

Relocation to Redress, ed. Roger Daniels, Sandra C. Taylor, and Harry H. L. Kitano, pp. 200–201. Salt Lake City: University of Utah Press.

Mirikitani, Janice. 1978. *Awaking the River.* San Francisco: Isthmus Press.

Miyamoto, S. Frank. 1939. *Social Solidarity among the Japanese in Seattle.* Seattle: University of Washington Publications in the Social Sciences 11.

——. 1972. An Immigrant Community in America. In *East across the Pacific: Historical and Sociological Studies of Japanese Immigration and Assimilation,* ed. Hilary Conroy and T. Scott Miyakawa, pp. 217–43. Santa Barbara, Calif.: ABC-Clio.

——. 1984. *Social Solidarity among the Japanese in Seattle.* Seattle: University of Washington Press.

——. 1986–87. Problems of Interpersonal Style among the Nisei. *Amerasia* 13:29–45.

Modell, John, ed. 1973. *The Kikuchi Diary.* Urbana: University of Illinois Press.

Moerman, Michael. 1965. Ethnic Identity in a Complex Civilization: Who Are the Lue? *American Anthropologist* 67:1215–30.

Montero, Darrel. 1980. Japanese Americans: Changing Patterns of Ethnic Affiliation over Three Generations. Westview Special Studies in Contemporary Social Issues. Boulder, Colo.: Westview Press.

Morgan, G. D. 1981. *America without Ethnicity.* Port Washington, N.Y.: Kennikat Press.

Myer, Dillon S. 1971. *Uprooted Americans: The Japanese Americans and the War Relocation Authority during World War II.* Tucson: University of Arizona Press.

Nagata, Donna K. 1990. The Japanese American Internment: Exploring the Transgenerational Consequences of Traumatic Stress. *Journal of Traumatic Stress* 3:47–69.

Nagata, Judith. 1974. What Is a Malay? Situational Selection of Ethnic Identity in a Plural Society. *American Ethnologist* 1:331–50.

Nahirny, Vladimir C., and Joshua A. Fishman. 1965. American Immigrant Groups: Ethnic Identification and the Problem of Generations. *Sociological Review* 13:311–26.

Nakano, Mei. 1990. *Japanese American Women: Three Generations, 1890–1990.* Berkeley: Mina Press and San Francisco: National Japanese American Historical Society.

Naroll, Raoul. 1964. On Ethnic Unit Classification. *Current Anthropology* 5:283–91, 306–12.

National Association of Japanese Canadians. 1985. *Economic Losses of Japanese Canadians after 1941.* Winnipeg, Manitoba: National Association of Japanese Canadians.

National Committee for Redress, Japanese American Citizens League. 1978.

The Japanese American Incarceration: A Case for Redress. San Francisco: National Committee for Redress, Japanese American Citizens League.

National Council for Japanese American Redress. 1979. Summary of Proposed Legislation. Unpublished paper. Seattle: National Council for Japanese American Redress.

North American Times. 1936. *1936 Edition Year Book*. Seattle: North American Times.

Novak, Michael. 1972. *The Rise of Unmeltable Ethnics*. New York: Macmillan.

O'Brien, David J., and Stephen S. Fugita. 1983. Generational Differences in Japanese Americans' Perceptions and Feelings about Social Relationships between Themselves and Caucasian Americans. In *Culture, Ethnicity, and Identity: Current Issues in Research*, ed. W. C. McCready, pp. 223–40. New York: Academic Press.

Odo, Franklin, Mary Uyematsu, Ken Hanada, Peggy Li, and Marie Chung. 1971. The U.S. in Asia and Asia in America. In *Roots: Asian American Reader*, ed. Amy Tachiki, Eddie Wong, and Franklin Odo, with Buck Wong, pp. 223–44. Los Angeles: UCLA, Asian American Studies Center.

Ogawa, Dennis. 1971. *From Japs to Japanese: the Evolution of Japanese American Stereotypes*. Berkeley: McCutchan.

Okada, John. 1976. *No-No Boy*. Seattle: University of Washington Press.

Okamura, Raymond. 1974. Background and History of the Repeal Campaign. *Amerasia* 2:73–94.

Okihiro, Gary Y. 1984. Religion and Resistance in America's Concentration Camps. *Phylon* 45:220–33.

Okubo, Mine. 1966 [1946]. *Citizen 13660*. New York: AMS Press.

Omi, Michael, and Howard Winant. 1986. *Racial Formation in the United States from the 1960s to the 1980s*. New York: Routledge.

Park, Robert E. 1950. *Race and Culture*. New York: Free Press.

Parsons, Talcott. 1965. Full Citizenship for the Negro American? A Sociological Problem. *Daedalus* 94 (4):1009–54.

———. 1975. Some Theoretical Considerations on the Nature and Trends of Change of Ethnicity. In *Ethnicity: Theory and Experience*, ed. Nathan Glazer and Daniel Moynihan, pp. 53–83. Cambridge: Harvard University Press.

Patterson, Orlando. 1975. Context and Choice in Ethnic Allegiance: A Theoretical Framework and Caribbean Case Study. In *Ethnicity: Theory and Experience*, ed. Nathan Glazer and Daniel Moynihan, pp. 305–49. Cambridge: Harvard University Press.

———. 1977. *Ethnic Chauvinism*. New York: Stein and Day.

Peterson, William. 1966. Success Story, Japanese American Style. *New York Times Magazine* Jan. 9, 1966.

Poyer, Lin. 1988. Maintaining "Otherness": Sapwuahfil Cultural Identity. *American Anthropologist* 15:472–85.

Quan, Martie. 1988. Redress! The American Promise. *Rafu Magazine*, Dec. 19, 1988, sec. 1, pp. 1–9.

Ranger, Terence. 1983. The Invention of Tradition in Colonial Africa. In *The Invention of Tradition*, ed. Eric Hobsbawm and Ranger, pp. 211–62. Cambridge: Cambridge University Press.

Reitz, Jeffrey. 1980. *The Survival of Ethnic Groups*. Toronto: McGraw-Hill Ryerson.

Reminick, Ronald A. 1983. *Theory of Ethnicity: An Anthropologist's Perspective*. Lanham, Md.: University Press of America.

Residents of Minidoka Relocation Center. 1943. Minidoka Interlude, September 1942–October 1943. Hunt, Idaho: Residents of Minidoka Relocation Center.

Rex, John. 1986. The Role of Class Analysis in the Study of Race Relations—a Weberian Perspective. In *Theories of Race and Ethnic Relations*, ed. John Rex and David Mason, pp. 64–83. Cambridge: Cambridge University Press.

Rex, John, and David Mason, eds. 1986. *Theories of Race and Ethnic Relations*. Cambridge: Cambridge University Press.

Roda, Anne. 1984. Death and Continuity among the Nisei. Ph.D. dissertation, University of Washington, Seattle.

Sandberg, Neil C. 1974. *Ethnic Identity and Assimilation: The Polish-American Community*. New York: Praeger.

Sanjek, Roger. 1990. *Fieldnotes: The Makings of Anthropology*. Ithaca: Cornell University Press.

Santos, Bob. 1983. Rebuilding Seattle's I.D.: The Story of Inter*Im. *East Wind* 2:3–7.

Sarna, Jonathan D. 1978. From Immigrants to Ethnics: Toward a New Theory of Ethnicization. *Ethnicity* 5:370–78.

Schlesinger, Jr., Arthur M. 1991. *The Disuniting of America*. New York: Whittle Communications.

Seriguchi, Karen, and Frank Abe, eds. 1980. *Japanese America: Contemporary Perspectives on Internment*. Proceedings of conferences held January–March 1980 in the State of Washington. Seattle: American Friends Service Committee and Combined Asian American Resources Project.

Shibutani, Tamotsu, and K. M. Kwan. 1965. *Ethnic Stratification*. London: Macmillan.

Shils, Edward. 1972. Intellectuals, Tradition, and the Traditions of Intellectuals: Some Preliminary Considerations. *Daedalus* 101 (2):21–34.

——. 1981. *Tradition*. Chicago: University of Chicago Press.

Simpson, George, and Milton Yinger. 1972 [1953]. *Racial and Cultural Minorities*. Fourth edition. New York: Harper and Row.

Smith, Anthony, D. 1981. *Ethnic Revival*. Cambridge: Cambridge University Press.

Smith, David H. 1975. Voluntary Action and Voluntary Groups. *Annual Review of Sociology* 1:247–70.

[225]

Sollors, Werner, ed. 1989. *The Invention of Ethnicity.* Oxford: Oxford University Press.

Sone, Monica. 1953. *Nisei Daughter.* Seattle: University of Washington Press.

Spicer, Edward. 1971. Persistent Cultural Systems: A Comparative Study of Identity Systems That Can Adapt to Contrasting Environments. *Science* 174:795–800.

Spicer, Edward H., Asael T. Hansen, Katherine Luomala, and Marvin K. Opler. 1969. *Impounded People: Japanese-Americans in the Relocation Centers.* Tucson: University of Arizona Press.

Starn, Orin. 1986. Engineering Internment: Anthropologists and the War Relocation Authority. *American Ethnologist* 13:700–720.

Stein, Howard F., and Robert Hill. 1977. *The Ethnic Imperative.* University Park: Pennsylvania State University Press.

Steinberg, Stephen. 1981. *The Ethnic Myth: Race, Ethnicity, and Class in America.* New York: Atheneum.

Stonequist, Everett V. 1935. The Problem of the Marginal Man. *American Journal of Sociology* 41:1–12.

Suguro, Ed. 1989. Good Times in Nihonmachi. *Northwest Nikkei* 1:1, 6–7.

Suzuki, Bob. 1980. Education and Socialization of Asian Americans: A Revisionist Analysis of the Model Minority Thesis. In *Asian-Americans: Social and Psychological Perspectives,* vol. 2, ed. Russell Endo, Stanley Sue, and Nathaniel N. Wagner, pp. 155–75. Palo Alto, Calif.: Science and Behavior.

Suzuki, Peter T. 1976. The Ethnolinguistics of Japanese Americans in the Wartime Camps. *Anthropological Linguistics* 18:416–427.

Tachiki, Amy, Eddie Wong, and Franklin Odo, with Buck Wong, eds. 1971. *Roots: An Asian American Reader.* Los Angeles: UCLA, Asian American Studies Center.

Takahashi, Jerrold Haruo. 1980. Changing Responses to Racial Subordination: An Exploratory Study of Japanese American Political Styles. Ph.D. dissertation, University of California, Berkeley.

Takasugi, Robert. 1974. A Legal Analysis of Title II. *Amerasia* 2:95–104.

Takeuchi, Kojiro. 1929. *Beikoku Seihokubu Imin-shi.* Seattle: Taihoku Nippo.

Takezawa, Yasuko Iwai. 1988. Ethnic Stereotypes in the U.S.A.: The Dynamics of Ethnic Group Images Seen in Advertising and Jokes. *Japanese Journal of Ethnology* 52:363–90.

——. 1989. "The Invention of Tradition" and Ethnicity among Japanese Americans. *Shikyo (En marge de l'histoire)* 19:53–66, 98–99. Tsukuba, Japan.

——. 1991a. Children of Inmates: The Effects of the Redress Movement among Third-Generation Japanese Americans. *Qualitative Sociology* 14 (1):39–56.

——. 1991b. Social and Cultural Byproducts of the U.S.-Japan Relationship— the Social Status and Ethnic Identity of Japanese Americans during World War II and under the Contemporary Trade War. *Gaiko Jiho,* no. 1283:35–51.

Tana, Daisho. 1976. *Santa Fe, Lordsburg, Senji Tekikokujin Koryujo-nikki.* Vol. 1. Tokyo: T. Tana, Y. Asaji, Yamaki Bo Futsu Shorin.

Tateishi, John. 1984. *And Justice for All.* New York: Random House.

———. 1986. The Japanese American Citizens League and the Struggle for Redress. In *Japanese Americans: From Relocation to Redress,* ed. Roger Daniels, Sandra C. Taylor, and Harry H. L. Kitano, pp. 191–95. Salt Lake City: University of Utah Press.

tenBroek, Jacobus, Edward N. Barnhart, and Floyd W. Matson. 1954. Prejudice, War, and the Constitution. Berkeley: University of California Press.

Thomas, Dorothy S. 1952. *The Salvage.* Berkeley: University of California Press.

Thomas, Dorothy, and Richard Nishimoto. 1946. *The Spoilage.* Berkeley: University of California Press.

Tonkin, Elizabeth, Maryon McDonald, and Malcolm Chapman. 1989. *History and Ethnicity.* London: Routledge.

Toren, Christina. 1988. Making the Present, Revealing the Past: The Mutability and Continuity of Tradition as Process. *Man,* n.s., 23:696–717.

Trottier, Richard. 1981. Charters of Panethnic Identity: Indigenous American Indians and Immigrant Asian Americans. In *Ethnic Change,* ed. Charles F. Keyes, pp. 271–305. Seattle: University of Washington Press.

Tsuji, Shinichi. 1990. *Nikkei Kanadajin: Redressing the Past.* Tokyo: Shoubunsha.

Turner, Victor. 1967. *The Forest of Symbols.* Ithaca: Cornell University Press.

Uchida, Yoshiko. 1982. *Desert Exile: The Uprooting of a Japanese-American Family.* Seattle: University of Washington Press.

United States Statutes at Large. 1988. Public Law 100-383. Aug. 10.

Uyeda, Clifford I. 1978. The Pardoning of "Tokyo Rose": A Report on the Restoration of American Citizenship to Iva Ikuko Toguri. *Amerasia* 5:69–94.

Uyematsu, Amy. 1971. The Emergence of Yellow Power in America. In *Roots: An Asian American Reader,* ed. Amy Tachiki, Eddie Wong, and Franklin Odo, with Buck Wong, pp. 9–13. Los Angeles: UCLA, Asian American Studies Center.

van den Berghe, Pierre. 1978. Race and Ethnicity: A Sociobiological Perspective. *Ethnic and Racial Studies* 1:401–11.

———. 1981. *The Ethnic Phenomenon.* New York: Elsevier.

Vincent, Joan. 1974. Brief Communications. *Human Organization* 33:375–79.

Wagner, Roy. 1975. *The Invention of Culture.* Chicago: University of Chicago Press.

Wallman, Sandra. 1979. *Ethnicity at Work.* London: Macmillan.

Warner, W. Lloyd, and Leo Srole. 1945. *The Social Life of a Modern Community.* New Haven: Yale University Press.

Washington State Commission on Asian American Affairs. 1982. *Countdown II.* Seattle: Washington State Commission on Asian American Affairs.

Waters, Mart C. 1990. *Ethnic Options.* Berkeley: University of California Press.

Wax, Rosalie. 1971. *Doing Fieldwork*. Chicago: University of Chicago Press.

Weglyn, Michi. 1976. *Years of Infamy: The Untold Story of America's Concentration Camps*. New York: Morrow Quill.

Wong, Buck. 1971. Need for Awareness: An Essay on Chinatown, San Francisco. In *Roots: An Asian American Reader*, ed. Amy Tachiki, Eddie Wong, and Franklin Odo, with Buck Wong, pp. 265–73. Los Angeles: UCLA, Asian American Studies Center.

Wong, Paul. 1972. The Emergence of the Asian-American Movement. *Bridge* 2:33–39.

Woodrum, Eric. 1981. An Assessment of Japanese American Assimilation, Pluralism, and Subordination. *American Journal of Sociology* 87:157–69.

Yamada, Mitsuye. 1989. The Cult of the "Perfect" Language: Censorship by Class, Gender, and Race. Paper presented at Parallels and Intersections: A National Conference on Racism and Other Forms of Oppression, University of Iowa.

Yanagisako, Sylvia. 1975a. Two Processes of Change in Japanese-American Kinship. *Journal of Anthropological Research* 31:196–224.

———. 1975b. Women-Centered Kin Networks in Urban Bilateral Kinship. *American Ethnologist* 4:207–26.

———. 1985. *Transforming the Past: Tradition and Kinship among Japanese Americans*. Stanford: Stanford University Press.

Yanagisako, Sylvia, Donna Leonetti, Jay McGough, and Laura Newell. 1977. *The Japanese American Community Study*. Olympic, Wash.: State Superintendent of Public Instruction.

Yancey, W. L., E. P. Ericksen, and R. N. Juliani. 1976. Emergent Ethnicity: A Review and Reformulation. *American Sociological Review* 41:391–402.

Yinger, J. M. 1983. Ethnicity and Social Change: The Interaction of Structural, Cultural, and Personality Factors. *Ethnic and Racial Studies* 6:395–409.

———. 1985. Ethnicity. *Annual Review of Sociology* 11:151–80.

Zaibei, Nihon jin-kai. 1940. *Zaibei Nihon jin-shi*. San Francisco: Zaibei Nihon-jin-kai.

Index

Abe, Frank, 42, 49
African Americans, 70–71, 128, 135–36, 138, 147–48, 150, 158, 167, 182, 202, 206, 212; black power movement, 145–48, 150
Alba, xvi, 19, 211
Aleuts, 37, 50
alien, ineligibility for citizenship, 6, 30, 61, 73
Alien Fishing Law, 73
Alien Land Laws, 6, 72
American government, 83–94, 96, 100, 171, 186–87
Americanism, 39, 69, 96, 209–11
Americanization, 68–69, 70, 110–11, 116–19, 125–26, 136–38, 148–49, 153, 184, 190–91, 194, 201, 204, 208–12
American Promise, 40–41
American public school, 65, 68–70, 128, 132, 194, 198, 201–2
Anglo-conformity, 81, 119, 125, 148, 211
annual events, 63, 107, 130
anti-Asian sentiments, 189, 200
"Appeal for Action to Obtain Redress for the World War II Evacuation and Imprisonment of Japanese Americans, An," 39, 209
Asian American identity, 13, 18, 143–44, 147–49, 152–53, 182, 203–8
Asian American movement, 144–53, 203–6
Asian Americans, 10–12, 71, 124, 139–53, 169, 180–82, 200, 204, 207–8

Asian American studies, 145–47, 149
Asian Family Affair, 147, 150
Asian population trends, in Seattle, 8–9
Asian Student Coalition, 145, 147–48
assembly centers, 1, 30, 86–90
assimilation, xvi, 19, 116, 118–19, 126, 141, 152, 177, 195–96, 200, 209
association and friendships, among Japanese Americans, 62, 67, 69–71, 118–19, 127–29, 134–41, 144, 201–2

Bainbridge Island, 78
banzai, 67
barracks, 31, 86–93
Barth, Fredrik, 13
Beacon Hill, 9–10, 70, 127, 139, 141, 202
Beacon Hill Boys, 147
blacks. *See* African Americans
"Blood," concept of, 64, 66, 193
bon-odori (folk dances), 62, 130–31, 198–99
Boys' Day, 130
Breaking the Silence (Louis), vii, 21, 53–54, 166
Buddhism, 62, 75, 99, 112, 116, 130
Bush, President George, 28, 58, 187

Cambodians, 182
Camp Harmony, 2, 43, 84, 86–91
Canadian government, 57, 187
Carter, President Jimmy, 47
Caucasians. *See* European Americans

[229]

Anthropology of Contemporary Issues

A SERIES EDITED BY
ROGER SANJEK

From Working Daughters to Working Mothers: Immigrant Women in a New England Industrial Community
BY LOUISE LAMPHERE

Sunbelt Working Mothers: Reconciling Family and Factory
BY LOUISE LAMPHERE, PATRICIA ZAVELLA, AND FELIPE GONZALES,
WITH PETER B. EVANS

Creativity/Anthropology
EDITED BY SMADAR LAVIE, KIRIN NARAYAN, AND RENATO ROSALDO

Cities, Classes, and the Social Order
BY ANTHONY LEEDS, EDITED BY ROGER SANJEK

Lesbian Mothers: Accounts of Gender in American Culture
BY ELLEN LEWIN

Civilized Women: Gender and Prestige in Southeastern Liberia
BY MARY H. MORAN

Blood, Sweat, and Mahjong: Family and Enterprise in an Overseas Chinese Community
BY ELLEN OXFELD

The Magic City: Unemployment in a Working-Class Community
BY GREGORY PAPPAS

State and Family in Singapore: Restructuring an Industrial Society
BY JANET W. SALAFF

Uneasy Endings: Daily Life in an American Nursing Home
BY RENÉE ROSE SHIELD

Children of Circumstances: Israeli Emigrants in New York
BY MOSHE SHOKEID

History and Power in the Study of Law: New Directions in Legal Anthropology
EDITED BY JUNE STARR AND JANE F. COLLIER

"Getting Paid": Youth Crime and Work in the Inner City
BY MERCER L. SULLIVAN

Breaking the Silence: Redress and Japanese American Ethnicity
BY YASUKO I. TAKEZAWA

City of Green Benches: Growing Old in a New Downtown
BY MARIA D. VESPERI

Renunciation and Reformulation: A Study of Conversion in an American Sect
BY HARRIET WHITEHEAD

Upscaling Downtown: Stalled Gentrification in Washington, D.C.
BY BRETT WILLIAMS

Women's Work and Chicano Families: Cannery Workers of the Santa Clara Valley
BY PATRICIA ZAVELLA